CONFRONTING CHALLENGES TO THE LIBERAL ARTS CURRICULUM

Comparative research on higher education in developing and transitional countries is often focused on such issues as access, finance, student mobility, and the impact of globalization, but there has been little attention to curriculum and the forces that shape it. *Confronting Challenges to the Liberal Arts Curriculum* fills an important gap in the literature by examining the context, content, challenges, and successes of implementing liberal arts coursework within undergraduate curriculum. In order to fully understand the place of liberal education in each location, chapter authors have employed a wide lens to investigate the influences upon curricular content in China, India, Mexico, Pakistan, Poland, Russia, South Africa, and Turkey. Thus, this volume explores how curricular content is decided, how educational programs are being structured, and whether countries are viewing higher education as more than just the preparation of students for specialized knowledge.

By providing detailed case studies of these countries at crucial transition points in their higher education systems, each chapter outlines the state of higher education and the government's role, the impact of imported models, the presence of a liberal education, the curricular formation, and best examples of successful programs. Ultimately, this volume depicts how global influences have come to rest in developing countries and how market forces far removed from faculty and students have shaped the undergraduate curriculum. This valuable book will be of interest to scholars and researchers in higher education as well as practitioners working to foster student and faculty exchange and raise awareness of curricular issues.

Patti McGill Peterson is Presidential Adviser for Global Initiatives at the American Council on Education.

CONFRONTING CHALLENGES TO THE LIBERAL ARTS CURRICULUM

Perspectives of Developing and Transitional Countries

Edited by Patti McGill Peterson

Routledge
Taylor & Francis Group

NEW YORK AND LONDON

First published 2012
by Routledge
711 Third Avenue, New York, NY 10017

Simultaneously published in the UK
by Routledge
2 Park Square, Milton Park, Abingdon, Oxon OX14 4RN

Routledge is an imprint of the Taylor & Francis Group, an informa business

Library of Congress Cataloging in Publication Data
Confronting challenges to the liberal arts curriculum : perspectives of developing and transitional countries / edited by Patti McGill Peterson.
   p. cm.
   Includes bibliographic al references and index.
   1. Education, Humanistic–Curricula–Cross-cultural studies. 2. Education, Higher–Curricula–Cross-cultural studies. 3. EDUCATION / Higher I. Peterson, Patti McGill.
   LC1011 .C672 2012   370.11/2–dc23

ISBN: 978-0-415-50605-2 (hbk)
ISBN: 978-0-415-50606-9 (pbk)
ISBN: 978-0-203-12732-2 (ebk)

Typeset in Goudy
by Wearset Ltd, Boldon, Tyne and Wear

CONTENTS

PREFACE AND ACKNOWLEDGMENTS

This book is the culmination of a 30-year conversation with Julie Johnson Kidd in which we explored the broad issues of higher education but always returned to the purpose and quality of undergraduate education. At its heart was the role of liberal education and its emphasis on providing a wide spectrum of thought from multiple academic disciplines, the interrelatedness of knowledge from different cultures, and the basic habits of inquiry and critical thinking. Over the years, each of us moved from a primary involvement with American higher education institutions to an engagement with higher education in other countries. This development enriched our conversation and made us eager to bring a global dimension to it by inviting others to contribute their ideas and perspectives.

Through the generosity of the Christian A. Johnson Endeavor Foundation and its President, Julie Johnson Kidd, it was possible to develop a comparative investigation of the role of the liberal arts in undergraduate education outside the United States. Her intellectual curiosity and openness to new ideas have supported this research. The purpose was neither to promote a monolithic view nor to criticize from an American perspective. It was above all to learn from others about this topic and ultimately to illuminate our collective understanding of the status of undergraduate education and the extent to which liberal education plays a part in its design and structure.

Without preordaining any specific outcomes for the collection of country case studies, we knew there would be significant differences with the U.S. experience. This intuition was immediately signaled when we began to identify authors. Colleagues from developing and transitional countries indicated that there was not much to describe. They reported a lack of attention to undergraduate education and few if any publications, scholarly or otherwise, about the place of the liberal arts and general education in curricular design. We quickly understood that we would need to broaden our investigation and that the case studies would need to address the larger context of higher education and the forces that were driving its form and structure in our targeted countries in order to help us understand the differing national scenarios.

It was, therefore, a welcome part of our process in developing this edited volume that I was able to meet in person with all the contributors to discuss these ramifications. This opportunity was supported by the Rockefeller Foundation through its Bellagio Center with supplemental support from the Christian A. Johnson Foundation. Nestled above Lake Como in northern Italy, the Center provided an ideal setting—quiet and hospitable—for a valuable cross-cultural discussion. The Bellagio seminar allowed in-depth examination of our topic, constructive inquiry, and an accompanying critique of our work. The comments I received from contributing authors helped me to frame the volume's introductory chapter. Ultimately, we were very fortunate to assemble such a capable group of authors. Their case studies form the *sine qua non* of this endeavor.

Many others contributed to the completion of this book. Our supporting cast included: Kate Woodward, partner in all things, who has provided essential assistance to every aspect of this volume; Susan Kassouf, at the Christian A. Johnson Endeavor Foundation, who offered valuable advice at various stages of the project; Lavina Fielding Anderson, editor extraordinaire, who missed her calling as a diplomat; and Robin Helms, whose support at the beginning of the project was critical to a strong start. Others who have been strong supporters are Philip G. Altbach, Director of the Center for International Higher Education, and Michelle Cooper, President of the Institute for Higher Education Policy.

All of us who have been part of this project look forward to the possibility that this volume will stimulate a global discussion about the purpose of undergraduate education and the role of the liberal arts. That discussion is long overdue.

1

A GLOBAL FRAMEWORK

Liberal Education in the Undergraduate Curriculum

Patti McGill Peterson

Introduction

Demand for higher education worldwide is growing exponentially. Much of the enrollment growth in recent years has come from developing and transitional countries. Historically, many students from these countries have been part of a global migration to developed countries for access to high-quality education. While this pattern continues to be a characteristic of international higher education, there are growing indications that sending nations wish to take more direct responsibility for educating future generations of their students. A current sign of economic and political maturation in developing nations is a strong desire to improve and expand their own education infrastructure to meet the burgeoning demand for access to higher education (Altbach & Peterson, 2007).

The strategies to strengthen higher education vary by country, but a common imperative for the development of higher education is to align it with priorities for nation building and modernization. The case was made strongly by post-independence leaders in Africa, such as Kwame Nkrumah of Ghana and Julius Nyerere of Tanzania, who stated clearly that they wanted universities first and foremost to address the interests and priorities of their nations (Mwiria, 2003). Invariably, as part of the emphasis on the centrality of the state's interests, there are high-level discussions about the need to build "world-class" universities and to promote fields of study deemed essential for economic development (Altbach, 2006). Science, especially applied science, and technology fields receive paramount attention. Allied fields of business and management science, as well as applied economics, also receive special consideration.

Comparative research on higher education in developing and transitional countries is often focused on such issues as access, funding models, the mobility of students, research agendas, public and private institutions, and the impact of globalization. In general, there has been very little focus on the content of academic programs and the kinds of investments governments are making in specific programs and disciplines. This omission was much in evidence at both the 1998 and 2009 UNESCO World Higher Education Conferences, which assembled delegations from all its member nations to discuss the progress of tertiary education worldwide (World Conference on Higher Education, 1998, 2009). Yet curriculum development and the major forces that are shaping it in various national contexts are topics that merit focused attention. Analysis of the variables that influence curriculum development in different national and cultural settings is very scarce in published research. Related issues, such as the role of academic governance, the involvement of faculty in curricular reform, and the relationship between the expansion of higher education and students' personal and intellectual development, likewise receive scant attention.

This neglect creates a very challenging environment for examining the role of liberal education outside the United States where the topic is often written about and discussed. To understand the presence or absence of liberal education and the liberal arts in a country's educational system, it is important to understand how curricular content is decided, what forces of choice are at work, whether breadth of exposure to subject matter is considered, and to what extent there is a desire to see one of higher education's responsibilities as preparing the student for more than specialized knowledge.

To address this omission, in 2008 the Christian A. Johnson Endeavor Foundation supported the initiation of a comparative, multinational project: "Liberal Learning in Global Perspective." It was a direct result of long-term association with liberal arts colleges in the United States and my tenure as head of the Council for the International Exchange of Scholars, which administers the worldwide Fulbright Scholar Program. The latter provided an education on the importance of national and cultural context in understanding how higher education is organized, the differing roles of faculty, and the ways students are educated at the undergraduate level. It became clear that the reasons for the presence or absence of liberal education in different countries needed to be examined both in historical terms and also through the lens of more current realities facing higher education. This kind of cross-cultural examination meshed well with the foundation's long-term interest in liberal education and its efforts to support culturally attuned liberal education initiatives in countries outside the United States.

The choice to focus the project's case studies in developing or transitional countries was influenced significantly by the World Bank's 2000 report on higher education in developing countries. After outlining the many pressures facing tertiary education in these countries and addressing the importance of such high-profile issues as science and technology, the report offered a chapter on the importance of general (liberal) education. It began with a quotation from Alvin Toffler, "The illiterate of the 21st century will not be those who cannot read and write, but those who cannot learn, unlearn, and relearn," then went on to deal realistically with the obstacles to liberal education (Task Force on Higher Education and Society, 2000, p. 83). It also argued persuasively for the merits of including some form of general education for all students. The report's basic premises were that developing nations needed citizens who could help build the nation in many ways and that narrowly educated specialists might find themselves outmoded by rapidly changing economies and the forces of globalization. What was missing in the report, except for a few selected examples, was whether countries were heeding this admonition as they expanded their systems of higher education.

The continued silence in the decade that has passed since this report signals the need for in-depth case studies representing different regions at varying stages of higher education development that would examine these issues and provide insight into whether liberal education could rise above the obstacles in order to grow and flourish beyond the United States. Ultimately, authors were identified for the case studies in China, India, Mexico, Pakistan, Poland, Russia, South Africa, and Turkey. The charge to these authors was to address several areas as part of their examination of the presence (or absence) of liberal education in their countries, including background on the state of higher education and the nature of secondary education as a prelude to each case study's major focus: curricular formation and the role of liberal education in higher education.

Bringing together such a richly divergent group of countries, each with its own history of higher education, dictated the importance of finding common ground. Among other things, it meant that choice of terms and their origins had to be carefully understood.

In Search of Meaning: Historical Wellsprings

The concept and practice of the liberal arts has been primarily associated with Classical Greco-Roman and European origins. When searching for answers, we invariably go to the wellsprings in our quest for descriptive language. For those who have not watched the modern morphing of liberal education, the term implies a classical education geared cumulatively to the great works of the West, particularly from the Greco-Roman, Renaissance humanist, and Enlightenment periods of European history. Bruce Kimball (1995) has written a very thorough history of the complicated trajectory of the idea of liberal education, which makes oversimplification about the derivation of terminology a dangerous exercise. What seems clear, however, is that the language referring to liberal education among free Athenians can be identified by the fifth century BCE. There are all kinds of etymological debates and varying degrees of emphasis on different branches of Greek thought during this period as it relates to liberal education.

Those debates notwithstanding, it was the ideals associated with being an educated person that have become interwoven with our modern conceptions of liberal education. These include the ability to be self-aware and self-governing and the capacity to respect the humanity of all human beings (Nussbaum, 2003). Using Socrates as a model yielded two fundamental elements of liberal education: the habit of critical thinking and taking responsibility for one's own thought and speech. The Socratic notion of the importance of the examined life as well as the Aristotelian sense of the importance of trying to understand the nature and principles of the universe combined to reinforce the idea of critical inquiry in the study of all things. However one interprets the classical history or the players during this period, these ways of learning and habits of mind encouraged by a liberal education had a profound and long-lasting influence on what it meant to be a well-educated and civically involved person.

What began in Greece was reinforced and consolidated by Rome's succession to global dominance. When Rome took up colonial residence in far-flung parts of the ancient world and encountered the richness of culture and education in such subject colonies as Egypt, it projected to the empire's subjects the hegemony of Rome backed by the culture and education of Greece. The general education of young Roman elites included a corpus of Greek and Latin epic poetry, history, philosophy, and political oratory that changed little between the first and the fifth centuries CE (MacCormack, 1989).

Later in 16th-century Europe, medieval universities have expanded their offerings to include Judeo-Christian foundations along with those of the Greco-Roman period. The Greco-Roman canon of texts was configured into the seven liberal arts that constituted the core of medieval education, while the Judeo-Christian branch of Europe's heritage from classical antiquity became the separate discipline of theology. The latter was grounded in the Bible as its principal text. These intellectual, cultural, and religious perspectives constituted liberal education and became the bedrock of "the West" and its educational traditions.

Britain absorbed these traditions and exported them to its colonies—the future United States of America—in the late 17th century. The "Laws, Liberties, and Orders" of Harvard College had their origin in the Elizabethan statutes of the University of Cambridge (Ashby, 1964). Like the young upper-class Romans who looked to Greece for their education, the young men privileged to enter a colonial college focused on Greek and Latin classics as the core of their liberal education. This situation held steady for nearly 200 years. As late as 1828, Yale College issued a report in its defense. Liberal education, it argued, provided the discipline and furniture of the mind and pointed proudly to Yale's success in training young men from the upper classes who would serve as society's enlightened leaders and decision-makers (Lane, 1987). This classical curriculum remained remarkably consistent well into the 19th century. In an era when Latin and Greek were believed to be essential to any man who considered himself liberally educated, the forces of stability were a powerful influence in the American college (Bastedo, 2005).

A major point of this mini-history of liberal education is the spectacular tenacity of the core curriculum over a significant period of time. The treasure trove of knowledge came from the West—advanced by the Romans and institutionalized by the medieval universities. What was taught to entering students at America's first colleges reflected this lineage. There were also other tenacious features. Notably, only a very small proportion of the population was considered eligible for a liberal education. The students were exclusively male, mainly the sons of wealthy colonists. The privileged nature of a liberal education was underscored by the fact that the colonial colleges combined yielded only about 100 graduates annually (Bastedo, 2005). The education they received did not seek wisdom in locally produced knowledge. Rather, liberal education of this vintage was based on the great works and thoughts of other civilizations and held up as the ideal, defining an educated person.

Contemporary Realities/Understandings

Higher education in the United States is currently the largest repository of the modern version of liberal education. Today the nature of liberal education at its universities and colleges is extremely varied—very far in both form and years from the classical liberal arts education of 18th-century Harvard College. American educators use "liberal education" somewhat loosely to describe a variety of educational models. Only vestiges of the classical *artes liberales* are part of contemporary liberal education in its U.S. manifestations. The ideals of living an examined life and educating enlightened citizens remain, but a core of courses and texts common to many institutions no longer exists. Many, but not all, four-year undergraduate institutions now offer some kind of general education component before students begin their majors. At one extreme, it can consist of a few basic core distribution course requirements; at the other, it can be represented by highly structured programs that integrate curricular with co-curricular offerings. Given this diversity, it is not surprising that its contemporary meaning is difficult to convey in other national settings.

For many colleagues outside the United States, particularly among developing countries, there is little familiarity with the term, which sometimes even has pejorative connotations. The fact that historically it accompanied the domination of one country over another has meant that it is associated with the legacy of colonialism in many places. Reserved for a few elites, it habitually disregarded the local culture. In colonized India, for example, English was deemed more important than Sanskrit; Shakespeare more relevant than the Mahabharata; the teachings of Milton and Burke more appropriate than the teaching of Buddha. It was Thomas B. Macauley as an agent of the British Empire who wanted to create in India through liberal education "a class of persons Indian in blood and colour, but English in tastes, in opinions, in morals and intellect" (quoted in Ashby, 1964, p. 2). Ironically, many of those who led the fight against colonial domination had been educated in European universities and often quoted the political philosophers of the West in laying out the grounds for civil disobedience. The experience in the countries of Sub-Saharan Africa is generally similar. In addition to its colonial connotation, liberal education is often still seen as superfluous in the context of nation building. Having thrown off the shackles of colonialism, countries dealing with the enormous demands of economic development tended to view liberal education as a luxury reserved for elites, one that the country could ill afford.

In short, in countries with no significant experience with liberal education, the words and the concepts tend to raise more questions than answers in cross-cultural conversations. Does it imply a political orientation? Is it just a superficial hopscotch over a number of subjects? Is it designed for those who do not have the ability to undertake a serious program of study in a particular academic field? Questions about course content are common and are accompanied by inquiries about what exactly the curriculum is and specifically what subjects are taught. After all, for those who know something about the historical origins of liberal education, very specific content and texts were revered over many generations for what they taught, weren't they? Yet the answers do not lie in the past, nor are they easy to provide, neatly packaged, in the present. Part of the reason is that liberal education in the 20th and 21st centuries in America has always been a work in progress.

A colleague from a German university, pondering the direction of American higher education, remarked that the curriculum of U.S. universities and colleges is always under debate, a marked departure from his experience at his own institution. At the heart of much of this debate is the question of what the nature of undergraduate education should be and how general education should be introduced prior to a student's undertaking specialized study. A good illustration of the seriousness with which this matter is taken was the debates that began in the 1980s and which continue, though with less intensity, to the present. At their center was the battle over moving from a Western-oriented canon to a more multicultural one.

The Western core and perceived narrowness of the curriculum of liberal education was the object of student protests in the 1980s. This resistance was symbolized by the chant of students at Stanford University: "Hey, hey. Ho, ho. Western Civ has got to go." As colleges and universities (Stanford among them) became responsive to these protests, the canon of the core curriculum expanded significantly to include a multicultural spectrum of texts (Heller, 2002). The movement away from an exclusive core of Western texts, in turn, caused considerable backlash from conservative academics. They blamed liberal academics for opening the curriculum to an "anything goes" approach and were especially unhappy with interdisciplinary and multicultural studies that supplanted the traditional core curriculum focusing on time-honored classics and a more homogenized West (Heller, 2002).

The so-called "culture wars" of American academe ensued. E. D. Hirsh's *Cultural Literacy* (1987) defended what for him were essential texts, including those of the ancient Greeks. Allan Bloom followed shortly with *The Closing of the American Mind* (1987) and later by Harold Bloom's *The Western Canon* (1994). Overall the argument was that liberal education should deliver core information to students with a strong (some argued exclusively) Western orientation. Groups like the Association for Core Texts and Courses sprang up to promote a return to a core curriculum informed by the great works of the Western world (Zelnick, 2002). While groups like the Association of American Colleges and Universities (AAC&U) (n.d., 2010) argued for a broader, more inclusive core curriculum, the National Endowment for the Humanities, under its director, Lynne Cheney, made its support clear for curricular projects that adhered more closely to the West and to the traditional texts of an earlier America (Menand, 2010).

Charges of elitism, cultural hegemony, and a curricular *idée fixe* on one side were met passionately by those who warned of loss of cultural identity, illiterate students, and general education running amok. Nevertheless, many academic institutions moved forward to revise curricula. The end result was a broader canon of knowledge as the keystone of general education programs. As noted earlier, what is offered in terms of content varies so widely that it would be very difficult to describe a typical liberal education curriculum or general education program, except for its basic commitment to general education followed by a concentration in a major field of study. This characteristic is the most unique feature of U.S. higher education in comparison to the rest of the world.

The sound and fury that characterized the culture wars had some salutary outcomes. First and foremost, it highlighted a general agreement on the importance and centrality of undergraduate education in American higher education. Lack of agreement about the content of general education programs also shifted the nature of the debate from what subjects it should include to what it should produce. Colleges and universities now describe the attributes their educational programs wish to foster. Instead of listing core texts, mission statements and catalogues describe aims and objectives—for example, the graduate should be able to think and write clearly and effectively; be articulate in at least one language, if not more; have deep insight into his or her culture and a broad understanding of other cultures; know something about research and the nature of scientific discovery; and have depth of knowledge in a particular discipline. Many of these attributes align well with the seminal ideals of a liberal education expressed in ancient Greece.

Settling on Descriptive Terminology

The overall effect of the ongoing debate about liberal education is that the tent housing the enterprise has become a very big one, encouraging broad cultural engagement and a wide range of educational activities. As a result, the terminology associated with liberal education is as varied as its myriad manifestations (Schneider, 2008). Many terms are used interchangeably: liberal education, the liberal arts, liberal arts education, liberal learning, and general education. While these terms do not always have clearly demarcated boundaries, it is important for this project to propose some basic distinguishing characteristics. We do not assume uniformity of approach to liberal education among the countries in this project, but the use of terms needs to be relatively consistent among the case studies.

The AAC&U, a national higher education association in the United States devoted to the theory and practice of liberal education, has attempted to clarify terminology by offering some definitions. These definitions are in keeping with the "big tent" approach that allows an array of cultural contexts and a variety of models. They also help to make distinctions between several commonly used terms:

> *Liberal Education*: An approach to learning that empowers individuals and prepares them to deal with complexity, diversity, and change. It provides students with broad knowledge of the wider world (e.g., science, culture, and society) as well as in-depth study in a specific area of interest. A liberal education helps students develop a sense of social responsibility as well as strong and transferable intellectual and practical skills such as communication, analytical, and problem-solving skills, and a demonstrated ability to apply knowledge and skills in real-world settings.
>
> *Liberal Arts*: Specific disciplines (the humanities, social sciences, and sciences).
>
> *General Education*: The part of a liberal education curriculum shared by all students. It provides broad exposure to multiple disciplines and forms the basis for developing important intellectual and civic capacities. General education may also be "the core curriculum" or "liberal studies."
>
> (AAC&U, n.d.)

The Task Force on Higher Education and Society (2000) convened by the World Bank and UNESCO focused its report on the realities of developing nations in its discussion of liberal education. Among other things, it argued for the introduction of liberal education in a differentiated system of higher education. It discussed the value and importance of liberal education and described its general education component as an excellent form of preparation for the flexible, knowledge-based careers that increasingly dominate the upper tiers of the modern labor force. It described general education as a curriculum aimed at imparting general knowledge and developing general intellectual capacities. It went further by saying that, depending on the student and his or her goals, different levels of general education are possible. These included:

> A basic grounding for all higher education students, whatever type of institutions they attend or course they study;
>
> A discrete and substantial component of general education, which helps broaden the experience of students engaged in specialist, professional, or technical study;
>
> An intensive general education curriculum that provides exceptionally promising, intellectually oriented students with a solid basis for their careers or for advanced specialist study.
>
> (*Task Force on Higher Education and Society*, 2000, p. 87)

This approach adds to the idea that the definitions of liberal education and general education need to be flexible enough to allow sufficient adaptation to different national and cultural realities. The Task Force report widens the permutations for general education and how it might be used in different curricular settings.

For the purpose of this comparative project, we have adopted a broad concept of liberal education as a student-centered education that offers both breadth and depth of study. It provides core knowledge that fosters understanding of one's own culture as well as that of others; strengthens skills of critical inquiry, thinking, and articulation; cultivates social responsibility and civic values; and ultimately creates a basis for lifelong learning, engaged citizenship, and professional competency. By its nature, liberal education is global and pluralistic through the diversity of ideas and experiences that characterize the social, natural, and intellectual world (AAC&U, n.d.) Fundamental to the idea of liberal education is the concept that a student's field of specialization needs to be accompanied by a commitment to engaging with a broad spectrum of knowledge.

"General education" as we use it refers to part of the liberal education curriculum shared by all students. It is a core curricular component that is required of everyone regardless of the student's area of specialization. The rationale for what is required should align with the philosophy and purposes of the liberal education by which it is framed.

This definition of general education does not necessarily mean that all students take the same courses. Louis Menand in his discussion of general education describes two basic systems that have emerged: the distribution model and the core model. The former normally requires students to select three departmental courses in each of the liberal arts divisions (humanities and arts, the social sciences, and the natural sciences). They are often referred to as "service courses," designed by academic departments for non-specialists as part of their participation in general education. The idea behind a distribution system is that liberal learning is the sea in which the departmentalized fields all swim whereas a core general education program requires all students to take the same core courses. Some are less elaborate in their design than others, with a beginning course in common followed by a guided distribution requirement while others may be a full extra-departmental program such as the one offered at Columbia University (Menand, 2010).

These models and definitions leave out some important elements frequently associated with liberal education. Jonathan Becker (2003), co-author of this project's Russia case study has written about liberal arts education as a curricular system. The working parts of that system are: a flexible curriculum that allows for student choice and which demands both breadth and depth of study; and a student-centered pedagogy that is interactive and requires students to engage directly with critical texts within and outside the classroom. This may be a tall order for institutions trying to serve massive numbers of students, especially if those institutions have little experience either in developing educational programs in which students have significant choices or with dynamic pedagogical standards. Realistically, the entire system might not be adoptable or adaptable in some countries, but its elements can be separately undertaken. Very importantly, it underscores good teaching and a commitment to interactive learning as vital elements of liberal education.

In the United States, undergraduate education is the platform upon which liberal education is built. Normally the first two years of a four-year undergraduate program are focused on general education. This stage is followed by selecting a major field of study and concentrating on course work in that field over the next two years. Even in the second two years, it is possible to take elective courses outside one's major field. This curricular approach is radically different from programs in most countries; typically, immediate specialization in a subject area follows completion of secondary education. While the nature of graduate education in the United States is much admired and imitated in many countries, its model for undergraduate education is an outlier in the global context.

Liberal Education and Transplanting Educational Models

As important as it is to carefully define the terms related to liberal education so that the concept can be understood in other parts of the world, this aspect of American higher education is not its primary attraction for the rest of the world. What are generally admired and imitated most are its research universities and graduate education programs. The mass migration of students from around the world to the United States is mainly to its research institutions and not to its undergraduate colleges. There is, however, a history of liberal arts colleges being established in other countries as part of America's earlier international outreach. The establishment of liberal education institutions in such faraway places as Japan, Turkey, Lebanon, and Egypt in the late 19th century and the early 20th century owe their existence to a certain level of missionary zeal among those responsible for these educational exports. A number of them, such as the American University of Beirut and the American University of Cairo have become highly respected institutions in their regions, educating the elite not only in their host country but also throughout the Middle East.

For the most part, these institutions have not had a great deal of influence in the way that publicly supported higher education has developed in other parts of the world. While Roberts College in Turkey and the American University of Cairo are highly visible and well regarded, they have not been particularly influential in shaping undergraduate education in those countries. For the most part, these transplants of liberal education have remained privileged islands in a massive sea of students moving quickly to their specialties without benefit of general education programs in public institutions.

It can be argued that the shape of higher education in developing and transitional countries has, until recently, been influenced more by Europe than by the United States. The continental European model of higher education is characterized by six-year programs of specialized study that are geared toward specific professions or research with no clear separation between undergraduate and postgraduate studies. This model became pervasive for much of the world as part of the process of colonization. Europe's history of colonial domination had an educational component, a legacy that remains significant for both secondary and higher education. In the realm of higher education, many of the transplanted universities had less commitment to liberal education because of that model's influence, whether it was the Napoleonic version or the later Humboldt version. The British had a major influence on higher education in India and Sub-Saharan Africa. While early transplants of British universities offered a broader educational experience for students, they, too, eventually turned to increased specialization. Eric Ashby noted that there was a time when most British university students aimed at a general degree covering a range of related subjects and only a minority specialized by taking "honors" in one subject. He reported that, by the early 1960s, about 81% of students in the universities of England and Wales were taking courses for honors degrees, about two-thirds of them in one subject only. At the time when Britain was exporting universities to tropical Africa, the fashion of specialization was at its height (Ashby, 1964). Specialization in one subject and the pre-professional nature of European higher education thus had a profound influence wherever a European country was the colonial master. Whether select students were able to study in the universities of the metropole or in the colonial universities that were established, "sitting to read" a single subject was the pattern.

Insurrection against colonial masters did not reinstate liberal education. Newly independent countries found their infrastructures, including the universities, in shambles when the colonial civil servants retreated to their home countries. Other developing countries were in disarray as a result of World War II. When India was attempting to deal with its post-colonial challenges, China in another part of Asia faced deep poverty left by a long war with few prospects for economic development.

While some countries were throwing off colonial domination, other parts of the world were experiencing its imposition by the Soviet Union. The influences of the Soviet higher education model were far reaching and have left a heavy imprint on education that is still in evidence in many of the former "Iron Curtain" countries. Even in non-Iron Curtain countries, the model was powerful. It exhibited an extreme aversion to liberal education, instead emphasizing departmentalization, segmentation, overspecialization, and the separation of teaching from research.

In China, Soviet influence in the 1950s took academic specialization to a new extreme. There were a total of 60 ministries in the central government, each operating its own higher education institution; for example, Beijing Agricultural University was overseen by the Ministry of Agriculture; Beijing Chemical College was supervised by the Ministry of Chemical Industry, etc. Some comprehensive universities became specialized engineering institutes, while their schools of arts and sciences were pruned away. The traits of segmentation and hyper-specialization shaped the structure of Chinese higher education until the 1990s and became the main targets of reform (Weifang, 2004).

Foreign aid from developed countries in the West influenced curricular development as part of their intention to help developing countries modernize. Indeed, the term "developing nations" was coined by donor agencies. Many strings were attached to the funds being disbursed. Organizations like the World Bank often set the national agenda in terms of what should receive the most attention. Literacy programs and access to elementary-level education were high on their agenda, leaving higher education to its own devices for the most part. With few resources, universities languished.

As higher education became part of the development equation, the specialization of the continental European model was joined by an emphasis on vocational education that reflected perceived development and workforce needs. Higher education was often referred to as "tertiary education" to foster the existence of a less exclusive group of institutions as an alternative to traditional universities. Donor policy focused on what higher education could contribute to economic development, not to individual students or to civil society. An important part of the development syndrome was the prioritization of fields of study. In traditional universities, fields such as engineering and applied fields in technology and science were favored over the disciplines of the liberal arts.

Two of the principal authors involved with producing the World Bank's report *Higher Education in Developing Countries: Peril and Promise* sum up the situation concisely:

> Donor policy has abetted this focus on vocational training. Organizations such as the World Bank have traditionally promoted infrastructure and strong institutions as keys to development. These require skilled workers. Building physical and transport infrastructure requires engineers; setting up a strong financial system requires bankers and accountants; and establishing a health system requires personnel trained in modern medicine. It is not surprising, therefore, that higher education systems in many developing countries have been geared toward early specialization aimed at producing "job ready" graduates.
>
> (Bloom and Rosovsky, 2003, p. 39)

The orientation of big-donor organizations to market forces helped forge an alignment between national development priorities and academic specialization. They became a powerful combination for shaping higher education. Donor agencies routinely expected a workforce study as a prelude to funding higher education development. The United States contributed to this trend through projects funded by USAID. Having been bound by the colonialism of the late 19th and early 20th centuries, the newly independent states now faced a similar phenomenon in the form of foreign donors' good intentions but restrictive outcomes, since funding was offered on condition that higher education moved in specific directions.

In the post-colonial period, the World Bank played a powerful role in educational development. The bank, through the International Development Association (IDA) in the 1970s, provided credit to developing countries to expand and improve educational services (Kiernan, 2000, p. 198). For many countries, this credit later imposed a heavy burden on their national budgets through debt repayment. During this period, the bank had adopted a "basic needs" philosophy that focused on basic education. By the 1980s, however, this approach was overshadowed by Structural Adjustment Programs (SAPs) designed by the bank in partnership with the International Monetary Fund (IMF) for developing countries. The SAPs had an extraordinary influence on the direction of education at all levels. The bank emphasized tertiary education based on manpower needs assessment. As a consequence, it focused on vocational and technical education that would provide the skilled manpower necessary for an industrial economy. The SAPs initiated a period of great austerity in many countries that depended on the World Bank and IMF for loans (Kiernan, 2000). Higher education opportunity actually shrank during this time, and "brain drain" became a common phenomenon in the developing world.

The more recent entry of bilateral partnership donors, particularly by the Scandinavian countries, is more respectful of the views of national governments and engages in cooperative goal setting. However, throughout all of these phases the model of higher education being supported is that of the European university with an emphasis on its research function and vocational specialization. In this respect, the emphasis is no different from that of the World Bank. Undergraduate education—and certainly liberal education—are not part of the picture.

The culmination of all of these helping hands, as noted earlier, aligned symmetrically with other forces that had been at work to reinforce specialization, emphasize vocationalism, marginalize liberal arts disciplines, and limit the possibilities of liberal education. In this convergence, the model of higher education that was being embraced all over the world by the 1960s was the research university. It was not just a phenomenon for the higher education history of developing countries; it pushed higher education development in the United States in that direction as well. In the last third of the 19th century, U.S. institutions of higher learning had began to emulate the German universities, dividing themselves into specialized disciplines and emphasizing expertise and the discovery of new knowledge. The German model had as its purpose the advancement of knowledge principally through graduate study and research. The broad encounter with the multiple disciplines of the liberal arts was overshadowed by specialization (Barker, 2002; Deneen, 2009/2010).

Globalization, Competitive Market Forces, and Liberal Education

The ideas that countries needed both useful knowledge and cutting-edge knowledge to be active participants in the community of nations were powerful drivers. In developing nations, the focus was primarily on pragmatic knowledge related to economic development; but among the superpowers, the race was on for cutting-edge research—to land a man on the moon, to build the fastest plane, or to design the submarine that could dive the deepest. These were high-status projects that assured superpower positioning. In this scenario, liberal education was viewed as a luxury that even developed nations could ill afford. For developed countries, it meant a period of extraordinary investment in science that contributed substantially in the United States to the rise of the "multiversity" that depended for its growth and existence on huge government contracts.

Clark Kerr, in his 1963 Godkin Lectures, coined the term "multiversity" and talked about the need for an entity that would be central to the economic development and productivity of the nation, produce greater affluence and better quality of life for the citizenry, and contribute to worldwide military and scientific supremacy (Kerr, 1963). He was speaking of his aspirations for the University of California, Berkeley, but he could have been speaking for the aspirations of those who presided over universities and were responsible for their development anywhere in the world. Kerr correctly predicted that the research enterprise would take priority over undergraduate education and that the humanities would lose out to science in the competition for resources. He was also prescient about the challenges facing undergraduate education: the needs for its coherence and improvement and the creation of a more unified intellectual world (Barker, 2002).

The international circulation of students and scholars has reflected many of Kerr's predictions. It also set the stage for what the rest of the world found most compelling about higher education in the United States: its multiversities, research concentration, and graduate education. Philip Altbach (2006) notes that the influences and relationships for the flow of students is complex; however, looking at the subjects that students and faculty from developing and transitional countries study in developed countries, it is not difficult to see a clear and consistent pattern. By and large, they are not coming to study philosophy, literature, or the other disciplines of the liberal arts. They are coming to work in specialized fields that have been marked as "valuable" to their countries of origin. Whether that field is an agricultural bio-engineering lab at the University of Wisconsin or a nanotechnology center at the State University of New York at Buffalo, they are filled with students and scholars who have come to the United States to acquire the latest knowledge and skills in scientific and technical fields. The majority of these students are bypassing the disciplines of the liberal arts and the opportunity to learn about the value of general education as a component of undergraduate education.

Given the fairly steady marginalization of the liberal arts disciplines and the impact on liberal education by market forces in developed and developing countries, including the international student market, we need to ask what the prospects are for liberal education in a global context.

New Developments and New Models

In various parts of the developed and developing world are indications of revitalized liberal education in some quarters. Among the wealthier countries and regions, one of the most noteworthy examples is the Netherlands. Over the past decade, eight liberal arts colleges have been established as part of the university system. In Hong Kong, the territory's government has made a commitment to undertake a major reform of undergraduate education by moving away from the three-year degree inherited from the British to a four-year American model. This reform represents a clear rejection of hyper-specialization at the undergraduate level in favor of liberal education with a core curriculum shared by all students. Singapore is seriously considering setting up a liberal arts college to add differentiation to its higher education system, and the National University of Singapore has developed a partnership with Yale University to create a Yale–NUS residential liberal arts college in Singapore (Wildavsky, 2010). Australians are also revamping their degree programs. The University of Western Australia is currently planning to eliminate nearly all professional undergraduate degrees (which students begin directly after secondary school) and require baccalaureate-level students to take a broader range of courses in the arts and the sciences before specializing (Overland, 2008).

Very innovative versions of liberal education are also appearing. Gotland University in Sweden has established liberal education programs with an emphasis on trans-disciplinary and cross-cultural studies. In Japan, which has a mixed history of liberal education in its institutions, Waseda University's School of International Liberal Studies, founded in 2004, is committed to a broad, cross-cultural education with no specialization at the undergraduate level.

A newer type of transplant from the United States has also been appearing recently around the world. The approach here is substantially different from the mode of transplant in earlier years. For example, Qatar's Education City has invited specific U.S. institutions to develop a branch campus there. Many of these invitees are institutions offering graduate and professional programs, such as Cornell University's School of Medicine. Qatar provides substantial financial incentives for U.S. universities to establish a presence in the country. Similarly, New York University recently established a residential American liberal arts college with select graduate programs in Abu Dhabi. Its core curriculum is organized around four themes: "Pathways of World Literature," "Structures of Thought and Society," "Art, Technology, and Invention," and "Ideas and Methods of Modern Science." The Abu Dhabi government covers financial aid and all other costs associated with the NYU campus.

With fewer financial incentives, Bard College has, with local partners, helped to establish a number of liberal education initiatives in different places in the world. In Russia, through Smolny College, it offers dual degrees from Bard and St. Petersburg State University. Dartmouth has a partnership with the American University of Kuwait with the support of Kuwait's government that requires students to complete 45 general education credits. Those credits may emphasize communication skills, effective leadership, aesthetic appreciation, and cultural awareness (Inside Higher Education, 2009).

A number of European venues are sponsoring noteworthy new institutions with a liberal education mission. Two examples are Slovakia's Bratislava International School for the Liberal Arts and Germany's European College for

Liberal Arts. A U.S. foundation, the Christian A. Johnson Endeavor Foundation, has been the primary financial supporter of both. Rather than a "transplant philosophy," the foundation has encouraged an indigenous endeavor with Europeans responsible for institutional development. This approach differs significantly from the early days of Americans setting up institutions on foreign soil, deciding the curriculum, and populating the faculty and the administration.

Less well-developed countries are also showing some budding experiments with liberal education. One example is the BRAC University initiative in Bangladesh. Another impressive undertaking in liberal education in that country is the Asian University for Women. Planning documents refer to developing a curriculum that will enhance critical thinking and writing skills and provide a knowledge of world history, religion, the ethical issues surrounding globalization, and the problems facing developing countries (Nussbaum, 2004). Lady Shri Ram College is an example of a long-standing and highly regarded women's college in India with a liberal education mission. The Aga Khan University network is promoting education for more civic engagement in its institutions. Through its Muslim Studies programs and the Aga Khan Humanities Project in Central Asia, it is emphasizing the fundamental importance of the social sciences and the humanities.

These examples notwithstanding, they represent a very small proportion of the enrollment in higher education across the world. It is not clear what kind of influence these more recent initiatives will have on the larger higher education systems around them. For individual institutions with a liberal education mission, the crucial question is whether they will remain isolated phenomena in higher education or models for reform for other institutions. The answer depends largely on whether the philosophy and practice of liberal education is possible broadly in developing and transitional countries facing the enormous pressures of scarce resources and massive enrollments.

If we embrace a broad definition of liberal education and the space for the different interpretations that it provides, we may see some interesting possibilities. We will also see the important interaction of national culture and history in the formation of curriculum and educational practice. A grasp of these dynamics will ultimately help us understand whether liberal education can gain any traction in places where it has heretofore truly been a foreign concept.

The case studies in this volume offer a kaleidoscopic response to the questions raised above. While each country's experience is different and deserves its own analysis, there are certain commonalities among them. The legacy of the continental European model of higher education combined with the forces of nation building, economic development priorities, and global competition have left little space for liberal education. Stand-alone liberal arts colleges in the countries of this comparative study, whether transplanted from the United

States or modeled on those kinds of institutions, have heretofore had very little influence on the overall direction of higher education in those countries. Outside donors and market forces have been dual and often integrated factors that have reinforced the marginalization of liberal education in favor of promoting more "economically relevant" higher education. The European model of higher education has, until recent times, set the course for academic programs and has been the model in which specialization has flourished. These commonalities notwithstanding, as higher education expands and reform movements proceed in these countries, ministries of education and institutions will have increasing opportunities to consider what value liberal education may bring to the content and quality of higher education.

In several of the countries, this reappraisal is already in evidence. As noted earlier, Hong Kong is vigorously pursuing liberal education as part of its reform efforts. What may be less well known is that the rest of China is also poised to try to integrate a general education component into undergraduate education programs. While Turkey and India have largely moved to a heavy emphasis on academic specialization, they also show evidence that some institutions focused on applied science and other professional fields, such as business education, are seriously considering the alignment of different kinds of general education requirements with professional education. In contrast, the extreme influence of specialization in the Soviet model of higher education would make it seem very unlikely that liberal education could take hold in any form in Russia and Poland. The facts that Smolny College, a liberal arts college, is now part of St. Petersburg State University and that Poland has an important and highly visible liberal education initiative underway are both noteworthy developments.

Several of the case studies show deep and pervasive obstacles to the adoption of forms of liberal education in some higher education systems. Analyzing and understanding those factors is of equal importance to this comparative project. In post-colonial Latin America, as evidenced by the study for Mexico, there is very little evidence that higher education will move away from a focus on academic specialization at the undergraduate level. Yet the possibility remains that, as these countries consider a more highly differentiated higher education system, liberal education might be part of the mix. Pakistan's inherited focus on academic specialization and the imposition of Islamiyat as a narrow configuration of Islamic studies for all students pose another set of challenges to establishing liberal education in that country's institutions. South Africa offers a very complex case study because liberal education found in the universities of the apartheid era is associated with racial segregation. As the country continues its process of integration and healing, the question remains open whether a model of liberal education could be a valuable component of higher education and nation building.

Conclusion: Setting a Course for the Future

The usefulness and relevance of higher education's content is held up as an important standard for its support by governments around the world. How specifically can we or should we measure those factors of usefulness and relevance? Does it mean that whoever receives a degree should be immediately and fully employable upon graduation? Should the curriculum be aligned with the priorities of the nation? What if the field in which the student has taken his or her degree is bypassed by the forces of globalization and new discoveries that make the graduate's professional knowledge obsolete? What if national priorities change by virtue of the pressures of political and market forces? The mega question among many questions that ministries of education and institutions must consider is what kind of educated human capacity countries need to become modern, successful nation states. Is it narrow specialization focused on solving immediate problems, or is it education for the long journey of national, societal, and individual development? As a partial answer to these questions, some fundamental issues and assumptions need to be reexamined.

One of the arguments against liberal education is that it does not address economic development issues. It falls into the "luxury we cannot afford" category. There are relevant counter-arguments that challenge this opinion. The CEOs of multinational companies who are responsible for a substantial amount of economic development are increasingly pointing out the need for a more broadly educated workforce and especially for management personnel who can think critically about challenges that were not covered in their textbooks. A study at AT&T indicated that technically trained rising executives knew how to answer questions but that those who were liberally educated knew what questions were worth answering (Baum & McPherson, 2010). The explosion of knowledge, global competition, and the rapidity of change demand a prescient mind that is educated to understand larger issues and trends. A 2010 survey of major employers in the United States found that they did not want linear thinkers who could work in only one area of the company. Over 90% of the respondents indicated that they wanted universities and colleges to educate students at the undergraduate level to communicate effectively both orally and in writing and to use critical thinking and analytical skills. Nearly half would like to see their employees more knowledgeable about democratic institutions and values (AAC&U, 2010). Major business schools that attract students from all over the world are engaged in curricular reform. Stanford instituted its reform efforts because it concluded that students were being trained too narrowly within artificial specialties. Yale and Harvard are making similar changes (Kaplan, 2009). It seems clear that those responsible for economic development in any country will need a broad education that fosters the skills and understandings that are attributes of a liberal education.

The impact of rapidly expanding knowledge and the forces of globalization could have an unforeseen tragic consequence. The possibility is omnipresent that narrow training will leave companies and countries atop the slag pile of human obsolescence. Generations of engineers and scientists can easily be left behind in the whirlwind of new discovery and invention. Those who are trained for a particular profession may find that fundamental knowledge for that profession is changing at nano-speed. Knowing how to assess the tsunami of change, understanding its origins and implications, and addressing ways to adapt to it will be based on finding a balance between training and education, rote learning and critical inquiry, and science and the other liberal arts disciplines. Striking that balance will need to be fundamental in planning the direction of higher education and the future of the nation.

Nation building is a very complicated matter and cannot be defined in narrow terms. It is far more complex than just economic development. Dismissing the importance of connecting education to building a country's physical infrastructure or being able to produce enough food to feed a hungry population would be supremely negligent in the face of the basic needs facing developing countries. However, all nations move historically through a hierarchy of needs that also include food for the minds and the souls of its leaders as well as for the citizenry as a whole. In this process of maturation, a host of other issues arise. Among them are the challenges of defining the common good, the concept of equal opportunity for all, the right to security and safety in one's home and in the workplace, and the need to protect the environment from degradation, to name only a few. Educating citizens to participate meaningfully and peacefully in national discussions about these issues and many others would benefit immensely from their exposure to the basic tenets of a liberal education through carefully crafted models of general education. Whether seen in the light of professional capability or civic responsibility, liberal education in these contexts seems much more like a necessity than a luxury.

As noted at the beginning of this chapter, much of the comparative research available for the study of higher education deals with subjects other than curriculum design. As the devolution of authority for higher education moves more responsibility for governance closer to governing boards and institutions, administrators and faculty will have more opportunities to consider what curricular reforms will improve the content and quality of their academic offerings. In many countries where a central ministry of education has made decisions about the curriculum, this will be uncharted territory. While each country should be able to determine its own course of action, looking past old ways of doing things will require innovative thinking and a better understanding of alternative models that seem to be working well within as well as outside the country. One size will not fit all; but if liberal education and its deeply rooted values are to take hold in some form, commitments must be made, not only to national economic priorities, but also to the full role that institutions of higher education can play in any society, to their students, and to the faculty who teach them.

One important lesson stands out in trying to construct the history and meaning of liberal education. It is not static. The Socratic ideal of the examined life through critical inquiry and respectful argument is now joined by a more modern commitment to an understanding of the pluralistic societies in which we live our personal and professional lives (Nussbaum, 2003). Surely it is not just the development of individual nations but also the coming together of many nations that, with increasingly intertwined destinies due to globalization, will characterize this era of humankind's experience. Finding ways to educate our students now and for generations to come to be good national citizens through their contributions to national development in its fullest measure (economic, civic, and cultural) will be one important goal. Another equally important goal will be to foster a sense of global citizenship in our students through an understanding of the history and culture of others. While we cannot teach them everything about the rest of the world through liberal education, giving them skills of inquiry and the sensitivity to ask before assuming commonalities or differences will mark an important new level of maturity for all nations. It is, as Martha Nussbaum suggests in her book of the same name, ultimately about cultivating our humanity through our educational choices.

References

Altbach, P. G. (2006). *International higher education: Reflections on policy and practice*. Chestnut Hill, MA: Boston College Center for International Higher Education.

Altbach, P. G., & Peterson, P. M. (Eds.). (2007). *Higher education in the new century: Global challenges and innovative ideas*. Rotterdam: Sense.

Ashby, E. (1964). *African universities and western tradition*. Cambridge, MA: Harvard University Press.

Association of American Colleges and Universities. (n.d.). What is liberal education? Retrieved on June 3, 2010, from www.aacu.org/leap/What_is_liberal _education. cfm.

Association of American Colleges and Universities. (2010). *The quality imperative: Match ambitious goals for college attainment with an ambitious vision for learning*. Washington, DC: AAC&U.

Barker, C. M. (2002). *Liberal arts education for a global society*. New York: Carnegie Corporation of New York.

Bastedo, M. N. (2005). Curriculum in higher education: The historical roots of contemporary issues. In P. G. Altbach, R. O. Berdahl, & P. Gumport (Eds.), *American higher education in the twenty-first century* (pp. 462–485). Baltimore, MD: Johns Hopkins University Press.

Baum, S., & McPherson, M. (2010). Money isn't everything. *Chronicle of Higher Education*. Retrieved on July 6, 2010, from http://chronicle.com/blogPost/Money-Isn-t-Everything?25328/.

Becker, J. (2003). What a liberal arts education is and … is not. Bard College, Institute for International Liberal Education. Retrieved on September 25, 2008, from http://www/bard/edi/iile/general/becker.shtml.

Bloom, A. (1987). *The closing of the American mind*. New York: Simon & Schuster.

Bloom, D. E., & Rosovsky, H. (2003). Liberal education: Why developing countries should not neglect it. *Liberal Education*, 89(1), 38–44.

Bloom, H. (1994). *The western canon*. Boston, MA: Houghton Mifflin Harcourt.

Deneen, P. J. (Fall 2009/Winter 2010). Science and the decline of the liberal arts. *New Atlantis*, 26, 60–68.

Heller, M. (2002). Questioning our western tradition. In B. Cowan, & S. Lee (Eds.), *Uniting the liberal arts: Core and context* (pp. 157–167). Lanham, MD: University Press of America.

Hirsh, E. D. (1987). *Cultural literacy*. Boston: Houghton Mifflin.

Inside Higher Education (2009). The liberal arts abroad. Retrieved on August 4, 2010, from www.insidehighered.com/layout/set/print/news/2009/02/16/liberalarts.

Kaplan, D. A. (2009, October 27). MBAs get schooled in ethics. *Fortune*, pp. 27–28.

Kerr, C. (1963). *The uses of the university*. New York: Harper and Row.

Kiernan, M. (2000). The role of donors in educational reconstruction and transformation. In T. Mebrahtu, M. Crossley, & D. Johnson (Eds.), *Globalisation, educational transformation, and societies in transition* (pp. 195–207). Oxford, UK: Symposium Books.

Kimball, B. A. (1995). *Orators and philosophers: A history of the idea of liberal education*. New York: The College Board.

Lane, J. C. (1987). The Yale report of 1828 and liberal education: A neorepublican manifesto. *History of Education Quarterly*, 27, 325–338.

MacCormack, S. (1989). The "West," the liberal arts and general education. *Viewpoints: American Council of Learned Societies*. Occasional Paper, No. 10, 13–17.

Menand, L. (2010). *The marketplace of ideas: Reform and resistance in the American university*. New York: W.W. Norton & Co.

Mwiria, K. (2003). University governance and university–state relations. In D. Teferra & P. G. Altbach (Eds.), *African higher education: An international reference handbook* (pp. 32–44). Bloomington: Indiana University Press.

Nussbaum, M. C. (2003). *Cultivating humanity: A classical defense of reform in liberal education*. Cambridge, MA: Harvard University Press.

Nussbaum, M. C. (2004). Liberal education and global community. *Liberal Education*, 90(1), 42–47.

Overland, M. A. (2008). Australian universities revamp degree programs to become more like those in the U.S. *Chronicle of Higher Education*. Retrieved on October 9, 2008, from http://chronicle.com/daily/2008/09/4803n.htm.

Schneider, C. G. (2008). Liberal education takes a new turn. In *The NEA 2008 almanac of higher education*. Washington, DC: National Education Association.

Task Force on Higher Education and Society. (2000). *Higher education in developing countries: Peril and promise*. Washington, DC: The World Bank.

Weifang, M. (2004). Chinese higher education: The legacy of the past and the context of the future. In P. G. Altbach, & T. Umakoshi (Eds.), *Asian universities: Historical perspectives and contemporary challenges* (pp. 53–85). Baltimore, MD: Johns Hopkins University Press.

Wildavsky, B. (2010). Can Yale help liberalize Singapore? *Chronicle of Higher Education*. Retrieved on September 22, 2010, from http://chronicle.com/blogPost/Can-Yale-Help-Liberalize/27036/?ais+=at&utm.

World Conference on Higher Education. (1998). *Higher education in the 21st century: Vision and action.* Paris: UNESCO.

World Conference on Higher Education. (2009). *The new dynamics of higher education and research for societal change and development.* Paris: UNESCO.

Zelnick, S. (2002). Practically educated: The ACTC director's address. In B. Cowan, & S. Lee (Eds.), *Uniting the liberal arts: Core and context* (pp. xiii–xxi). Lanham, MD: University Press of America.

2

CHINA

General Education Grounded in Tradition in a Rapidly Changing Society

Kathryn Mohrman, Jinghuan Shi, and Manli Li

In China, education is seen as essential for national development. Colleges and universities are particularly important in terms of training the next generation of leaders, creating the innovative products and practices that will move China forward, and contributing to the betterment of society in general. Although much work remains to be done, over the last 30 years Chinese higher education has been transformed from a centralized, closed, and specialized collection of a few universities for a small elite, to a more open, flexible, and diversified mass higher education system. A recent government report, "Outline of China's National Plan for Medium and Long-Term Education Reform and Development (2010–2020)," not only positions education as a national strategic priority but also gives particular emphasis to fostering creativity and innovation through higher education as China seeks to become less dependent on foreign ideas, research, and corporate practices (State Council of the People's Republic of China, 2010). The introduction of general education requirements throughout Chinese higher education, starting in the 1990s, is designed to help prepare students to meet the demands of a rapidly changing, increasingly global environment.

Historical Background

China, as a country with a long history of civilization, has a rich culture that provides the core elements of its education. More than 2,000 years ago, a Confucian text outlined the purposes of education: "What the great learning teaches is to illustrate illustrious virtue, to renovate the people, and to rest in the highest excellence."[1] The purpose of traditional Confucian education was to nurture in students a willingness to become actively engaged in society, to develop a sense of social responsibility, and to become fully involved members of society and citizens of the country. In other words, this type of education focused on nurturing morally upright and politically mature human beings instead of teaching professional or instrumental knowledge and skills. As its basic goal, it laid a foundation of humanistic values and ethics. The content of education was very broad, non-professional, and non-instrumental. Since education in China has always aimed at fostering virtue and cultivating character, general education in the Western sense presents no contradictions with the traditional values of Chinese learning. In this regard, education in China has always been integrated with social and political needs.

Chinese reformers after 1840 saw borrowing knowledge from foreign countries as a shortcut for strengthening their nation. Such subjects as the natural sciences, applied technology, and foreign languages, which were not in the traditional Chinese knowledge system, were particularly welcomed. However, also starting in the late 19th century, more and more Chinese realized that foreign education was not just a collection of various facts, but a whole system of teaching and learning that China could use as an instrument of intellectual and moral formation for a new nation.

Systems of education built on separate subjects and disciplinary knowledge were brought from Western countries by foreign missionaries, by Chinese students returning from study in the West, and by Chinese intellectuals who wanted to replace traditional education with modern systems. Although officials and literati often tried to isolate Western learning, the new subject-based knowledge broadened the horizons of Chinese intellectuals and gradually created a new philosophy of scholarship in Chinese society.

As a result, Chinese intellectuals looked to the Japanese model of education in the early 20th century, the American model in the 1920s, and the Soviet model in the early 1950s. When the People's Republic of China (PRC) was created in 1949, the structure of the Chinese higher educational system resembled the American system, but the knowledge patterns were closer to those of the Soviet Union. Special emphasis was put on science, engineering, and other applied fields to meet the needs of industrialization and modernization. Although these importations, as Marianne Bastid (1987) pointed out, were in no way imposed by foreign powers, there were still contradictions between the traditional knowledge system and the modern approach in which disciplinary subjects form the core of school curriculum.

The 1980s marked an era of change in Chinese higher education. After a period of isolation from most of the world, China moved to a policy of reform and opening up to the rest of the world. In its approach to education, the Chinese government sought to prepare high-level human resources for professional, technical, and administrative positions; to generate new knowledge through research; to extend that knowledge to the society at large; and to promote the building of a harmonious society through service to economic, political, and social spheres. Thus, Chinese education today has several goals. Its economic aim is to sustain and stimulate national economic development by cultivating highly qualified citizens and by providing innovation in science and technology. Its political aim is to educate citizens with both a strong sense of national identity and a world perspective. And the cultural aim is to engage students with knowledge both from Chinese civilization and from all humanity, and to clarify the interrelationship of the local and the global.

These goals required a new structure and governance system. Starting in the late 1980s and early 1990s, the old system of centralized control was changed to a two-level system in which the state provides general supervision while provincial and local governments manage most of the delivery of educational services (see Figure 2.1). Whereas in the past, the central government was the sole provider of financial support, current funding streams are diverse, with institutions taking more responsibility for providing their own resources. Through these reforms, the autonomy of individual institutions of higher education has been enlarged.

The relationship between the state and students has also changed. All students are expected to make a reasonable financial contribution to their own higher education, while scholarships are available for those with excellent academic and moral records. Students in economic distress may apply for loans and part-time jobs. Graduates are responsible for finding their own employment, a major change from the old central planning model, which assigned students to work units, often for life.

Generally speaking, reform and development are the major trends of higher education in China over the last century. In the past 30 years, the system has

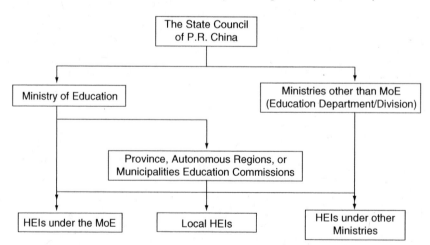

FIGURE 2.1 China's higher education administrative system (source: based on information in Ministry of Education (2008), *Education Statistics Yearbook of China*).

evolved from a unified, centralized, closed, and static system to one character-ized by diversification, decentralization, openness, and dynamism, stimulating the involvement of local governments and non-state sectors. These reforms coincide with worldwide trends of massification, marketization, and increasing globalization in higher education. The process of change will continue, however, as education must keep pace with a rapidly developing society in which reform seems to be a priority for the Chinese people.

Current Situation

In 1997, five million students were enrolled in tertiary education of all kinds; but this number increased steadily until, in 2007, it had reached 30 million, accounting for a gross enrollment ratio of 25%. Paralleling the move to mass higher education, the Chinese Ministry of Education has also emphasized quality through the national Quality Raising Project started in 2005. In addi-tion, the government provides targeted funding for the enhancement of the 39 top universities that are being positioned to be nationally and internationally competitive. Improving tertiary vocational education has been put on the pri-ority agenda in recent years, with local governments and non-governmental agencies given particular responsibility for developing vocational programs.

China has both public and private institutions of higher education, differ-entiated by four tiers of administration. First are those universities under the direct control of the Ministry of Education. Second are institutions adminis-tered by provincial governments. The third tier is institutions affiliated with various ministries or departments of the state—for example the Commission of Science, Technology, and Industry for National Defense. The fourth tier of administration is joint supervision by both central and local authorities. As part of the larger reform of the Chinese governmental system, many institu-tions of higher education were moved from the national Ministry of Education to provincial and local authorities. In addition, many smaller universities with specialized missions were combined with other institutions to form compre-hensive universities. Table 2.1 shows the number of different types of higher education institutions (HEIs) in China, and Table 2.2 depicts institutions based on disciplines.

Several of the current criticisms of Chinese higher education are related to its history. For example, the desire to create new models of general education and interdisciplinary learning is a reaction against the highly specialized pro-grams of the past (Chen, 2004; Dello-Iacovo, 2009). From the 1950s to late 1970s, Chinese higher education policies focused on training experts in differ-ent fields, especially in applied science and technology, which were needed in the period of early industrialization. Curricula were divided into detailed knowledge and skills needed in specialized labor markets; general knowledge for college students was limited to political studies and foreign languages. The

TABLE 2.1 Number of higher education institutions by institutional type, 2008

	Total	HEIs under central ministries and agencies			HEIs under local authorities			Non-state/private
		Total	HEIs under Ministry of Education	HEIs under other central agencies	Total	HEIs under local education ministries	Run by non-education departments	
Institutions providing postgraduate programs	796	374	73	301	422	359	63	–
Regular HEIs	479	98	73	25	381	358	23	–
Research institutes	317	276	–	276	41	1	40	–
Regular HEIs	**2,263**	**111**	**73**	**38**	**1,502**	**852**	**650**	**638**
University	1,079	106	73	33	604	533	71	369
Colleges with specialized courses	1,184	5	–	5	910	326	584	269
Vocational and technical colleges	1,036	2	–	2	770	260	510	264
HEIs for adults	**400**	**14**	**1**	**13**	**384**	**159**	**225**	**2**
Other private HEIs	**866**	–	–	–	–	–	–	**866**

Source: Ministry of Education (2008), *Education Statistics Yearbook of China*.

TABLE 2.2 Number of different types of regular HEIs on the basis of disciplines, 2008

	Total	Universities and colleges	Short-cycle colleges	
			Regular	Tertiary vocational/technical colleges
Total	2,263	1,079	1,184	1,036
Comprehensive university	533	246	287	281
Natural sciences and technology	801	320	481	458
Agriculture	83	41	42	40
Forestry	18	7	11	11
Medicine and pharmacy	159	103	56	14
Teacher training	188	140	48	4
Language and literature	48	21	27	26
Finance and economics	237	110	127	112
Political science and law	69	23	46	32
Physical culture	30	16	14	13
Art	80	39	41	41
Ethnic nationality	17	13	4	4
Non-state/private colleges	638	369	269	264

Source: Ministry of Education (2008), *Education Statistics Yearbook of China*.

case studies of general education reforms in this chapter reflect a response to this history.

A second criticism of the education system, especially at the secondary level, is linked to the rigid, selective examination system for university admissions. China has more applicants than places in its higher education institutions. Students and teachers give priority to the memorization of material for the tests, while placing less emphasis on analysis, innovation, and critical thinking. Many reformers are trying to change this balance, but the examination system still dominates.

As a third example, senior high school students are divided into two tracks. In social sciences, students focus on history and geography. In the natural sciences, students emphasize physics, chemistry, and biology. Both groups are required to study common subjects such as Chinese literature, mathematics, physical training, and a foreign language. Reforms of elementary and secondary education have brought changes, not only in curricula, but also in the development of new textbooks and the adoption of new teaching and learning methods. New trials and experiments are flourishing in schools. New concepts such as student-centered, activity-based, and integrated learning are becoming more widely accepted, not only in schools but also by the whole society. Reforms at the senior secondary level have included elective courses, research opportunities, and interdisciplinary courses. Integrated learning of science combines physics, chemistry, and biology while comprehensive social learning emphasizes practical knowledge and skill in social life. These new courses are considered complements to the subject-based curricula, while test-oriented education still predominates. However, these changes reflect a greater awareness of the importance of general education in the basic requirements for high school students. While this approach to general education is not as broad as the situation in some countries, these innovations will continue as China pursues higher quality education and international competitiveness.

In 2003 the Ministry of Education published an influential report, declaring that China should move from being the country with the largest population to a country with richer human resources (Project of Education and Human Resources, 2003). In 2010, the Fourth National Conference on Education issued a 10-year plan for education. This plan describes the challenges facing Chinese education in the 21st century, including strengthening the reform in basic school education, increasing enrollment, expanding access to higher education, and making institutional structures and curricula reform better fit the country's social and economic development. Among hot issues in higher education debates today are the two-track system in senior secondary education, reforming the college entrance examination system, and expanding general education at the college level. The nationwide discussion surrounding the new national strategy will certainly bring a new tide of educational reform for Chinese education at all levels.

Curricular Reform on the Undergraduate Level

Under the old command-and-control system, most academic decisions were made by the national Ministry of Education. Students applied for a specific major and studied nothing else for their four undergraduate years. The curriculum was totally required and unified. Students entered as a cohort, everyone in a given major took the same courses at the same time, and it was very difficult for students to select courses not included in their major.

Faculty, too, conformed to a rigid system. They taught courses prescribed by the Ministry of Education with little room for creativity or personal preferences. The standard pedagogical approach was a teacher lecturing from a raised platform at the front of the room while students sat in rows taking notes. Memorization was the standard way to study for examinations that often demanded recall of facts more than the application of knowledge or creative problem solving. Required courses sometimes remained the same for a number of years, leading to yellowed lecture notes and outdated information.

Much of the reform of higher education has focused on the curriculum. More autonomy has been granted to individual colleges and universities, especially top institutions, to develop their own academic programs and courses. As a result, many specialized institutions have become comprehensive universities; some have created new campuses and even quasi-private colleges with curricula different from the main institution. Departments and individual faculty members have more freedom to choose textbooks, devise syllabi, create new courses, and pursue interdisciplinary innovations. While government officials must still approve new academic programs, these programs need not follow a single path as before.

Given these reforms, students also have more freedom. While China still has a national college entrance examination system, more students are admitted because of special achievement or secondary school recommendations. As described in detail in the next section of this chapter, Chinese colleges and universities are expected to offer a series of general education courses outside the students' majors, usually in the form of distribution requirements in which students can choose from a long list of courses and earn a certain number of credits in different disciplinary areas. Some elite institutions even allow students to enroll without declaring a major until the end of the first or second year of undergraduate study. Most majors now allow some choice of courses within the major, providing more opportunities for students to exercise their academic preferences (Kai, 2005; Kirby, 2008).

In addition to academic flexibility for both students and faculty, institutions and undergraduates are highly sensitive to the labor market. With massification, Chinese universities are turning out millions more baccalaureate graduates than they did a decade or two ago, leading to significant unemployment or underemployment among college graduates. Students and their families think hard about job prospects when considering what major to choose, although both students and government have favored regular institutions of higher education over vocational/technical schools. Universities, too, look at the labor market in creating new programs, allocating resources, and positioning themselves in a more market-oriented higher education system. Greater flexibility also means greater uncertainties for everyone involved.

Case Studies of General Education

In the last two decades, the Ministry of Education has strongly encouraged universities, colleges, and vocational schools in China to develop general education programs. As a result, all college students in China experience general education, at least in theory. The motivation for reform was the acknowledgment by both government and universities that narrowly trained graduates would not be productive in a rapidly changing job market nor would they have well-balanced personalities (Feng & Guo, 2007). Each institution determines its curricular specifics depending on faculty interest, institutional priorities, and academic strengths (Li, 1999; Wang & Li, 2001). The case studies provided here give a good sense of the range of academic and extracurricular structures employed by some of the leading universities in China. In addition, many other institutions look to the top universities as models for their own reform programs and sometimes wait to see what the leading institutions have done before developing their own general education curricula, so these universities have an influence that goes beyond their own faculty and students.

Although traditional Chinese education was more holistic than subject-based learning, only in the last century has the Western philosophy and practice of liberal education become familiar in Chinese higher education circles. With increasing contacts between China and the United States in the first half of the 20th century, American concepts of general and liberal education became popular in China. Colleges and universities founded by foreigners were especially likely to implement Western—often American-style—liberal arts curricula. For more than two decades after the creation of the People's Republic of China, however, the government followed a model of higher education that emphasized rigid subject-based knowledge plus moral-political studies.

In the reforms of the 1980s and 1990s, many Chinese universities revised their undergraduate programs to include general education as a crucial element to strengthen academic excellence. The term most often used is *wenhua suzhi jiaoyu*, which means cultural quality education and harkens back to traditional concepts about the importance of educated individuals in Chinese society.

In Mainland China, the typical undergraduate program in higher education institutions has three components: (a) Ministry of Education compulsory courses, (b) *wenhua suzhi jiaoyu* courses, and (c) courses required for the major. In some cases, students have free electives as well. Specialized courses for the major are provided as courses of concentration/major by academic departments such as Chinese literature, mathematics, or electrical engineering.

This chapter refers to courses required by the Ministry of Education (e.g., political theory, military training, English language, and sports) as "Ministry of Education compulsory courses." The *wenhua suzhi jiaoyu* courses are determined by individual institutions. Different universities use different terms for this part of the curriculum; for example, some universities name *wenhua suzhi jiaoyu* courses as "general education elective curriculum," while others call these courses the "cultural quality curriculum." Both the Ministry of Education compulsory courses and the *wenhua suzhi jiaoyu* courses fall outside the students' field of concentration and have the primary goal of cultivating the whole person.

The Ministry of Education compulsory courses are the same at all institutions of higher education in China. The goals of *wenhua suzhi jiaoyu* are shared by all universities, but the implementation of the goals and the exact configuration of courses differ from one campus to another depending on faculty interests and institutional strengths. The case studies below demonstrate the philosophy and practice of *wenhua suzhi jiaoyu*, as well as the Ministry of Education compulsory courses, through curricular offerings, extracurricular activities, and organizational structure in different universities.

Structure of the Common Courses

In most major universities in China today, undergraduate students must fulfill required credits in both Ministry of Education compulsory courses and in *wenhua suzhi jiaoyu* courses. Chinese academics consider these non-specialized, non-major courses as general education, even though that description is different from the definition used on other countries represented in this volume. Table 2.3 presents the undergraduate program of several leading universities in China. At Tsinghua University, for example, with its traditional strength in engineering and technology, non-major courses account for 22% of a typical undergraduate's program, while at Zhejiang University the comparable figure is 33%. Overall, non-major education represents between one-quarter and one-third of the undergraduate program at the universities represented, which is not too different from the American experience.

Distribution of the Common Courses

As already noted, the Ministry of Education compulsory courses are mandated by the Ministry of Education and implemented by all colleges and universities. The newer *wenhua suzhi jiaoyu* courses, designed to broaden students' knowledge and perspectives, are usually based on current faculty interests and available academic resources. For example, at Peking University, the *wenhua suzhi jiaoyu* curriculum offers more than 300 choices in five categories: mathematics

TABLE 2.3 General education curriculum in three Chinese universities (by credits required)

Distribution of common courses	Course categories	Peking University	Zhejiang University	Tsinghua University
Ministry of Education compulsory courses	Common English series	8	9	6
	Political series	12	13.5	14
	Military sports series	6	5.5	7
Wenhua suzhi jiaoyu courses	Mathematics and natural sciences	2	3	2
	Social sciences	2	3	4
	History	2	3	1
	Language, literature, and arts	4	1.5	2
	Philosophy and psychology	2	0	2
	Communication and leadership	–	1.5	3
	Technology and design	3	2	–
Total credits required for bachelor's degree		140–150	116	175
Percentage of total in non-specialized, non-major courses		25–27%	33%	22%
Percentage in wenhua suzhi jiaoyu courses		8–9%	10%	7%

Notes
Course guides for undergraduate programs: Peking University (2008), Zhejiang University (2007), Tsinghua University (2006).

and sciences; history; philosophy and psychology; social sciences; and language, literature, and arts. These courses are the responsibility of the relevant departments—physics, history, economics, art, and so on. Every student must take at least two credits in each of the five categories, as well as the Ministry of Education compulsory courses.

These reforms at Peking University draw on the institution's history as a multidisciplinary comprehensive university with well-known professors committed to offering courses to cultivate students' broad educational experience. As early as the 1920s and 1930s, students were encouraged to choose courses from different disciplines outside their majors (Wang, 2005). In the early stages of reform in the 1990s, Peking University set up a number of cross-school elective courses that combined liberal arts with science. Many of the general education courses are taught by top academicians and famous researchers at the university.

In contrast, Tsinghua University has created eight groups of courses: four credits in language and art, at least one of which must be in the art curriculum; history and culture; literature, philosophy, and life; science and technology; technology and society; contemporary China and the world; arts education; and law, economics, and management. Students in science and engineering must earn at least 13 credits in the eight categories, while liberal arts students must take certain courses in science and technology. In order to raise the quality of *wenhua suzhi jiaoyu* courses, Tsinghua has strengthened the process of review before offering the courses and has also given greater attention to students' evaluations of their courses and professors.

Zhejiang University divides its approximately 300 courses into 10 categories: ideology, military sports, and language (the Ministry of Education compulsory courses); basic computer, history and culture, literature and art, economics and society, communication and leadership, science and research, and technology and design (the *wenhua suzhi jiaoyu* courses). All students must earn three credits in history and culture, but they may choose among more than 40 courses in this category, including Chinese philosophy, architectural history, PRC history, Western art history, the Silk Road and Mo Gao Grottoes art, and Chinese tea culture.

Administrative Approaches

Chinese universities bear the responsibility of creating their own approaches to general education. Most institutions' current programs have followed the successes of pilot programs introduced by the Ministry of Education in 1999, usually coordinated by the undergraduate education staff in the provost's office. Curricular offerings are enhanced on some campuses by two administrative approaches: strengthening the educational impact of extracurricular activities and creating new management systems for undergraduate education.

For example, in 1994 Huazhong University of Science and Technology instituted a series called Humanistic Quality Education Lectures, which has since offered more than 1,400 events with a total audience of more than 50 million people. Many influential professors, scholars, and political figures have given speeches in this series, allowing students to benefit from their teaching style and knowledge, absorbing their positive thoughts and culture.

At Tsinghua University, student associations have flourished. In 2007, more than 100 student groups involved about 20,000 members in such activities as sports, science and technology, arts, humanities and social sciences, and the commonweal. These organizations have developed into one of the important aspects of cultivating students' interests, encouraging healthy growth, providing space for self-education, and developing an active cultural life on campus. At the same time, these student associations play an important role in the development of school values, moral education, the popularization of scientific knowledge and practice, employment guidance, harmonious campus building, and voluntary social service. Coordinated with Tsinghua's *wenhua suzhi jiaoyu* courses, the associations create a favorable atmosphere in which the students can grow.

Fudan University exemplifies the second approach—the establishment of new management systems for general education. Fudan takes the intellectual approach that general education first and foremost is an educational philosophy. Operationally, Fudan believes that general education is a system; the implementation of general education reform requires its own system both for curriculum as well as for activities outside class. In 2007, Fudan University reformed its management system, promoting general education as the core and creating Fudan College as the mechanism for these reforms.

Fudan College is an undergraduate teaching unit as well as a student affairs unit with four residential colleges. All undergraduate students (including international students), regardless of discipline, are members of Fudan College, usually for one year but two years for students in the eight-year clinical medicine program.

The four residential colleges are the basic units of student management. They also continue the cultural tradition of the Chinese *shuyuan* academy while drawing upon the experiences of residential colleges in foreign universities. The four colleges are named after the school's most respected past presidents. Each college has a uniform, school song, unique plaque and couplets, separate apartment buildings, and a museum that showcases the former president's deeds to strengthen students' recognition of school culture and history. Students of different backgrounds, interests, talents, expertise, and locales all live together, promoting multi-cultural integration and international exchanges while overcoming emotional alienation. This reform at Fudan is designed to encourage students to gain an education that fully and effectively combines the universal and the specialized, the curricular and the extracurricular.

The most recent experiment in general education is at Zhongshan University (Sun Yat-sen University) in the south of China. Its new Liberal Arts College was established in 2009 with, as dean, Professor Gan Yang, a scholar well known for actively promoting general education in China (Gan, 2006). The goal of the college is the cultivation of elites equipped with well-organized general knowledge and the creation of leaders in the fields of liberal arts, humanities, and social sciences. The students are admitted through a highly selective process and live together at the Nanshan campus separate from the main campus of Zhongshan University. The curriculum for students during the four-year undergraduate program includes classic Chinese, Greek, Latin, and other foundations of ancient civilizations.

According to the ideas of both the president of Zhongshan University and Gan Yang himself, the Liberal Arts College is not just a separate program for a small group of students, but a pilot project for the transformation of the whole university, leading to reform in the country's higher education system. It is too early to evaluate the program and to predict the influence it may bring, but there is no doubt that it represents a challenge to the entire university system. The continuing emphasis on innovation in undergraduate education, and especially in general education, freely predicts more such reforms in higher education in China.

The Special Case of Hong Kong

In 2004 the University Grants Committee of Hong Kong (the equivalent of a ministry of education) announced that its higher education undergraduate degrees would henceforth require four, rather than three, years, while secondary education would shrink from seven to six years. The total number of spaces in tertiary education would also increase. A comprehensive planning process is now underway, with the new system due to commence in the fall of 2012. The change, commonly referred to as "3+3+4," has eight goals: to align with four-year first degrees in Mainland China, North America, and Europe; to give students a broader academic experience, including more exposure to disciplines outside the student's major field; to give greater attention to non-academic learning and extracurricular experiences; to increase opportunities for foreign study; to focus on the development of the whole student; to promote tighter linkages to the workplace; to require outcomes-based assessment; and to develop graduates who are capable of succeeding in the global knowledge economy and able to meet society's rapidly changing needs.

As the chairman of the University Grants Committee (UGC) stated, "Extending the normative length of undergraduate study is not simply shifting one year of secondary education to the tertiary level, or add[ing] one foundation year to undergraduate studies" (Cha, 2008). "Hong Kong higher education is being asked to do nothing less than 're-invent' itself—a tall order!"

declare two American observers (Finkelstein & Walker, 2008, p. 3). The change is seen by many as a major shift in educational philosophy, moving away from a focus on specialization to a more holistic approach to the educational experience (Stone, 2008).

While Hong Kong is a Special Administrative Region of the PRC, it is largely autonomous in matters of higher education. Thus, the Hong Kong government, not Beijing, is directing the reforms described here. Hong Kong's independence in these matters also means that the Ministry of Education requirements for Mainland students are not applicable in Hong Kong's universities; faculty and administrators in Hong Kong institutions of higher education determine their own curricular reforms and design their own course structures.

Hong Kong has eight baccalaureate-granting universities and a host of two- and three-year institutions (see Table 2.4). As Finkelstein and Walker (2008) point out, the missions and histories of the eight lead to different curricular approaches to the common goal. At the three historic research universities (University of Hong Kong, Chinese University of Hong Kong, and Hong Kong University of Science and Technology), faculty and administrators are focusing on the first-year experience as well as on the middle and latter parts of the undergraduate program. This dual focus is shared to a lesser extent by Hong Kong Polytechnic University and City University of Hong Kong. Within these institutions, the professional disciplines such as medicine and law (both fields are undergraduate programs) tend to emphasize the ending years in terms of articulation with postgraduate professional practice.

In the past, Hong Kong Baptist University and Chinese University have offered four-year degrees based on their American origins. Lingnan University and Chinese University also have a long history of general education requirements which most Hong Kong institutions lack because they have followed a British model. While different institutions use different terminology, their planned curricula certainly move in the direction of greater attention to general and liberal education as defined in this volume.

What are Hong Kong universities planning in anticipation of 2012? The University Grants Committee and the Hong Kong legislature have supported a series of workshops and conferences on the 3+3+4 reform, as well as significant funding for internal planning activities. While the overall goals are shared, each institution is charged with developing a curriculum and student support program in line with its own mission and history. The similarities are great, however, across the eight universities, perhaps because of the strong role played by the University Grants Committee. Finkelstein and Walker (2008, pp. 11–15) observe six commonalities: approximately 120 course credits for the four-year undergraduate degree; distribution requirements of approximately 30 credits over four to six broad areas such as science and technology, arts and humanities, and society and human forms of organization; language

TABLE 2.4 Responses of Hong Kong universities to the 3+3+4 reforms

	HKU	CUHK	UST	Poly U	City U	HKBU	Lingnan	IED
New core course	–	X	–	–	–	X	X	–
New university distribution requirement	X	–	X	X	X	X	X	X
IT literacy	–	X	–	–	–	X	–	–
Chinese heritage	–	X	–	X	X	X	X	–
Residential education	X	X	X	–	–	–	–	–
Internships	X	–	–	X	X	X	X	X
Service learning	X	–	–	X	–	X	X	–
Foreign study	X	X	X	X	X	X	X	X
Interdisciplinary focus	X	X	X	–	–	–	X	–
Capstone experience	–	X	–	X	–	X	–	–

Source: Finkelstein & Walker (2008).

Notes
HKU, University of Hong Kong; CUHK, Chinese University of Hong Kong; UST, Hong Kong University of Science and Technology; Poly U, Polytechnic University; City U, City University of Hong Kong; HKBU, Hong Kong Baptist University; Lingnan, Lingnan University; IED, Hong Kong Institute of Education.

requirements in Chinese and English of six to 12 credits (the University of Hong Kong, as the historic colonial university, continues to teach only in English, while the Chinese University of Hong Kong emphasizes its role as a bridge between East and West, teaching in English, Cantonese, and Mandarin); a common core course required of all first-year students on some campuses; expanded foreign study options and an increase in the intake of foreign students; and increased internship and service-learning opportunities.

An examination of the planned curriculum on two Hong Kong campuses— the University of Hong Kong and the Chinese University of Hong Kong— gives a sense of current thinking about general and liberal education. The University of Hong Kong describes its goals as enabling students to develop their capacities to pursue academic/professional excellence, critical intellectual inquiry, and life-long learning; tackle novel situations and ill-defined problems; enact personal and professional ethics, self-reflection, and a greater understanding of others; acquire intercultural understanding and become global citizens; develop skills in communication and collaboration; and provide leadership and advocacy to improve the human condition (Tsui, 2009).

This new undergraduate curriculum requires 240 credits, with one credit equaling 20 to 30 student workload hours. Required of all students will be 12 credits of English, six credits of Chinese, and 36 credits in the common core (details below) totaling 23% of the four undergraduate years. Specialization through majors will require 30–40% and through minors 15–20%. Electives will round out students' programs.

A campus steering committee describes the common core's goal as seeking

> to help students see the interconnected and the interdependent nature of human existence through exploring some common human experiences. The word "common" delimits the scope of the curriculum and the word "core" defines its essence. The former draws attention to the commonality of human experiences and the latter to those matters that have been, and continue to be, of deeply profound significance to humankind.
> (Tsui, 2009)

The common core follows the familiar distribution pattern of four broad areas: scientific and technological literacy; the humanities; global issues; and Chinese culture, state, and society. In addition, Tsui mentions attention to diverse modes of learning, including experiential, case- and inquiry-based learning, and small-group collaboration. The similarity to U.S. university practices is no accident; in several of the symposium programs posted on the Internet, American experts are prominent as invited speakers.

The Chinese University of Hong Kong has a slightly different approach, perhaps based in its long tradition of general education requirements. It will require all students to take two foundation courses—"Classics for Today:

In Search of a Good Life and Good Society" and "Science in Classics: Exploring the Universe and Life" (Wong & Chiu, 2009). The common goals of these courses are developing one's self-awareness as humans and the development of an authentic self through the cultivation of moral values. These two courses are envisioned as small, seminar-based discussions of great thoughts about perennial human concerns. The goal is to move from text-based courses to issue-based dialogue and discovery. All sections of the foundation courses will use the same syllabus and move at the same pace. Wong and Chiu (2009) outline readings and core questions in their presentation.

The two courses required of all undergraduates at the Chinese University of Hong Kong are designed to prepare them for the existing general education program of at least one course in each of four areas: Chinese cultural heritage; nature, science, and technology; society and culture; and self and humanity. In addition, it has four undergraduate residential colleges, with two more planned as part of the expansion in Hong Kong higher education. Each college requires six credits of college-determined general education courses, ranging in different colleges from an introductory course about the idea of the university to mandatory assemblies, senior seminars, high-table dinners, and elective college-based courses.

The combination of the fourth year of undergraduate study, plus larger enrollments, will require a significant increase in the number of teaching faculty on all eight campuses. Such growth is likely to pose difficult challenges for Hong Kong universities as they seek to raise their stature in the international arena (achieved largely through research and publications) while also providing a new, high-quality undergraduate experience for more students. There may be a temptation to follow some of the less desirable aspects of the American higher education system, such as heavy reliance on graduate students as teaching assistants and the tendency to develop a two-track/second-class faculty in which some professors are undergraduate-only or teaching-only. There is also a danger in distribution programs of developing a list of courses so lengthy that little commonality can be perceived. In addition, any new curriculum will require a concerted effort to maintain its enthusiasm and rigor once the initial excitement and novelty have faded. Despite these concerns, however, the Hong Kong experiment is a bold move in the direction of liberal arts and general education.

Contemporary Challenges in Higher Education

Higher education in China faces a series of challenges that have real implications for the long-term success of general education.

The Challenge of Social Transition and Marketization

Like most other countries in the world, China has looked to market forces to finance its higher education system. The recruitment and training of personnel reflects market demand, and students are increasingly attentive to the needs of the job market when selecting majors. The uncertainty and constant fluctuations of the job market have caused instability in higher education and have eroded the integrity of teaching and research. Many students and their parents favor the pursuit of a specialized education that equips the graduate with vocationally relevant knowledge and skills—with the result that such students neglect general education targeted at the cultivation of the whole person.

The System's Uniformity and the Unified Entrance Exam

As a large country with limited resources in higher education, China has a strict entrance examination system to select students for higher education. Passing the entrance exam with high scores seems to be the motivation for many students in secondary school. The exam-oriented system misappropriates students' time, constrains their interests and creativity, and even impacts their overall physical and psychological development. The original goal of education is distorted or forgotten. In the cases described in this chapter, Hong Kong has clearly addressed the linkage between secondary education and higher education, while institutions on the Mainland are working toward an overall reform of the system.

Making General Education Central to the Undergraduate Program

While Chinese students are required to take a significant portion of their undergraduate courses outside the major, many do not believe that these courses improve their comprehensive knowledge, ability, and quality and, as a result, do not take them seriously. In addition, in many universities, the general education curriculum lacks organic links and cannot be integrated into the total undergraduate program. Neither professors nor students consider general education courses as fundamental academic training but rather as an opportunity to expand knowledge and to learn a bit about everything; often these courses are relatively easy to pass. As a consequence, general education is too often seen as additional or marginal, the departments offering them do not take such courses seriously, and, at times, neither do the universities themselves.

Providing Organizational Structures that Link "Universal" and "Special"

The establishment of Fudan College and Liberal Arts College in Zhongshan University represent systematic breakthroughs that are both pioneering and creative. These new organizational units provide an institutional guarantee for the students regarding both general education courses and the larger goal of cultivation of the whole person. The Hong Kong experience, especially at the Chinese University of Hong Kong, is similarly motivated. In the long run, then, the development of general education in China's universities will continue to reach a new stage.

Prospects for the Future

Because of the strong desire to keep pace with the global trend and increase China's national capacity through education, the country's higher education can, in some respects, be seen as seeking to do everything at once—expand access to higher education, reform the curriculum, launch *wenhua suzhi jiaoyu* requirements, change the funding structure, encourage interdisciplinary work, become internationally competitive, do cutting-edge research, and more. These goals are laudable, but the country's ability to implement them for tens of millions of students simultaneously is questionable. National and local governments have invested substantial resources in higher education, especially in top universities, but the funding has not kept pace with the needs.

As a result, many Chinese academics believe that the overall quality of higher education has declined, especially at the undergraduate level. Massification has led to higher student/faculty ratios, overcrowded classrooms and laboratories, and fewer opportunities for meaningful academic interaction between faculty and undergraduate students—problems that China shares with a number of other countries seeking to expand their higher education systems.

Wenhua suzhi jiaoyu has always been conceptualized as a curricular structure that exposes students to disciplines and concepts outside their major fields. As such, it most closely resembles what Patti McGill Peterson describes in Chapter 1 as general education with distribution requirements described by themes or disciplines. Many universities are finding it a challenge, however, to offer enough high-quality courses for all students, especially when the incentives for faculty push in the opposite direction. True, all Chinese faculty members are expected to teach undergraduates; but, as is the case in other countries, most professors prefer to teach their specialties rather than non-major introductory courses. Departments with large numbers of students sometimes look upon general education courses as a burden when the students in those courses are not "their" majors. At least at comprehensive universities, faculty also are expected to produce more research and publications than ever before, so professors face the dilemma of multiple demands on their time.

The rapid expansion of *wenhua suzhi jiaoyu* to all institutions of higher education has not been matched by equivalent faculty development efforts. Comprehensive universities probably have the easiest time in implementing this reform since they can draw upon a broad array of departments and faculty expertise to offer a menu of general education courses. More specialized institutions, however, may not have faculty in the humanities or the natural sciences who can quickly assume these responsibilities. While in theory all Chinese college students are exposed to disciplines outside their majors, the reality may differ widely.

Issues of pedagogy are only beginning to be discussed in most Chinese universities. Partly because of tradition and partly because of fiscal constraints, large lecture classes are the reality for most students. The experiment of freshman seminars at Tsinghua University is an exception, probably possible only at a few affluent top institutions. But regardless of the size of the classes, the question remains: "What is the teaching style? What kinds of interactions occur between faculty and students and among the students themselves?" The goals of liberal learning include creative inquiry, analysis, innovation, critical thinking, and written and oral communication skills. To date, most universities have not given systematic attention to these issues.

The 11th five-year plan for 2006–2010 calls for the nation to become an innovative society (National Development and Reform Commission, 2005). The English-language overview of the plan frequently uses such phrases as "independent innovation" and "abundant human capital" to describe China's direction. "The Outline of China's National Plan for Medium and Long-Term Education Reform and Development (2010–2020)," published in 2010, clearly identified education's general goal as promoting the all-around development of students. It is reasonable to expect that, with the implementation of the national plan, *wenhua suzhi jiaoyu* in higher education will be strengthened. New trials in broadening knowledge bases, integrating subject-based learning, and stimulating innovation through overall capacity building are important steps in reforms that will bring China to a new stage of development.

In conclusion, then, general education in China is both a long tradition and an imported Western concept. As a result, the current situation is complex because of conflicts between Chinese culture and Western influence. The concept of educating the whole person has deep historical roots in China, but the general education curriculum in today's universities draws strongly on Western approaches (Ma, 2009). The first generation of Chinese intellectuals who turned their eyes to Western education was especially attracted to subject-based knowledge, especially in applied science and technology, for strengthening and modernizing the nation. Western concepts of general education seemed unclear and often ambiguous, especially when tinged with religious overtones. The recent history of university development in China, following different models from Europe, the United States, and the Soviet Union at different times, has further confused the real meaning of general education.

The second characteristic of Chinese higher education is the close connection with social change and therefore its susceptibility to outside influences. For example, Chinese reformers a century ago sought to master Western engineering and sciences in order to resist foreign aggression. General education has not been linked in the same way to broader social objectives; most of the debate has occurred within educational circles, not in the whole society. The reforms that began in the 1980s, however, have the potential for connecting general education to larger national goals of economic development and a harmonious society. Adopting international standards and developing Western-influenced curricula are bridges connecting China with other parts of the world, as well as strengthening the national identities of Chinese young people. General education in this context is responding to the changing society and confronting the multiple needs of national development. This perspective helps to clarify the real meaning of general education in the Chinese context.

The third characteristic is the need to create a new model of general education with Chinese characteristics, building on the tradition of education as the all-around development of the whole person. Currently both government and ordinary people have realized that China's social progress requires different kinds of talents and that a well-organized general education system will produce graduates with higher levels of knowledge, ability, and character. As a result, Chinese universities are experimenting with different approaches to higher education overall and to general education programs specifically. But they are still experiments and are often limited to the most prestigious national universities. General education will achieve its full potential in China only with further reforms that will transform all aspects of the largest tertiary education system in the world.

Note

1 This quotation comes from the *Great Learning*, Chapter 42 in the *Book of Rites*, one of the classics of Confucianism. Cheng Hao and Cheng Yi, scholars in the Song Dynasty, pulled out the *Great Learning* and edited it as a separate volume. Later, Zhu Xi, another scholar in the Song Dynasty, combined the *Great Learning* with the *Doctrine of the Mean*, the *Analects of Confucius*, and the *Mencius* to create the *Four Books*.

References

Bastid, M. (1987). Servitude or liberation? The introduction of foreign educational practices and systems to China from 1840 to the present. In R. Hayhoe, & M. Bastid (Eds.), *China's education and the industrialized world: Studies in cultural transfer* (pp. 3–20). Armonk, NY: M. E. Sharpe.

Cha, L. M. (2008). *Partnering for excellence in education.* Speech at Partnering for Excellence in Education Symposium at the Hong Kong Institute of Education, Hong Kong. Retrieved on July 16, 2009, from http://ugc.edu.hk/eng/ugc/publication/speech/2008/sp20081206.htm.

Chen, X. (2004). Social changes and the revival of liberal education in China since the 1990s. *Asia Pacific Education Review, 5*(1), 1–13.

Dello-Iacovo, B. (2009). Curriculum reform and "quality education" in China: An overview. *International Journal of Educational Development, 29,* 241–249.

Feng, H., & Guo, M. (2007). General education curriculum reforming [sic] advance in the universities of China Mainland. *US–China Education Review, 4*(7), 23–25.

Finkelstein, M. J., & Walker, E. W. (2008). *The progress of Hong Kong's universities in implementing the 3–3–4 reforms: A status report on preparations and prospects.* Wah Ching Center for Research on Education in China (University of Hong Kong) and the Hong Kong-America Center. Retrieved on July 18, 2009, from www.hku.hk/chinaed/Finkelstein/HK.FINAL%20REPORT.version1.2.03SEPT08%20final.pdf.

Gan, Y. (2006). *Da xue tong shi jiao yu de liang ge zhong xin huan jie* [Two key links in the general education in universities]. *Du Shu, 4,* 3–11.

Kai, J. (2005). The centre-periphery model and cross-national educational transfer: The influence of the U.S. on teaching reform in China's universities. *Asia Pacific Journal of Education, 25*(2), 227–239.

Kirby, W. C. (2008, Summer). On Chinese, European, and American universities. *Daedalus, 137,* 139–146.

Li, M. (1999). *Tong shi jiao yu: yi zhong da xue jiao yu guan* [General education: A view of higher education]. Bejing: Tsinghua University Press.

Ma, W. (2009). The prospects and dilemmas in Americanizing Chinese higher education. *Asia Pacific Education Review, 10,* 117–124.

Ministry of Education of the People's Republic of China. (2008). *Education statistics yearbook of China.* Beijing, China: People's Education Press.

Ministry of Education of the People's Republic of China. (2009). *Education statistics (higher education).* Retrieved on July 15, 2009, from www.Ministry of Education.edu.cn/edoas/website18/level2.jsp?tablename=1261364343113580.

National Development and Reform Commission of the People's Republic of China. (2005). The outline of the eleventh five-year plan for [the] national economic and social development of the People's Republic of China. Retrieved on August 17, 2009, from http://en.ndrc.gov.cn/hot/W020060531535873293851.jpg.

Project of Education and Human Resources in China. (2003). *Striving China from a country with the largest population to a country with richer human resources.* Beijing: Higher Education Press.

State Council of the People's Republic of China. (2010). Outline of China's national plan for medium and long-term education reform and development (2010–2020). Retrieved on August 8, 2010, from www.gov.cn/jrzg/2010-07/29/content_1667143.htm.

Stone, M. V. (2008). *The university grants committee and "3+3+4."* Keynote speech at Partnering for Excellence in Education symposium, Hong Kong Institute of Education, Hong Kong. Retrieved on July 9, 2009, from www.ugc.edu.hk/eng/ugc/publication/speech/2008/sp2008120602.htm.

Tsui, A. B. M. (2009). *HKU common core curriculum: What is "common" and what is "core?"* Presentation at the 3+3+4 Symposium on "Core Curriculum," University of Hong Kong. Retrieved on October 8, 2009, from www.ln.edu.hk/334symposium/files/Keynote-What-is-Core-Prof-Amy-BM-Tsui.pdf.

Wang, Y. (2005). *Tui jin tong shi jiao yu, cui sheng yi zhong xin de jiao shi mo shi* [A model of cross-disciplinary education]. *Journal of Peking University (Philosophy and Social Sciences)*, 5, 191–197.

Wang, Y., & Li, M. (2001). The concept of general education in Chinese higher education. In R. Hayhoe, & J. Pan (Eds.), *Knowledge across cultures: A contribution to dialogue among civilizations* (pp. 311–321). Hong Kong: Comparative Education Research Centre.

Wong, W.-h., & Chiu, J. (2009). *Teaching core texts.* Presentation at the 3+3+4 Symposium on General Education, Chinese University of Hong Kong. Retrieved on October 15, 2009, from www.cuhk.edu.hk/oge/gesymposium/presentation/Julie_TeachingCoreText.pdf.

Zhou, M. (2005). *Zhong guo gao deng jiao yu gai ge yu fa zhan de zheng ce cuo shi* [Policies of higher education reform and development in China]. *China Higher Education Research*, 5, P4–P6.

3

INDIA

Structural Roadblocks to Academic Reform

Pawan Agarwal and Rajashree Srinivasan

Introduction

Higher education in India has received significant attention in recent years, much of it focused on widening access and ensuring equity in access. There is some interest in relevance and quality as well, due to an intensifying lack of crucial skills despite the growing incidence of graduate unemployment. Issues of relevance and quality are, however, viewed in the limited context of career training and concentrate on training students in narrowly marketable skills rather than on graduating well-rounded people. This perspective raises doubts about whether there is clarity on the objectives of higher education itself.

The role of higher education in India has evolved over time. During the colonial era, it served the interests of the British. During the early years of independence, higher education was assigned the task of nation building. Now higher education provides India with a competitive edge in the global knowledge economy. It is now increasingly recognized that higher education in India has failed to align itself with the priorities for nation building and modernization, raising concerns about whether it can achieve the task currently assigned to it.

This chapter looks at trends in the Indian higher education with particular reference to general education, an approach that provides broad exposure to fields of knowledge and that forms the basis for developing intellectual and civic capacities. It examines the issue of flexibility in curriculum that allows for student choice, student-centered pedagogy, and the demands for breadth and depth of study both within and outside the classroom. These elements are usually associated with liberal arts education, which is geared to building good human beings and responsible citizens and to imparting universal intellectual values that transcend subject boundaries. Liberal arts education is now seen as an essential force for building and maintaining a modern economy and a modern society.

The chapter begins with a discussion of the origins of and influences on the country's education system. It then provides an overview of secondary education with particular reference to curricular issues, following up with a review of the country's higher education, its stated goals, existing academic arrangements, and innovative practices at the national and institutional level. Finally, the chapter draws conclusions from the country's experience with academic reforms and provides a prognosis about the future.

Higher Education's Origin and Influences

The modern Indian system of higher education is largely based on the British model, but it also has elements from the oriental culture, in which learning historically was pursued for its own sake without reference to economic or other external factors. According to the fascinating accounts by Chinese scholars Xuanzang (AD 602–644) and I-Ching (AD 635–713), the famous ancient Indian universities of Nalanda and Vikramshila developed pedagogical systems largely devoted to widening their students' spiritual horizons. In ancient and medieval India, education was mostly religious and literary in character, being based on the ancient religious and philosophical literature in Sanskrit, Arabic, and Persian languages (Dongerkery, 1967, p. 21).

The foundations of modern Indian higher education were laid in the early 19th century when India was a British colony and T. B. Macaulay in 1835 sweepingly dismissed "Eastern" knowledge (all their books would fit on one shelf of an English library). This widely shared view accepted the model of the British university and also accepted English as the medium of educational instruction for India. In those times, higher education essentially served the political and economic interests of the British rulers. The most favored subjects were the humanities and languages rather than the sciences or technical subjects.

India's first universities were founded at Calcutta, Bombay, and Madras (now, renamed Kolkata, Mumbai, and Chennai respectively) in 1857—incidentally, the year of a popular uprising against British rule. All three followed the British model, and all three had, as their main goal, according to the preamble of their enabling legislation "pursuit of a regular and liberal course of education." Not surprisingly, as unrest about British rule spread throughout India, students and even teachers from these universities led the country's struggle for freedom. Historian Ramachandra Guha (2008) notes that their influence on India's destiny was as profound as the popular uprising. Students and graduates of these universities questioned the logic of colonial rule and held up, as a mirror to their British rulers, the ideals of liberty and justice that provided intellectual ammunition for the popular movement for independence.

Sociologist Andre Béteille (2007) notes that the universities in colonial times "opened new horizons both intellectually and institutionally in a society that had stood still in a conservative and hierarchical mould for centuries" (p. 442). He continues by noting that they were often the first open and secular institutions in a society that was governed largely by the rules of kinship, caste, and religion. Thus, even though the age-old restrictions of gender and caste did not disappear in the universities, they came to be questioned there.

August 1947 brought independence to India; and the country became a federal, democratic republic after its constitution came into effect on January 26, 1950. The principles of equality, tolerance, and religious freedom preached and practiced by Mahatma Gandhi, who played a key role in the country's struggle for freedom, left a powerful imprint, not only on the minds of those actively interested in politics but also on the mind of the population in general.

With a high degree of syncretism and cultural pluralism, religious tolerance and peaceful coexistence define India's cultural tradition. The ideal of tolerance among the Hindus, who constitute four-fifths of the country's population, is aptly captured by Swami Vivekananda (1893) in his famous address at the World Parliament of Religions in Chicago:

> I belong to a religion which has taught the world both tolerance and universal acceptance. We believe not only in universal toleration, but we accept all religions as true. I am proud to belong to a nation which has sheltered the persecuted and the refugees of all religions and all nations of the earth.

Hence, even with a large Hindu majority, India is a secular nation; and despite occasional threats to that character, it has steadfastly held to its strong secular values.

India is also a multilingual nation with no fewer than 1,652 spoken languages. India was born as federation of states, and language played an important role in defining its internal state boundaries. It has no national language. Even though Hindi is the most widely spoken and primary tongue of 46% of the people, there are also 22 other "major" languages. English is used extensively in business and administration and has the status of a "subsidiary official language." It is also important in education, especially as a medium of instruction in higher education.

India seeks to achieve social and economic equality through democratic processes. It adopted universal suffrage soon after independence, long before achieving economic prosperity. Thus, political freedom coexists in India along with sharp economic disparities and deeply entrenched caste hierarchies. Observers have sometimes seen democracy in India as faltering; but with the country's strong commitment to liberal values, Indian democracy has only become stronger with time. Overall India has a strong tradition of basic human rights, free and fair elections, multiparty democracy, social justice, and tolerance. Modern conceptions of liberal education that include the ability to be self-aware and self-governing and which possess the capacity to respect the humanity of all human beings have guided its education system.

Secondary Education in India

Secondary education has been the ignored middle level of education in India. The secondary gross enrollment rate (GER) is 40%, significantly lower than that in East Asia (70%) and Latin America (82%). Furthermore, its quality is poor. However, dramatic growth at the elementary level with improvements in retention and transition rates over the past decade has increased the demand for secondary education considerably. A recent World Bank (2009) report estimates this increased demand at 17 million with enrollment growing from 40 million in 2007–2008 to 57 million students in 2017–2018. To address the problems of poor access and low quality, the Indian government is currently planning a massive investment in secondary education.

Secondary Curricula

India's educational system is termed a 8+2+2+3 pattern, meaning that eight years of compulsory elementary education are followed by two years each at the secondary level and the higher secondary level, and three years at the first-degree level in higher education. All but two small Indian states have their own boards of education, and one of their responsibilities is determining secondary curricula. Three national boards have overlapping all-India jurisdiction with one of them meant for open schooling. Some schools offer the International Baccalaureate (IB) secondary program. Even though there is a coordinating mechanism, the Council of Boards of Secondary Education, it has virtually no role in curricular matters.

With only minor variations, most states provide general education without differentiation for the first 10 years, using the National Curriculum Framework developed by the National Council for Education Research and Training in 2005 (NCERT, 2005). At the primary stage, this framework provides training in the use of one language (the regional language), mathematics, and principles of healthy and productive living in the first two years. Environmental education is added for the next three years. From the sixth year onwards, a comprehensive syllabus covers three languages, math, science, social science, work experience, health and physical education, and art.

At the secondary stage, the National Curriculum Framework provides a greater emphasis on math, science, and social science. The subject matter covered in the years 6–12 is shown in Table 3.1.

Secondary curricula and pedagogy in India are often criticized for their emphasis on rote learning of facts as opposed to developing the students' higher-order thinking skills, a critique corroborated by a World Bank (2009) study. Even before this study, however, the National Council for Education Research and Training implemented a curriculum framework in 2005 that was devised to connect knowledge to life outside the school, to shift the emphasis from memorization to higher-order thinking, synthesis, and application of knowledge; to move away from textbook-centric learning; to make examinations more flexible and perhaps better integrated with classroom life; and to nurture an overriding identity informed by caring concerns within the country's democratic polity. This curriculum makes a conscious effort to promote a healthy work ethos and the values of a humane and composite culture (NCERT, 2005).

Unfortunately, the new curriculum received a lukewarm response from most school boards. Even if they agreed in principle to these changes, finding resources and motivating teachers to implement these changes were major handicaps. It is true that a few well-resourced schools and boards, such as the Council for Indian School Certificate Examinations (CISCE) that caters to schools in urban centers, follow the innovative curriculum. They have a greater choice of courses including vocational courses. In the CISCE schools, while environmental education is compulsory, there are as many as 32 electives in a wide range of areas from languages to performing arts and yoga.

After the IB was approved as an entry qualification to the Indian universities in 1994, more than 60 IB schools have been established, offering globally benchmarked curricula. Building international issues and approaches on the foundation of an Indian ethos, its curriculum offers a broad-based education. Such schools are popular among students preparing to go abroad for higher education. Both the CISCE and IB schools use English as the medium of instruction and cater to a small section of the urban elite.

Despite these promising indications, such innovations are limited; and most of the schools operating under other school boards have not fulfilled the expectations of the new curriculum. Much of the education in these schools is geared toward enabling students to pass high-stake board examinations or to do well on competitive tests for entry to a small number of quality higher education institutions. Several reputable colleges in Delhi accept only students with aggregate marks of 90% or higher. Entrance to the Indian Institutes of Technology at the undergraduate level is extremely difficult, with only one in 60 applicants achieving admission. In addition to their regular school classes, serious students undergo grueling coaching, sometimes for years, to assure that they will score well in these tests. Coaching centers have mushroomed all over

TABLE 3.1 The 2005 National Curriculum framework for years 6–12

Upper primary stage (3 years)	Weightage*	Secondary stage (2 years)	Weightage	Higher secondary stage (2 years)	Weightage
Three languages (regional, modern Indian, and English)	32	Three languages (regional, modern Indian, and English)	30	Foundation courses: language and literature, work education, health and physical education, games and sports	40
Mathematics	12	Mathematics	13		
Science and technology	12	Science and technology	13		
Social sciences	12	Social sciences	13	Three elective courses, usually grouped as science, commercial, humanities, etc.	60
Work education	10	Work education	9		
Fine, visual, and performing arts	10	Fine, visual, and performing arts	9		
Health and physical education	10	Health and physical education	9		

Source: NCERT (2005).

Note
* Weightage refers to its relative importance in the curriculum.

the country since the 1990s; but reflecting the reality of the examinations themselves, they concentrate on rote rather than broad-based learning. Hence, a huge "shadow education" in the form of coaching centers is growing that has a debilitating effect on the learning environment in schools.

Even though physical education, music, and the arts (fine, visual, and performing) appear in curriculum descriptions written by most school boards, these areas often receive only slipshod instruction. The CISCE's recent attempt to introduce electives in music, cultural heritage, crafts, creative writing, and translation studies at the higher secondary level failed to attract many students. Vocational options suffer from poor quality and low esteem; they are seen as being designed primarily for students from marginalized sectors of society. As a result, very few schools offer vocational courses. With higher secondary level as a terminal point for many people, the neglect of vocational options puts the country at risk of having an unskilled and poor quality workforce.

Interestingly, India's open schooling system, the National Institute of Open Schooling (NIOS), caters to nontraditional students, school dropouts, and students living in remote areas. It offers a very innovative curriculum; provides flexibility in the choice of subjects, courses, and place of learning; and, to ensure continuity, allows the transfer of credits to and from other systems. It offers life enrichment and vocational credit-based courses in a wide range of subjects (85 as of 2010) with multi-entry, multi-exit options. NIOS currently serves 1.4 million students; but unfortunately, these students face problems in attempting to enter formal higher education institutions due to the image that open schooling offers poor education and to unresolved issues of equivalence with other boards.

Future Prospects

The government of India in 2009 announced an ambitious program to universalize secondary education for which massive public investment and the use of innovative public–private partnership models are envisaged. Its target is to achieve a 75% rate of secondary enrollment by 2015 in the next five years, ensure universal access by 2017, and aspires to the ideal of universal retention by 2020 (GoI, 2009b). It aims at removing gender and socio-economic inequities and having a secondary school within a reasonable distance of the entire population. All schools would conform to prescribed norms and quality. Six thousand model schools with private partners at all levels of education are planned to serve as benchmarks of excellence.

The new program also proposes a coordinated plan for curriculum reforms. Greater flexibility in the choice of subjects would be promoted by "clustering" schools—pooling the resources of several nearby schools—and introducing different levels of difficulty. For example, subjects could be offered at two levels with students doing at least two or three of the six subjects at a standard level and the remaining three or four at a higher level. This twofold common core curriculum would be available until Class 10, or the end of the lower secondary level. It would incorporate job-preparation pedagogy to aid competencies such as critical thinking, the transfer of learning, creativity, communication skills, aesthetics, work motivation, work ethic, and entrepreneurship-cum-social accountability. The possibility of placing vocational education structurally and administratively outside the existing school system is being explored.

To address the problem of over-emphasis on year-end board examinations, continuous and comprehensive evaluation and internal assessment with grading systems are being introduced. Such evaluations would primarily focus on the diagnosis, remediation, and enhancing of learning. It would take into account the social environment of learning and facilities available in schools. Modes of assessment based on oral testing, group work evaluation, open-book examination, and examination without time limits would be considered (GoI, 2009b).

As the country moves toward the universalization of secondary education, it faces several challenges with regard to the content and organization of its curriculum and choice in offerings given the complexity and diversity of the educational environment. The current reforms address many of these challenges and augur well for liberal and broad-based learning in the formal system of education.

Higher Education in India Today

As stated earlier in this chapter, at the time India achieved its independence in 1947, it had a deep commitment to liberal values, particularly equality, despite the society's economic disparities, religious and linguistic diversity, and deeply entrenched social hierarchy. Education was valued for its own sake, and linkages of education with economic development were weak.

Stated Goals

The stated goals of higher education in India have been guided by liberal values. A visitor to any Indian university would almost certainly encounter a famous quotation from India's first Prime Minister, Jawaharlal Nehru. Addressing the students of the Allahabad University in 1947, he said:

> A university stands for humanism, tolerance, reason; adventure of ideas and for the search for truth. It stands for the onward march of the human race toward higher objectives. Universities are places of ideas and idealism. If universities discharge their duties adequately, then it is well with the nation and the people.
>
> (Nehru, 1950, p. 118)

In 1948, as chairman of India's University Education Commission, Dr. Sarvepalli Radhkrishanan reaffirmed the country's steadfast loyalty to the core elements of respect for other human beings, freedom of belief and expression for all citizens, a deep obligation to promote human well-being, and faith in reason and humanity. While the commission's report recognized the need for vocational and professional education to meet the needs of economic development, Dr. Radhkrishanan promptly added that the aim of education is "not the acquisition of information, although important, or acquisition of technical skills, though essential in modern society, but the development of that bent of mind, that attitude of reason, that spirit of democracy, which will make us responsible citizens" (quoted in GoI, 1948, p. 2).

Thus, the ideal of liberal education has been the bedrock of higher education for India since independence—in important ways a continuation of the culture ingrained in the British colonial universities. As noted earlier, these universities were the seedbed of Indian independence; and ideas from history, philosophy, and Western literature played a role in shaping the culture and ethos of those universities.

Liberal education or "general education," as it is referred to in India, has been separated from "skill-based learning" right from the beginning. Even general education observed a separation among disciplines. This division was reinforced by the University Education Commission that proposed a distinction between facts, events, and values (or nature, society, and spirit), as the subject matters appropriate to the sciences, social sciences, and humanities respectively. This model of disciplinary compartmentalization exists today, more than 60 years since its conception (GoI, 1948).

At the time of independence, India had one of the largest and most sophisticated systems of higher education among developing countries. Since then, the system has expanded rapidly, with student enrollment growing at a rate about two-and-a-half times that of population growth. This was, however, with few exceptions a continuation of the same kind of growth, not genuine educational reform. The academic system and the fundamental ethos (core principles, administrative organizations, the professoriate, personal affairs, research organizations, curriculum, teaching methods, examination systems, and so on) have remained similar to those of the universities founded during the British colonial period. Universities and colleges and enrollment grew fast in the humanities and social sciences but less quickly in the sciences.

At the time of independence, about 100,000 students were enrolled in general arts colleges that followed the Cambridge model of liberal education. History, political science, and sociology were the main subjects with minor programs in psychology, mathematics, and the natural sciences. Later, with a more intense focus on economic development and growth in the private sector, economics, statistics, and commercial instruction were added.

Over time, the idea that general education should be the basis for higher education has come under attack by opposing forces. The most important competing model was utilitarianism, which required universities and colleges to be centers for practical professional training, and which has been so successful that general education is now completely marginalized, even though the stated goals of higher education continue to be the same.

Contextuality and relevance—qualities that are particularly important in the humanities and social sciences—are missing in the entire system. According to Pratap Bhanu Mehta (2009), the most serious threat to a broad humanities culture does not come from the market. It comes internally, when scholars no longer believe that the "purpose of education is to distinguish the truly valuable from the merely fashionable, the purely instrumental from the genuinely elevating thought." He further laments that "university culture discourages any serious engagement with deep and enduring questions and decries pedagogical protocols that have forgotten how to connect a rich body of texts with the emerging needs of social self-knowledge."

Overview of the Higher Education System

Indian higher education grew rapidly after independence, but this growth was unplanned. As a result, Indian higher education today is complex, highly fragmented, and riddled with many contradictions. In terms of absolute enrollment (around 13.6 million students), it is the third largest in the world, following only China and the United States; but it has one of the lowest gross enrollment ratios—around 12.4%. Female participation rates are lower, and there are large regional imbalances and wide disparities in the enrollment ratios of various socio-economic groups. In the post-independence rush for expansion, equity received greater attention than quality. Thus, replication rather than innovation became the norm. The expansion outpaced the availability of facilities and faculty; hence, quality deteriorated rapidly.

The system has a huge number of institutions (about 26,500), perhaps as many as the rest of the world taken together. However, only 525 universities, enrolling one-tenth of these students, award degrees; the remaining students are enrolled in about 26,000 colleges affiliated to the universities. Colleges deliver a university-prescribed curriculum, an arrangement that lowers quality, as discussed in the next section. The degree structure is similar to Great Britain's with a bachelor's degree taking three years in most subjects, four in engineering and some professional subjects, and five in medicine and architecture. Master's degrees take two years and do not necessarily involve research. Most of the students are enrolled full-time; 87.3% of them are undergraduates with only 11% in graduate programs and just 0.7% enrolled at the doctoral level.

In the country's federal system, higher education is the joint responsibility of the national and the state government, with the former taking care of a small number of well-funded institutions and the latter responsible for the most institutions, including a majority of universities and colleges that focus on humanities and social sciences. Setting and coordinating standards is the exclusive domain of the national government, and it discharges its responsibilities through the University Grants Commission and 13 professional councils. These bodies have their own rules and regulations. Thus, multiple bodies and a complex web of rules and regulations govern Indian higher education. Universities play a key role in the academic activities of their affiliated colleges. Indian higher education is believed to be overregulated and undergoverned. The public universities, although they enjoy enormous academic autonomy, perceive regulatory arrangements from all three levels (state, federal, and council) as intrusive, while colleges have little academic freedom.

Private institutions are now the main area in which institutional growth is occurring, but many of them engage in unfair practices, which the current system has failed to address. Thus, a current challenge is to reform the system. Finally, even though the country's voluntary accreditation system is more than a decade old, less than one-fifth of the universities and colleges have undergone the applications and reviews necessary to achieve accreditation. As a result, credible public information is lacking by which students and parents can make informed choices, nor do the institutions have much incentive for self-improvement.

Although most of the funding for higher education comes from the government, private financing is now important. Development assistance from overseas donors plays a minor role and is confined to the vocational training and technical education sector. Private institutions account for more than one-third of all higher education institutions and about four-fifths of the enrollment in professional higher education (Agarwal, 2009, p. 91). They are entirely tuition based. In contrast, programs in humanities and social sciences are mainly offered by government-funded universities and colleges that regularly face financial hardships and are unable to raise their tuition fees for fear of student unrest. To supplement government funding, many of them now offer self-financing professional programs, a development that has further marginalized the studies of the humanities and social sciences.

The government's 10th five-year plan (2002–2007) for higher education spent $2 billion, while the 11th five-year plan (2007–2012) will spend a projected $18 billion on higher education. This is a historic high-water mark, yet these funds are primarily meant for institutions under the direct supervision of the national government and focus mainly on professional studies. Thus, government funding is not only limited, but its distribution is uneven. Lacking a mechanism for rational fund allocation and without linking funding to accreditation, the government is unable to leverage public funds to improve quality, steer enrollment, and guide curricula formation according to national needs. Student financial aid is markedly inadequate and raises serious equity concerns.

Overall, Indian higher education faces the twin challenges of significantly expanding the supply and effectively regulating the quality. In the past, growth has been swift, yet chaotic and largely unplanned. This accelerated growth and the drive to make the system socially inclusive resulted in a dramatic increase in numbers without a proportionate increase in funding or intellectual resources. As a consequence, academic standards have suffered (Béteille, 2005).

According to Agarwal (2009), inadequate infrastructure and facilities, vacant faculty positions, many unqualified faculty, outmoded forms of instruction, declining research standards, unmotivated students, and overcrowded classrooms characterize Indian higher education. Given the poor employability of arts and science graduates, education in the basic sciences and the humanities has suffered more than engineering and business subjects, since the private sector has taken over these fields. Although the research performance of Indian universities has improved in recent years, it continues to be limited compared to that of its peers. The separation of higher education and vocational sectors, fragmentation within higher education between general and professional fields, and further fragmentation between subjects and specializations does not augur well for a broad-based education. Several structural, academic, and institutional issues must be addressed to meet the growing expectations from the country's higher education.

Defining Features of Indian Higher Education

Despite the strong British influence on higher education from colonial days, the United States has also influenced Indian higher education, especially since the 1960s, when the Indian Institutes of Technology and Indian Institutes of Management were set up (Agarwal, 2009, p. 1). Based on the old British university model, students studying for a general degree cover a range of related subjects; a minority of them sit for honors in one subject. Professional degrees—particularly engineering degrees—are based on the U.S. model.

However, over the past 60 years, academic structure, curriculum formation and evaluation, pedagogy and classroom interaction have all evolved away from foreign cultural influences. Distinctive Indian elements are its system of universities with affiliated colleges, tracking students into separate streams, and the resulting institutional segmentation. We briefly discuss these defining features below.

The Academic Structure

The academic structures for both the undergraduate (bachelor's) and graduate (master's) degree programs in India are rather inflexible in the arts, social sciences, natural sciences, and commercial faculties. The bachelor's programs take three years, the master's programs two. At the bachelor's level, the choice of subjects is limited, with no cafeteria-type offerings. For example, in the science faculty, for the first year the student studies compulsory English and a predetermined combination like physics–chemistry–mathematics, physics–chemistry–biology, or geology–geography–chemistry. In the arts faculty, the combination could be English–Hindi–linguistics and in the social sciences political science–economics–sociology. This rigid combination leaves little choice for students to select subjects according to their own interests. Very few colleges offer vocational courses, and students studying them face problems in lateral and vertical entry into the general stream.

The second and third years have two patterns yielding either a "pass" degree or an "honors" degree. In the pass-degree pattern, the subjects of the first year (excluding compulsory English) are repeated in the second and third years. In the honors-degree pattern, the subjects of the first year (excluding compulsory English) are repeated in the second year. However, in the third year, the student takes only one of the three subjects but studies it more intensively. Different universities may adopt one or more of these patterns. Universities that offer honors at the bachelor's level give preference to students with honors degrees when admitting students to the master's program.

Most of the universities and colleges in India have academic sessions spread over 10 to 12 months. Some universities and most of the professional and technical institutions have adopted a semester system that enlarges the curricular space and encourages and supports accelerated learning.

Curriculum Formation and Evaluation

In India, the curriculum is determined exclusively by university faculty and approved by the institution's various academic authorities. The government has no role. Unlike China, where a core curriculum in political theory and military training is mandated by the Ministry of Education, or Pakistan, where Islamic studies are compulsory, curriculum in Indian universities is not guided by any political or religious ideology.

The process of curricula revision is, however, cumbersome and painfully slow. A Working Group on Undergraduate Education set up by the National Knowledge Commission (NKC, 2006) noted that the large sizes of most universities and the structure and composition of their academic bodies responsible for curricular changes are a major impediment in the timely and speedy revision of curricula.

In recent years, several universities have attempted to make their curriculum more pertinent and academically sound. In 2004, the University of Delhi overhauled its B.A. (pass) curriculum, introduced internal assessment, and renamed it "the B.A. program." In 2008, the University of Delhi introduced the semester system at the undergraduate level, instituted a system of credits, and revised syllabi to ensure modularity that would enable students to move easily between different fields of study and make better transitions to the graduate level. This transition would also ensure better student–teacher engagement and more efficient utilization of the academic calendar. Such curricular reforms often involve a tortuous process in the Indian universities. According to Professor Deepak Pental (2010), who led these reforms in the University of Delhi, the main resistance to such changes came from the "competitive politics of teacher groups."

Another cause for the staleness and irrelevance of curricula in Indian universities is the segregation of research from teaching, with the former usually taking place in colleges and the latter mainly occurring in the universities or in exclusive research institutions. This segmentation undermines the holistic process of generating and delivering knowledge. Researchers in the new and exclusive research institutions have absolutely no occasion to engage with young minds. The humanities and social sciences suffer not only from this separation but also from weaknesses inherent in research in the humanities and social sciences due to poor student quality and less academic rigor.

Student evaluations by the universities are often impersonal and erratic, largely on the basis of end-of-term (semester or annual) examinations and on a scale of 101 points (marks). Generally 40% constitutes the minimum for passing, 50% for second class, 60% for first class, and 75% for first class with distinction. This classification was developed during colonial times when evaluations were much stricter and has little relevance today except on paper.

Pedagogy and Classroom Interaction

Archaic teaching methods dominate the Indian classrooms. Most universities and colleges have large class sizes that hinder intensive classroom interactions. Teachers use mostly the lecture method and tutorials. Project work, panel discussions, and case studies are uncommon, and the use of audio-visual aids or new technologies is rare.

Obedience and loyalty mark the classroom culture, and questioning the teachers is not encouraged. Most of the teachers do not explain the instructional goals, then elaborate each point systematically, encouraging student interactions and feedback, and then provide a synopsis and recapitulation of the lesson at its conclusion, even though such a method should be the usual practice. The emphasis is on disseminating information, which is very often outdated. Student evaluations are based on their retentive ability and not on any derived knowledge or wisdom. In the absence of critical enquiry, the learning experience encourages a conformist attitude among the students. Liberal learning that fosters student dialogue, analytical thinking, and course work across a wide range of subjects is essential in forming socially informed students, but such qualities are often missing from Indian higher education classrooms.

The academic staff colleges established in many universities to train teachers focus almost entirely on content, rather than pedagogy. Help books containing the previous year's examination papers with model answers are widely used. Teachers often dictate model answers in the classrooms. In this situation, graduates usually have little knowledge about their field of study and even less how to relate that knowledge to the outside world. The 1986 National Policy on Education aptly summarized the situation by noting:

> Against the small minority of quality products, the preponderant majority come out of institutions of higher education, perhaps with a little more of book learning and of course a degree, but with very little capacity for self-study, poor language and communication skills, a highly limited world view and hardly any sense of social and national responsibility.
>
> (GoI, 1986)

The System of Affiliated Colleges

As noted earlier, nine-tenths of India's total post-secondary enrollment is in the affiliated colleges. They have been the main venue for higher education growth, their numbers doubling from fewer than 13,000 in 2000 to about 26,000 in 2009. However, they play no role in curricular formation. Several universities affiliate large numbers of colleges—some as many as 800. Most of these colleges are small with poor facilities and just eight to 10 teachers, mostly without a Ph.D. The colleges teach uniform and often outdated curricula with the goal of preparing students for university entrance examinations. As a result, they operate like tutorial classes, leaving no scope for innovation or experimentation by their teachers.

The affiliation system is a "minimum demands system" that tends to lower the academic standards of those colleges that can offer better instruction standards. The affiliating university often negotiates curriculum as the "lowest common denominator," so that all colleges are able to implement the same courses. This arrangement leaves little scope for innovation by an individual college (NKC, 2006). The teachers have little flexibility to experiment, use local and contextual examples, or employ alternative teaching strategies. They come for limited hours, deliver lectures in a routine manner, and depart with little sense of participating in the institution's affairs. There is very little focus on teacher training. What is provided usually deals with subject knowledge rather than pedagogy. Universities that have many affiliated colleges function like glorified examination boards.

Tracking under Streams

As a British colonial legacy, most Indian students study for a general degree covering a range of related subjects (mainly the humanities, social sciences, and natural sciences). Some of them specialize by taking honors in a single subject. After class 10, students choose the arts (the humanities and social sciences), a commercial program, or the sciences. These subject streams are aligned to different career options (see Table 3.2).

Often students are required to have specific subject combinations at the school and the first-degree level for graduate studies in different areas. Even though some boards, like the Central Board of Secondary Education, put no restrictions on subject combinations, most schools allow little choice. Practical problems like timetabling and teacher recruitment foreclose the possibility of freer combinations of subjects and the schools resort to clustering around closely related subjects.

Since the early decades of independence—1950s and 1960s—arts colleges have proliferated, resulting in large enrollments in the arts stream (see Table 3.3). This situation exists, notwithstanding the poor employment prospects of arts graduates, because such colleges are easy and relatively inexpensive to set up. Except for a few prestigious colleges, the quality of students and learning in these arts programs is poor. Better-prepared students opt for the science or commercial stream and move on to professional studies. Art graduates usually have no specific employable skills and face a tight labor market. Attempts to equip arts graduates with vocational skills have not met with much success. A separate vocational stream advocated in the National Policy on Education (1986) has been a non-starter.

TABLE 3.2 Typical subject combinations and career options

Stream	Arts	Commercial	Science (with math)	Science (with biology)
Typical subject combination	History, political science, sociology	Accounts, business studies, economics	Physics, chemistry, mathematics	Physics, chemistry, biology
Typical career options	Law, fashion designing, interior designing, business management, languages, journalism, film and drama, event management	Business management, chartered accountancy, company secretary, actuarial sciences	Engineering, architecture, computer applications, agriculture, technology, armed forces, planning and design	Medicine, dairy technology, pharmacy, biotechnology, nursing

TABLE 3.3 Enrollment by subject: 2008–2009

Subject	Total enrollment	Percentage of total
Arts	5,875,532	43.07
Science	2,612,406	19.15
Commercial/management	2,486,901	18.23
Education	286,478	2.10
Engineering/technology	1,313,706	9.63
Medicine	446,087	3.27
Agriculture	80,482	0.59
Veterinary science	21,827	0.16
Law	381,971	2.80
Others	136,418	1.00
Total	13,641,808	100.00

Source: University Grants Commission (2009), *Annual Report 2008–2009*.

The demand for professional education is met by a large and growing private sector. Several thousand self-financing colleges with narrow specializations in engineering, medicine, management, nursing, and teacher education have been established since the early 1990s. Rather than holistic, broad-based education, these institutions focus their curriculum narrowly on specific areas. Several states have established exclusive affiliating universities to enable this growth. In professional fields, more than four-fifths of the post-secondary enrollment is in private institutions (Agarwal, 2009, pp. 66–114).

While empirical data to support any hierarchy of streams is lacking, anecdotal evidence and folk wisdom assigns bright students to the sciences or professional education. The next best opt for commerce, and the academically disadvantaged study the arts and humanities. The vocational stream is for poor students from marginalized regions and socio-economic sectors. From the initial stages of schooling, students receive the message, either subtly or overtly, that the natural sciences are superior to the social sciences and are the domain of "bright" students. As a result, low self-esteem governs the classroom-transaction process in the humanities and social sciences, with both teachers and students uninterested in comprehending its contents. Students who wish to pursue education in the humanities and social sciences have very few options of good institutions (NCERT, 2005).

Not only is the curriculum in Indian universities and colleges narrowly focused, but most institutions offer only one type of program, thus resulting in a high degree of institutional segmentation. While about 50% of the universities and colleges offer general programs, the remaining programs deal exclusively with a particular field. There are about 14 universities and about 3,000 colleges devoted exclusively to engineering. Similarly, there are a large number of exclusive medical, law, management, agriculture, and even animal husbandry and fisheries institutions.

In sum, academic arrangements in India's institutions of higher education are characterized by an inflexible academic structure, a slow process of curricular change, and a dysfunctional evaluation system. Affiliating and tracking into streams create further problems for broad-based education.

Curricular Reforms and Innovative Practices

Reform efforts have attempted to address various weaknesses in these academic arrangements, both at the national and at the institutional level. This section provides an overview of these efforts and evaluates their impact. Even though curricular formation is primarily a responsibility of the universities, the University Grants Commission (UGC) has periodically attempted to steer curricular reforms. In 1986, it established 27 curriculum development centers at universities to review existing syllabi, restructure courses into units, and develop alternative models. Model curricula developed by the centers were circulated to all universities with encouragement to make suitable modifications and adopt them. However, the universities were suspicious about the UGC efforts, interpreting the model curricula as iron-bound mandates imposed by the commission. A review committee in 1991 recommended that the work of the curriculum development centers should be decentralized and that the universities and colleges should initiate UGC assistance (GoI, 1991, 1992). Over time, as the UGC's enthusiasm for curricular reform waned, the curriculum development centers became defunct. The model curricula have also received a poor response on account of the unavailability of quality teachers, limited opportunities for practical training, and the absence of clear linkages between these courses and improved job prospects.

In 2001, Professor Hari Gautam, then the proactive UGC chairman, oversaw the creation of a model curriculum in 35 subject areas through different committees. Once again the response from the universities ranged from lukewarm to hostile. A draft law for setting up a National Council for Higher Education and Research to replace the UGC is currently under discussion. It suggests that the new council would "develop, from time to time, a national curriculum framework with specific reference to new or emerging or interdisciplinary fields of knowledge and to provide a vision and [to] guide universities in recognizing and revising course curricula." This proposed legislation, too, has been criticized. In effect, national efforts to steer curricula reform in the universities continues to receive a negative response and be mired in the rhetoric of university autonomy.

Experience of Autonomous Colleges

In order to overcome various shortcomings of the affiliating system, the Education Commission in 1966 conceived the idea of autonomous colleges as a freer and more creative association of universities with colleges. Such colleges could decide their own evaluation processes and offer a broad-based curriculum with more flexibility (GoI, 2005). The idea of college autonomy garnered enthusiasm slowly, and it was not until 1978 that the first few colleges in Tamil Nadu gained autonomy. The 1986 National Education Policy anticipated that large numbers of autonomous colleges would emerge and even recommended the creation of autonomous departments within universities on a selective basis. The idea spread only slowly to other states and universities. Even after 30 years, there are just 314 autonomous colleges in 58 universities of 16 states (UGC, 2009).

Teachers' associations have usually opposed autonomous colleges. Calling such a move elitist, they fear that it would bring arbitrariness in decision-making by management, funding crises, increased workloads, and irregularities in conducting internal examinations. Concerted efforts to allay such mostly unfounded apprehensions have not been made, and there is a near absence of clear incentives for teachers to embrace the autonomy move. Thus, only 314 out of about 25,900 colleges are autonomous today (UGC, 2009).

Notable examples of innovative curricula in two autonomous colleges are Vivekanand College in Mumbai and Mount Carmel College in Bengaluru. Vivekanand College has incorporated traditional values in its curricula through organized residential living. Physical exercises like yoga, karate, other ancient martial arts, and meditation three times a day are compulsory. Sanskrit teaching occupies an important place. This curriculum inculcates among the students a deep sense of the traditional values of the ancient Gurukula with the holistic discipline of the hand, the head, and the heart (NAAC, 2004, p. 30). Mount Carmel College has weekly value education classes, guest lectures, and interaction with non-governmental organizations. Field experience through visits to orphanages, old age homes, and remand homes are an integral part of study. Their focus is on creating tolerance, a cross-cultural outlook, social awareness, and motivation for service to society (NAAC, 2004, p. 53).

Student Development as Part of Curriculum Design

Usually, the curriculum does not have separate programs for the personal and social development of students. Recognizing this weakness, the National Policy on Education Review Committee in 1991 recommended that the curriculum should be designed to help foster personal and social development. Later the Central Advisory Board of Education Committee suggested providing academic credit for extension activities like social work and rural development (GoI, 1991, 1992).

Accordingly, the UGC advised the universities to introduce foundation courses at the undergraduate level with the expectation that such courses would promote human development and social change. Several universities introduced a set of core foundation courses.

St. Joseph's College in Tiruchirapalli was one of the first colleges to run a four-semester, compulsory foundation course for undergraduate students based on Gandhian philosophy. This initiative flowered under the leadership of Father Jesudasan, a researcher in Gandhian thought. Its first semester provides a course covering the principles of value education; personality; the power of positive thinking; intellectual, social, moral, spiritual, and emotional development; human sexuality; family and parenthood; and bio-ethics. The second semester, which focuses on social education, covers the concepts of social analysis, poverty, inequality, different approaches to development, and integrity in public life. The third semester covers religion and social change, secularism/communalism, terrorism and violence, national integration, environment and sustainable development, consumer education, mass media, and advertising. The fourth semester proposes a vision of a new world, science and technology issues, public health including drug addiction and AIDS, population education, human rights, fundamental rights and minority rights/ duties, and primary and adult education.

The contents are not only comprehensive, but the presentation is lucidly illustrated through case studies and action points. The curriculum is integrated with a compulsory outreach program—Science and Humanities for Peoples Development (SHEPHERD). The students are sensitized to the problems of the community, particularly those of the poor and the needy, and are enabled to apply what they learn in the classroom to improve community life in their neighborhoods.

Similar foundation courses, however, did not become popular. A review in March 1991 showed that only nine universities and 208 of their affiliated colleges had introduced foundation courses (GoI, 1992). At present, there is little discussion about foundation courses. It is not even known whether the universities and colleges that introduced the foundation course are continuing them.

Innovative Engineering Curriculum

Engineering education is the fastest growing segment of Indian higher education. It is growing 20% annually and currently enrolls about two million students in about 3,000 engineering colleges that are affiliated to universities—in most cases, exclusively technical universities. These colleges have an inflexible and narrow curriculum with little of the humanities and social sciences except for a few courses in English language and some in management. Some institutions have also included a core course in human values; but overall, the curricular approach in such universities and colleges lags behind the emerging role of professional engineer in society and economy.

There are, however, exceptions. The Indian Institutes of Technology (IIT), set up in the 1950s and 1960s have successfully integrated the humanities and social sciences in their engineering curriculum. The Indian Institute of Technology in Kanpur, established as a partnership with a consortium of nine leading U.S. institutions, led this initiative of innovative curriculum and was, in part, influenced by the American Society for Engineering Education's approach to engineering curriculum. Its philosophy is that an ideal engineer should be capable of taking human factors into account while innovating and finding alternate solutions to engineering problems. This curriculum has been periodically renewed, bringing in flexibility by introducing electives in the 1970s and introducing communication skills in 2000. It is increasingly recognized now that meta-skills like complex communication skills and interactive adaptability are permanent elements in the emerging service-based economy.

With the introduction of electives and other courses and with the conversion of five-year programs to four years, the share of the humanities and social sciences courses has gradually declined from almost one-fifth of courses in the 1960s to its current level of about one-tenth (see Figure 3.1). Apart from the innovative curriculum, the Indian Institute of Technology at Kanpur also adopted a student-centered pedagogy with greater focus on self-learning and peer-to-peer learning.

Besides, the IIT, the International Institute of Information Technology at Hyderabad not only has a humanities and social sciences component as 15% of its curriculum but has also introduced a compulsory program on "education of life" (*Jeevan Vidya*). The program consists of weekly discussions in small

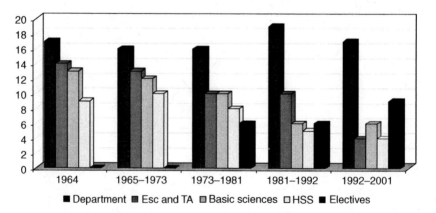

FIGURE 3.1 Undergraduate curriculum in the Indian Institute of Technology, Kanpur (source: Subbarao, 2008).

Note
Esc & TA = Engineering Sciences and Technical Arts.

groups on everyday issues in a free and frank manner, where arguments are self-verifiable without the appeal to faith-based or mystic elements. Once every year, such workshops are conducted over an entire week. This program has helped make students more responsible citizens with greater concern for family, friends, society, and nature (Ramancharla et al., 2009).

However, engineering curriculum integrated with student-centered pedagogic practices are confined to a very small number of institutions—perhaps 50 institutions enrolling 100,000 students.

Curriculum and Pedagogy at Lady Shri Ram College

Lady Shri Ram College at New Delhi, India's premier women's liberal arts institution, is a good example of an affiliated college that offers an innovative curricula and good pedagogic practices. The college has a focus on the humanities and social sciences but also offers programs in mathematics, statistics, elementary education, journalism, and conflict transformation and peace building. Short-term courses are available in art appreciation, women and political processes, communication skills, techniques of non-violence, publishing, mathematical skills, and legal literacy. The college reinforces the teaching–learning process through students' symposia, interaction with eminent scholars, fieldtrips, paper presentations, tutorials, and informal discussions.

According to Dr. Meenakshi Gopinath, principal of the college (personal communication), the college believes that such practices help students to develop critical thinking skills and build their capacity to discerningly organize detailed data and complex arguments on contemporary issues. Students are exposed to a rich cultural heritage, famous literary texts, music, and art—not only from India but also from other countries. Twenty-two student-run societies in music, dance, theater, the fine arts, debating, exposure to nature, creative writing, and public speaking provide a large choice of activities outside the classroom. Lady Shri Ram's efforts to make students socially responsible citizens is reflected in its attempt to ensure that students are part of either the National Service Scheme, the Voluntary Agency Placement Program, or Reaffirming Equity, Access, Capacity, and Humanism (REACH) with the goal of enhancing student sensitivity toward the underprivileged and on issues of gender, equity, and sustainable development. Thus, Lady Shri Ram follows the principle of liberal arts education guided by the conviction that women graduates of this college will play transformative leadership roles in society and actualize the idea of "Leadership with Social Responsibility," the college's motto, based on its initials of LSR.

The Foundation for Liberal and Management Education

The Foundation for Liberal and Management Education (FLAME) at Pune, founded in 2004 by two visionaries, Nemish Shah and Parag Shah, is a reaction to the rigid, syllabus-bound Indian academic system. The institute offers a four-year undergraduate program anchored to the concept of liberal education. This is a double qualification with a diploma in liberal education given by FLAME and a three-year B.A. degree awarded in association with a nearby university, Bharati Vidyapeeth. According to Parag Shah, the institution "revives the *Guru-Shishya Parampara* on which the ancient Indian teachings were based. The institution adopts an integrative and broad approach to learning that allows students to generate individual perspectives and draw from them relevant life values." The institute offers a wide range of subjects, including the sciences, social sciences, humanities, arts, and philosophy. Several fields of applied science enable students to choose career options. Thus, the students have flexibility in their choice of courses teamed with interdisciplinary learning.

Students' participation in the "Discover India" program helps them to anchor their learning on contemporary realities of the community/country as well as drawing from India's rich traditions. This is a six-credit compulsory course involving group work combined with experiential learning through fieldtrips of eight to 12 days. The residential campus has been designed with a "strong emphasis on integrating nature into all spaces and enables students from diverse backgrounds to experience living together in mutual tolerance and collaboration."

Indian Institute of Science at Bengaluru

Traditionally, the undergraduate program in arts and sciences at Indian institutions of higher education is three years. However, the Indian Institute of Science at Bengaluru, famous for its postgraduate program in science and engineering, has announced that, beginning in 2011, it will offer a four-year integrated bachelor of science. Its academic structure has a holistic interdisciplinary flavor, providing students with the opportunity to take courses in the sciences, engineering, and the humanities.

According to Professor P. Balaram (n.d.), director of this institute, the bachelor of science program carries a strong flavor of engineering and an exposure to social sciences. Since the program is offered in a primarily postgraduate institution, the students benefit from interactions with the postgraduate students, who could at times work as teaching assistants for the undergraduate classes. All students take core courses in physics, chemistry, mathematics, biology, engineering, and the humanities in the first three semesters of the undergraduate program. Specialization is introduced in the following three semesters even though students are encouraged to choose electives from streams other than their own specialization during this time. The program culminates with a research-oriented project in the fourth year (VII and VIII semesters). Apart from a broad curriculum with a multidisciplinary flavor, independent research at the undergraduate level is unique to this program.

New Policy Initiatives

As these examples show, innovative curricular and pedagogic practices have been confined to a small number of institutions. National initiatives have not been able to gain much momentum. In 2009, based on the recommendations of the Central Advisory Board of Education, the government launched academic reforms in five areas that include a shift from the annual to the semester system, a shift from year-end examinations to a combination of regular internal and external evaluations, periodic revisions of the curriculum, streamlined admissions, and the introduction of choice-based credits (GoI, 2009b). Further, it has been proposed that some curriculum revision be done every academic year and with substantial revisions occurring every three years for all courses. These changes would enhance student choice and allow greater flexibility.

The new credit system breaks the curriculum into small units and allows students to choose from various courses that would be revised regularly. The plans for the semester system should be implemented in all the central universities by 2011 and in all the state universities by 2012. These deadlines are unlikely to be met.

The choice-based credit system would enhance learning opportunities, allow students to better match their personal aspirations with their scholastic needs, ease their transfer between institutions, improve educational quality and excellence, provide flexibility for working students to complete their programs over an extended period of time, and make educational programs more comparable across the country. It is expected that these changes would increase the humanities and social sciences curricula even in professional programs. However, the impact of these renewed efforts for academic reforms will become apparent only as time passes (GoI, 2009b).

Another curriculum development has been a recent report of the Committee to Advise on the Renovation and Rejuvenation of Higher Education set up to advise on the renovation and rejuvenation of higher education. This report is a landmark in many ways. The report advocates a shift from discipline-based to interdisciplinary knowledge, advocates that students should study additional subjects beyond their major, and urges universities to adopt a curricular approach that treats knowledge in a holistic manner and that creates opportunities for different kinds of interfaces among disciplines from those possible in most universities today. Responding with concern to growing institutional segmentation, the report suggests creative and flexible mechanisms to ensure that the autonomy of the diverse institutional responses are not curbed, with the effect that autonomous institutions with little regulatory restriction should be allowed to grow within a university rather than outside it. But again, institutional mechanisms and resources for implementation of the report are nowhere in sight (GoI, 2009a).

Summary and Conclusions

Indian higher education is growing rapidly but falls far short of the country's expectations, particularly in terms of improved quality. Innovative curriculum and new pedagogy are the keys to the quality challenge. However, the country's higher education system has fallen captive to a number of problems: outmoded institutional and degree structures, an ineffective system of student tracking, and the inefficiencies of affiliated colleges, some of which are inherited from the British period. Recent growth has occurred largely in the narrowly focused private professional colleges. As a result, growth is occurring out of sync with current realities with the result that Indian higher education continues to be frustratingly compartmentalized.

A particular problem is the undesirable distinction between general education and professional education at the undergraduate level. This differentiation serves little purpose. Except for extremists, no one would object to exposing students to basic tenets of the humanities and social sciences so that graduates are good human beings and better citizens; at the same time, only purists would object to students acquiring the professional skills needed to obtain jobs upon graduation. The system of affiliated colleges, which tracks students into narrow streams early on, and institutional segmentation intensify this problem.

Thus, having an integrated curriculum and delivering it effectively is the key challenge confronting Indian higher education. A few institutions have succeeded in doing so, but these are exceptions. Good replicable institutional models that can integrate professional training with general education must be evolved. Flexibility in terms of content, syllabi, use of the semester system, a means of transferring credits, and an emphasis on multidisciplinary courses would help in such integration.

In the context of building socially cohesive societies and sustainable models of development, the humanities and social sciences can never be irrelevant. However, curriculum and methodology can certainly be outdated and would need to be constantly updated. For example, studies in psychology, sociology, and philosophy need to be reoriented to reflect new information and communication technologies and the redefined relationships among individuals and their roles as members of family and society characteristic of contemporary times.

There is a need to remove artificial barriers between science, the humanities, and commerce and to design interdisciplinary courses that widen the horizons and broaden the vision of students. It would be folly to constrain knowledge into mutually exclusive compartments. Such attempts would lead to the production of semi-literate individuals, not educated persons. Students need greater choice in terms of courses to discover their unique strengths and explore where their passions lie. They should be taught to question, discuss, and challenge the world and its values. They should not be inhibited by course structure, inane examinations, or faculty authoritarianism.

Academic reforms touching upon issues like content, the removal of superficial boundaries between disciplines, increasing student choice, and flexibility are receiving attention in the ongoing debates, but action on the ground remains limited. Such reforms have been talked about for decades but have faced stiff opposition from the strongly unionized faculty. A formidable challenge is to create incentives for the academic community that will encourage them to embrace these academic reforms.

With recent growth in and focus on professional education imparted in narrowly specialized institutions, which offer few, if any, liberal arts components in their curricula, India could face a future in which the workforce may be reasonably well trained but is narrow in its outlook. Higher education must be seen as a foundry for the development of more intelligent and able citizens, capable of contributions to the polity beyond their field of academic specialty.

Concerted efforts are required to make more liberal and student-centered learning part of the country's higher education. New curricular models like that in the Indian Institutes of Technology or the four-year B.S. program at the Indian Institute of Science at Bengaluru, or the four-year liberal arts bachelor at the Foundation for Liberal and Management Education (FLAME) at Pune are needed. Greater and wider international recognition of Indian degrees will depend largely on the holistic nature of programs offered and rigor in courses, teaching strategies and, evaluation procedures.

References

Agarwal, P. (2009). *Indian higher education: Envisioning the future*. New Delhi: Sage Publishers.

Balaram, P. (n.d.). Quoted in Indian Institute of Science at Bengaluru. Retrieved on December 16, 2010, from www.iisc.ernet.in/ug/.

Béteille, A. (2005). Universities as public institutions. *Economic and Political Weekly*, 40(31), 3377–3381.

Béteille, A. (2007, February 25). Universities at the crossroads. *Current Science*, 92(4), 441–449.

Dongerkery, S. R. (1967). *University education in India*. Mumbai: Manaktalas.

GoI. Government of India. (1948). *Report of the university education commission*. New Delhi: Author.

GoI. Government of India. (1986). *National policy on education.* New Delhi: Ministry of Human Resource Development, Department of Education.

GoI. Government of India. (1991). *National policy on education review committee report.* New Delhi: Ministry of Human Resource Development, Department of Education.

GoI. Government of India. (1992). *Report of the Central Advisory Board of Education (CABE) Committee on Policy.* New Delhi: Ministry of Human Resource Development, Department of Education.

GoI. Government of India. (2005). *Report of the Central Advisory Board of Education (CABE) on autonomy of higher education institutions.* New Delhi: Ministry of Human Resource Development, Department of Education.

GoI. Government of India. (2009a, January). *Report of the committee to advise on the renovation and rejuvenation of higher education in India.* New Delhi: Ministry of Human Resource Development, Department of Education.

GoI. Government of India. (2009b, August 31). *Background notes for the 56th meeting of the Central Advisory Board of Education (CABE).* New Delhi: Ministry of Human Resource Development, Department of Education.

Guha, R. (2008). Crucibles of modernity. In I. Pande (Ed.), *Beyond degrees: Finding success in higher education* (pp. 2–18). Noida: HarperCollins Publishers India.

Mehta, P. B. (2009, June 16). Century of forgetting. *Indian Express.*

NAAC. National Assessment and Accreditation Council. (2004). *Best practices in higher education.* Bengaluru, India: Author.

NCERT. National Council of Educational Research and Training. (2005). *National curriculum framework.* New Delhi: Author.

Nehru, J. (1950). *Independence and after: A collection of speeches, 1946–49.* New York: John Day Company.

NKC. National Knowledge Commission. (2006). Report of the Working Group on Undergraduate Education. Retrieved on June 10, 2010, from www.knowledgecommission.gov.in.

Pental, D. (2010, September 16). Our musty ivory tower. *Indian Express*, p. 10.

Ramancharla, P. K., Sangal, R., Mitra, A., Singh, N., & Karlapalem, K. (2009). An experiment on introducing human values course in undergraduate curriculum of engineering education. *Northeast American Society of Engineering Education Conference*, April 3–4, 2009, University of Bridgeport. Retrieved on July 10, 2010, from www.iiit.ac.in/techreports/2009_75.

Subbarao, E. C. (2008). *An eye for excellence: Fifty innovative years of IIT Kanpur.* Noida, India: HarperCollins Publishers India.

UGC. University Grants Commission. (2009). *Annual report 2008–2009.* New Delhi: Author.

Vivekananda, S. (1893). Retrieved on December 17, 2010, from www.swamij.com/swami-vivekananda-1893.htm.

World Bank. (2009). *Secondary education in India: Universalizing opportunity.* Washington, DC: World Bank.

4

MEXICO

Higher Education, the Liberal Arts, and Prospects for Curricular Change

Wietse de Vries and José Francisco Romero

Introduction

A chapter on liberal education in Mexico could at first sight be very brief: formally, it does not exist. The expression "liberal education" is missing from the Mexican vocabulary, and there is currently no debate about whether this type of education should be introduced. Likewise, the literature on higher education in Mexico does not mention the term.

However, the apparent difference between Mexico and other countries may be due to terminology. To illustrate the point, the American Association of Colleges and Universities (1998) provides this definition of what is judged as liberal education in the United States:

> Liberal education requires that we understand the foundations of knowledge and inquiry about nature, culture and society; that we master core skills of perception, analysis, and expression; that we cultivate a respect for truth; that we recognize the importance of historical and cultural context; and that we explore connections among formal learning, citizenship, and service to our communities.

This definition has many similarities with the mission statement of a major public university in Mexico, the Benemérita Universidad Autónoma de Puebla:

> We are committed to the education of a university community that is integrated with society, which leads us to create learning spaces that promote justice, equity, a better social balance, and human development. We promote dialogue and the development of critical and creative

thinking in our community. We educate citizens who possess social responsibility, are committed to democracy, and who are capable of managing their own learning in a critical and free way.

(BUAP, 2009, p. 38; our translation)

The commonalities between statements are not accidental; for decades, many Mexican universities have sought to offer an education that goes beyond a narrow preparation for a specific profession and that includes aspects such as preparing students for citizenship or for democracy. Thus, the topics that surround the debate on liberal education in other countries have been very present in discussions and reforms in Mexico, albeit under other banners, such as "general education."

But while the aims stated by several Mexican universities might be similar to those of other countries and universities, the solutions, reforms, and educational practices they have adopted—both in upper secondary schools and in higher education—may have worked out very differently. Moreover, in a highly diversified and deregulated system, each institution seems to have come up with its own answers.

In this chapter, we inventory these different institutional answers regarding the observed need for a more general education. We also explore the underlying logic of these answers—their history and philosophy. And finally, we discuss whether a liberal, or general, education is desirable, feasible, and perhaps even unavoidable, considering both the national and international contexts.

Inventory of General Education

Making an inventory of institutions in Mexico is not easy, given the current size and complexity of Mexican higher education. By 2004, the country had 1,533 institutions, with an additional 1,100 branch campuses (De Vries & Álvarez, 2005). These institutions offered nearly 8,000 undergraduate programs (majors) and 3,400 graduate options. This is not to say that all of these programs are unique or that they are evenly distributed. There are well over 1,000 options to study law, distributed among 1,000 institutions, but only a dozen options to study physics in a few universities.

The system has changed considerably since 1990, when it comprised some 700 institutions, mainly public universities and technological institutions, offering around 4,000 undergraduate majors and 1,600 graduate options. Enrollment, which stood at 1.2 million students in 1990, grew to 2.1 million in 2004. Even so, access remained limited to a fraction of the relevant age group. In 1990, 15% of Mexicans ages 20–25 were enrolled in an institution of higher education; by 2008, the percentage had reached 25%. Despite this increase, Mexican higher education continues to enroll fewer students compared to developed countries or even to other Latin American countries (De Vries & Álvarez, 2005).

Types of Institutions

An additional complication is that, over the last two decades, higher education has not only seen growth but also diversification and differentiation. Nowadays, the system is composed of several types of institutions.

Since the 1930s, the federal government has created several technological institutes, which offer a five-year education, generally in engineering. Until the 1990s, this sector was highly centralized. All decisions had to be approved by the federal Undersecretary for Technological Education. Since then, several technological institutes have been decentralized, which means that they depend on state governments for funding. Curriculum, however, has remained mostly a federal issue.

An additional sector of technological universities was created after 1990. These institutions offer two-year vocational degrees and are also regulated directly by the federal government, although they also require mandatory participation by the state government and the local business sector on their governing boards and in their daily operations. In the 2000s, the federal government also created polytechnic universities that offer extended education for graduates from technological universities and grant five-year degrees, and intercultural universities, designed to serve the indigenous population.

Furthermore, the preparation of teachers for elementary education takes place in teacher training schools (*Escuela Normal*). They are classified as higher education institutions, but most decisions regarding their curriculum depended until recently on the federal Undersecretary for Elementary Education.

In the sectors listed above, the federal government defines the curriculum and has focused on vocational training. Our review of these sectors found that no type of general education exists.

The university sector presents a very different situation. Public universities all have far-reaching autonomy. By law, they are free to create majors, decide on curricular content, hire faculty, admit students, and allocate funding internally. The recognition of degrees and curricula depends on the university council, not on outside parties. This means, in practice, that each university decides its curricular content. In many cases, these decisions are made by the department, or even by the body of professors that teach each major.

Private universities come in all shapes and sizes. Several large "elite" (selective and costly) universities offer a wide array of majors and many have branch campuses scattered around the country. But they operate alongside many other, generally very small, local institutions that offer only a few majors. Private universities are also modestly regulated. They operate with a permit from a variety of agencies, ranging from the federal Secretary of Education, to state Secretaries of Education, public autonomous universities, or presidential decrees. Private universities must submit their study plans to these authorities; but the initial recognition process is lax and practically no follow-up evaluation by outside parties exists. As private universities are not subject to public funding, they have not been subject to public policies either (de Vries, 2002). As a result, curriculum in the private sector is left to each university, to each department, or even to those teaching a specific major.

Thus, majors in the university sector have much operating leeway. There exist some tacit agreements about the number of courses or the number of hours students should spend in the classroom; but as to contents, university curricula are almost completely deregulated. Our chapter will therefore focus on the university sector, which currently comprises 70% of higher education enrollments.

Previous Levels of Education

Mexican elementary education includes primary education (grades 1–6) and lower secondary education (grades 7–9). Elementary education is mandatory and focuses on general topics (Spanish, mathematics, history, etc.). The federal government defines the curriculum and provides the textbooks, operating on the philosophy that a nationally shared curriculum is crucial to nation-building and that general education provides a common foundation at a basic level, while universities should train for a specific profession.

It can be debated, however, whether the elementary curriculum meets the criterion of "general education." In practice, rote learning of subject matters prevails, based on the national mandatory curriculum and textbooks. As a result, the curriculum basically defines what must be taught but gives no indication about what should be learned (Schmelkes, 1992). When it comes to learning assessment, Mexico shows poor results in mathematics, Spanish, and the sciences. Mexico's ratings in the Program for International Student Assessment (PISA) always show placement at very low levels. At the same time, nation-building goals seem to prevail over personal development or acquiring learning skills. As researchers have observed, an important part of school activities consists of preparing for ceremonies and parades, or memorizing historical facts. As the poet Octavio Paz (1985) once commented, Mexico is fond of "any pretext to stop the flow of time and commemorate men and events with festivals and ceremonies" (p. 47).

Upper Secondary Education

While the aims of elementary education are fairly clear and similar to those of other countries, the role of upper secondary education is far more complex.

It is not mandatory, and the government does not regulate the curriculum, even though the authority to operate can stem from the federal or a state government, or from either a public or private university. The result is that institutions of upper secondary education are something of a "no man's land."

An important characteristic is that many upper secondary schools are preparatory schools—created by universities with the purpose of recruiting and preparing future university students. As such, many preparatory schools are part of a university. The teachers are on the university payroll and many universities favor students from their own preparatory schools for admission.

This historical background has had important implications for curricular content. First, many schools are practically free to define their own curriculum and have done so over time, often in response to the particular perspective of the university of which they are a part. Further, federal and state governments have sought to create alternatives to university-owned high schools, such as vocational upper secondary schools. Such intervention has produced an impressive variety; by the 1970s, 187 different programs of study were formally registered by these upper secondary schools (Latapí, 1998).

Although most upper secondary schools prepare their students for tertiary education, this preparation has not taken the shape of a general or liberal education. Rather, upper secondary education mainly serves as a "rite of passage," bridging the three-year gap between lower secondary education and the university. This means that the typical curriculum tends to be "excessively inclusive of all types of contents," which "imperils the accomplishment of the formative and propedeutic character of this level [of education]" (Zorrilla, 2008, p. 203). Often it continues the rote learning typical of the primary level, sometimes even repeating the same subjects, such as Mexican history. Upper secondary education lacks an independent purpose. It does not prepare its students explicitly for the labor market, nor does it provide a general education; it mainly prepares for future university studies.

Recent policy documents (SEP, 2007) describe upper secondary education as problematic in terms of both content and efficiency. Many upper secondary schools have introduced entrance exams with the result that they reject some of their applicants. Of every 1,000 students who enroll in primary education, only 451 finish lower secondary education (Mexicanos Primero, 2010). Then, only about 65% of these students take the next step of enrolling in an upper secondary school. The huge quantity of ill-defined courses in the upper secondary schools creates an additional bottleneck: only 57% of students survive the three-year preparation (Diario Oficial de la Federación, 2008). As an upper secondary diploma is a requirement, this means that only 33% of the relevant age group obtains the credentials for entrance to higher education (Zorrilla, 2008). Furthermore, an upper secondary diploma is a requirement, but not a guarantee. An even smaller group manages to survive the university admission processes. Particularly perplexing is the fact that many students from the preparatory schools that are part of a university may successfully pass all courses but still fail the university's entrance exam.

Some changes are occurring. Several private schools have adopted such programs as the International Baccalaureate endorsed by UNESCO, which contemplates fewer unrelated subject matters. In the public sector, the federal government is currently urging schools to reorganize the huge number of separate subjects into general areas like the social sciences or the natural sciences and to work toward a simplified curriculum. But as this level of education has been unregulated for decades, changes are few and slow.

Historical and Cultural Influences on Higher Education

The debate about whether higher education should be specialized or general has a long history. A crucial aspect is that Mexican higher education originated from the European continental model of organization (Clark, 1983) and that it has mostly looked to Europe—and sometimes to Latin America—for model reforms, but very rarely to the United States.

Mirroring Europe, Mexican higher education traditionally prepares for a specific profession. This preparation takes around six years to complete, is specialized from the start, and leads to the degree of *licenciatura* or "license to practice." Except for medicine, where some supervision on practitioners exists, graduates are completely free to practice their profession. Within this model, no differentiation between undergraduate and postgraduate education existed until the 1980s. Master's and doctoral options were practically nonexistent, while the *licenciatura* was considered as final.

The organizational structure of universities also followed the European tradition. Universities were organized by Faculties (*Facultades*), not by departments. (We use "Faculty" (upper case) to refer to academic units and "faculty" for academic staff.) Each Faculty tended to offer just one or two study programs. For example, a university's Law Faculty offers a law program but operates completely separately from the Faculty of Administration. This form of organization means, as just one important consequence, that virtually no common courses exist between Faculties. Thus, students' programs resemble tunnels without side exits. It is impossible to take courses outside their Faculty; and given the absence of a credit recognition system, it is not possible for students to change to another program or university.

The consequence for faculty is that their careers largely depend on being hired to teach within a given Faculty, and then obtaining tenure. With strong unions, tenure was generally assigned automatically after two years, even for part-time faculty. As a result, curricular reform became something to be avoided since it would pose the threat of courses being cancelled. Each faculty member would staunchly defend his or her share of the curriculum. As a result, no tradition of a general education at the *licenciatura* level, followed by a specialization at the graduate level, emerged.

The History of Higher Education in Mexico

The Real y Pontificia Universidad de México, founded in Mexico City in 1595, ranks among the oldest in the world. This institution, and a dozen local colleges, were set up by the Catholic Church during the colonial era, replicating Spanish universities. They educated the elite through a small number of majors: theology, law, medicine, and the fine arts, which comprises a mixture of literature, history, and philosophy and is therefore akin to the liberal arts.

Following independence in 1810, however, these institutions underwent power struggles between conservatives and liberals, and between the government and the church. Starting in 1833, Mexico's President Gómez Farías closed the Pontificia Universidad, deeming it "useless and impossible to reform" (Garciadiego, 1996). His supporters took the position that building a modern state required institutions that taught civil law or modern languages instead of canonical law, theology, or Latin. As a result, the liberals created various public scientific and literary institutes and colleges to replace the Catholic institutions.

The conservatives considered these new institutions politically dangerous and tried to maintain the Pontificia Universidad, despite the president's efforts to close it. Still, they failed, and the university remained closed for several decades. Finally, in 1855, its main building was permanently converted into the first licensed *cantina* (bar). However, its professionally oriented colleges of law and medicine, and the College for Commerce and Agriculture continued to operate in other quarters. In addition, the government opened the Escuela Preparatoria (Upper Secondary School) in 1867, designed to provide general preparation at the upper secondary level, based on "scientific methods" (positivism) in order to prepare México for modern times (Garciadiego, 1996).

Over the next four decades, several political leaders tried to establish a new university that would be national, public, and secular. Plans did not prosper until the founding in 1910 of the university now known as Universidad Nacional Autónoma de México.

One result of the confrontation between liberals and conservatives was that the Catholic Church was banned from education at all levels. Until the 1980s, higher education remained essentially public and secular. Institutions were created, funded, and managed by government entities.

A second consequence was that nation-building, through the preparation of the local elite, became the central task for higher education. Given this logic, the organizational model adopted was that of France (hence, the term "Napoleonic model"). This type of organization typically consisted of the highly independent Faculties or Schools already described. They were grouped loosely within universities and tended to concentrate on the professions (law, medicine, and civil engineering). Only occasionally were other possible models, such as that of Berkeley or the University of Berlin, considered. One reason for the dominance of the Napoleonic model was the almost total absence of research in the sciences and the humanities, thus effectively excluding the Humboldt ideal. A second reason was that several dominant participants in the debate had studied in France.

Twentieth-Century Emphases

During the 20th century, three factors defined the character of Mexican higher education: (a) the Mexican Revolution (1910–1918) and the ensuing efforts to set up a new administration that altered the role of the state; (b) the Reform of Córdoba (Argentina) of 1918 that spurred universities to claim autonomy and to limit government intervention; and (c) growing enrollments, especially after 1970, that changed the nature of national education in various ways.

The Mexican Revolution with its focus on nation-building, particularly in the 1930s and 1940s, deemphasized the preparation of an educated elite in favor of educating peasants and workers. Vocational training became a paramount issue. In the 1930s, the federal government created the Instituto Politécnica Nacional and the first technological institutes as more "practical" alternatives to the universities. These initiatives related clearly to the nationalization of oil and Mexico's growing industrialization. Of course, industrialization reinforced the position of traditional professionals. However, their role did not remain limited to the practice of independent lawyers, physicians, or engineers. Many graduates from these programs went on to become politicians, administrators, business people, or public intellectuals. The National University, in particular its Law Faculty, became an important training ground for politicians and bureaucrats (Camp, 1995). As such, public universities attained a crucial role as "state-building institutions" (Odorika & Pusser, 2007). Furthermore, an increasing number of lawyers, physicians, engineers, and teachers became employees in the rapidly expanding government offices that included public health services and many state-owned industries.

Interestingly, José Vasconcelos, Mexico's first Secretary of Education, launched an initiative in the 1920s to provide all Mexicans with a "universal culture." Its most visible part was the translation of the canon of Western literature into Spanish with the books being distributed at a very low cost among the general population.

At the same time, small colleges of arts and letters flourished in several states, just like the discussion clubs that operated in cafés around the main square. However, intellectual and political life did not originate in a university-level education in the liberal arts but rather as an adjunct to a traditional profession. Those who discussed politics, literature, or the arts on a Friday afternoon tended to be the village lawyer, doctor, or teacher.

The Mexican university system also reflects this historical trend. During the first half of the 20th century, universities offered the traditional professions, but not the sciences or the arts. In most public state universities, these options were created only after the 1950s. Some universities never did offer these majors with these emphases; and even today, they are absent from most private universities. Where they do exist, enrollments always remained very small, compared to the professions.

A second defining force in Mexican higher education in the 20th century has been autonomy. The Reform of Córdoba called for institutional autonomy, seeking to limit government intervention in such matters as governance, academic content and curricula, and the hiring of faculty and staff. It proposed the participation of both faculty and students in governance and stressed the importance of research and collaboration with society.

During the 20th century, most Mexican public universities achieved autonomy with far-reaching results. The hiring of faculty and staff, curriculum development, and admissions policies became the exclusive realm of each university. Within institutions, university councils became very powerful. At the same time, their membership changed radically, many including equivalent numbers of students and faculty. Some universities even introduced a one-person one-vote procedure to elect the rector and other authorities. Academic freedom also took extreme forms. It became a common practice for faculty members to individually define the contents, instructional method, and evaluation forms for their courses, banning any outside influence from the classroom. As Fuentes observed regarding academic freedom: "There has been an extended tendency towards feudal isolation and the sovereignty of improvisation and arbitrariness" (Fuentes, Gago, & Ortega, 1991, p. 11). The results spilled over to research with each researcher claiming freedom to set his or her own agenda. Research also tended to be carried out in institutes, separate from the Faculties.

This form of institutional autonomy, however, clearly favored the traditional majors. In the numerous decisions that required voting, a Law Faculty with thousands of students wielded far more power than the Faculty of Philosophy, with a few hundred.

The third 20th-century influence—expanding enrollments—further heightened the dominance of traditional majors. After student protests in 1968, the government and most public universities opted for an "open door policy," admitting everyone with an upper secondary school diploma, without restrictions on fields of study. This liberalization caused a massive inflow into the public universities, with students clustering mainly in the traditional majors. The upshot was not, properly speaking, a system of mass education, as national enrollments remained under 15% of the relevant age group (Throw, 1974). However, many public universities saw their enrollments increase rapidly.

In some cases, the Faculty of Law grew to have as many students as a typical university had had 10 years earlier, while enrollments in the sciences or the humanities remained limited.

This trend further bolstered the traditional model of the university, characterized by separate Faculties. Politics played a major role in higher education. Several public universities became strongholds of opposition to the local or federal government, and the threat of calling students out in protests or on strikes became an important weapon in negotiating public funding. But politics was equally important within universities. Faculty directors negotiated their share of the institutional budget based on student numbers, with the result that students were increasingly considered as potential votes, not as young people who attended the university to learn something.

As public universities grew rapidly, they mainly did so following the traditional organizational structure. Most faculty members were hired on a part-time basis, combining academia with their professional practices. Faculties remained closed compartments, and majors continued to operate separately from each other. Such internal isolation made any idea of a general education implausible. However, some reform attempts were made, ranging from the creation of a new public university in México City (Universidad Autónoma Metropolitana) with a department structure and a strong research priority, to efforts within institutions to create alternative majors or to develop research expertise. Over the years, more faculty became full-time, new majors were established in the sciences and the humanities, and research grew in importance. These changes led to proposals that universities should become agents of change in society, not just preparations for a profession. Starting in the 1960s, the concept of the Humboldt research university became more important, stressing the link between research and teaching.

The Emerging Private Sector

Emerging from the historical trends that characterized the 20th century was the creation of private universities beginning in the 1980s. The first wave of these universities can be characterized as the "departure of the elite" who established private universities because they considered that public universities no longer met their needs (Levy, 1986). Some of these private universities had religious inspirations, while others were set up by business sectors.

Unlike the public universities, most elite private institutions were organized with a department structure, facilitating collaboration or mobility between similar majors. Several also started to offer a more general education, at least during the first years of each major. Not all of them shared the same motivation for this approach. Some religiously inspired institutions stressed a humanistic education, while others consciously modeled themselves on U.S. colleges and universities.

A second wave of private institutions surged mostly after 1990 and is best described as "demand absorbing" (Levy, 1986). For the most part, they catered to students rejected by the public universities and offered programs that were virtually identical to the most demanded professional programs.

Even when private universities looked to foreign models, they remained oriented toward traditional majors, in response to student demand. A first reason is that most private universities started out with Faculties of law, business administration, and engineering, where most of their students were concentrated. Because they do not receive public funding, they are highly dependent on tuition fees. Second, receiving authorization to operate from federal and state authorities, or from public autonomous universities, tended to be easier if study plans resembled those of the public universities.

Thus, despite the undeniable changes of the 20th century, enrollments remained concentrated in only a few majors. Law, accountancy, administration, and medicine account for 40% of students and engineering for another 35%, but the humanities and the sciences combined total less than 5%.

Higher Education Today

By 1990 it was clear that higher education in Mexico was in crisis and that the problem was not only financial. The federal government proclaimed that public universities did not respond properly to societal or labor market demands, a critique with which public opinion and most universities concurred (Gago, 1992). As a result, several federal policies attempted to reform the system. These initiatives, however, did not promote a liberal or general education. Although the results have been called a sort of "neo-liberal education" (Villaseñor, 1994), a primary goal for many federal policies has been meeting the needs of the labor market by fostering vocational training.

Various international organizations contributed to this perspective. A report from the Economic Commission for Latin America (CEPAL-UNESCO, 1992) stressed the urgent need for a renewed relation between higher education and the labor market. The World Bank (1994) and the Organization for Economic Cooperation and Development (1997), of which Mexico became a member in 1993, highlighted vocational training and improved human capital as essential for economic development.

These recommendations triggered important changes. One was the creation of a wholly new sector of technological universities, offering two-year vocational programs. A second initiative concerned the expansion and decentralization of the technological institutes. Third, the federal government urged public universities to stop growing, to introduce enrollment caps for the saturated traditional professions, and to create new majors that were better oriented to the labor market (Cabrera, de Vries, & Anderson, 2008). Universities responded with a rapid proliferation of new programs. While most universities typically offered some 20 majors in 1990, by 2010 most offered well over 50. Each university retained autonomy in deciding what majors to create and what the curriculum would include, but the proliferation of options was certainly triggered by financial initiatives from the government. Every new major provided the political opportunity to ask for more faculty positions and funding.

At the same time, the federal government introduced a deregulation of the private sector, spurring the rapid growth of institutions. Many small private institutions sprang up, offering mostly the supposedly saturated majors on which public universities had placed enrollment caps. Private participation grew from 17% of enrollments in 1990 to 35% by 2010. In the traditional majors, however, private institutions represented well over 50% of the total enrollment (Gil, 2005).

The general dissatisfaction with a university's ability to prepare its graduates adequately for the labor market led to a renewed focus on the vocational utility of majors. This approach, however, also led to the inclusion of majors that a few decades before would have been deemed as "unscientific"—for example, programs in fashion design, tourist administration, gastronomy, or folkloric dance.

A second set of views and policies, however, points to a somewhat different trend. Since 1990, several federal policies have stressed that public universities must become research universities. The most prominent policies in this area are those aimed at improving faculty credentials. At the beginning of the 1990s, most faculty members (75%) were part-time and had only a *licenciatura* degree. The federal government defined this faculty profile as a crucial problem and introduced a program that provided financial support to already-hired faculty in the public sector, so that they could obtain postgraduate degrees, become full-time, and carry out research (Rodríguez, 2002).

In many aspects, this support officially endorsed the Humboldt model. For the most part, universities and faculty warmly welcomed this program. However, the encouragement of the research university also raised new issues. One is the emergence of postgraduate studies, resulting in a European–U.S. hybrid in Mexican higher education. The traditional, long-term, specialized *licenciatura* came to be considered as some sort of undergraduate education that needed to be complemented by postgraduate studies.

A second question concerns the compatibility between a research university and the stress on vocationally or professionally oriented programs. Public policies started to create tensions within academe with the introduction of merit pay programs that mostly favor full-time faculty with a Ph.D. who are dedicated to research. These programs also clearly favor researchers from the sciences and humanities over part-time teachers involved in undergraduate professional programs. And while most students and faculty remained concentrated in the professionally oriented *licenciaturas*, many full-time faculty started to move from undergraduate to graduate education and, consequently, to spend less time on teaching (Comas, 2003).

Policies enacted since 1990 thus reflect conflicting demands. On the one hand, they clearly stress the need for more vocationally oriented programs. On the other hand, they seek to convert universities with a traditional orientation toward the professions into research universities (Acosta, 2000). Neither of these conflicting demands, however, acknowledges a need for a general education.

The Prospects for General Education

While public policies since the 1990s have not promoted general education, many universities have developed initiatives tending in that direction. But given Mexico's highly deregulated system, the initiatives have played out differently in each institution. To make an inventory of general education initiatives, we sampled curricular contents across all sectors of the higher education system and in several parts of the country.[1] In general, we can distinguish between general education by design and by default.

General Education by Design

In referring to "general education by design," we mean courses included in the curriculum with the explicit aim of offering something different from preparation for a specific profession. We found that the curriculum of the technological institutes and universities is strictly vocational, without any general education courses—except, perhaps, for one or two general introductory courses (DGEST, 2010).

In contrast, the university sector displays a bewildering variety of courses. Almost all of them offer courses, mainly in the students' early semesters, which do not directly relate to a specific major. The most frequent types of such courses are (a) remedial, (b) reflections of institutional missions and visions, and (c) general competencies.

Remedial. Such courses aim to compensate for insufficient prior preparation, rather than to provide a general education per se. Examples are reading/writing skills, information and communication technology, mathematics and statistics, and Mexican history, society, and culture.

Reflections of institutional missions and visions. This category is both the most varied and the most institution-specific. Popular topics are professional practice and ethics, social responsibility, ecology, sustainable development, globalization and human development, politics, and issues of faith and science. It seems that, through these courses, each institution seeks to put a particular stamp on its majors and to make its program distinctive in the growing competition for students. It also seems to us that some of these topics (e.g., globalization, social crises, or sustainable development) were somewhat faddish rather than genuine innovations. They have been added during the last decade, and some tend to have a short lifespan. For example, a course on globalization can be rapidly replaced by one on sustainable development.

Instruction in general competencies. This third area focuses on emerging expectations of skills that modern higher education should provide. Examples are complex and/or critical thinking, communication skills, interpersonal skills, and learning to learn. Our appraisal of these courses noted that some (e.g., critical thinking or communication skills) have been added recently because the international literature on education devotes considerable attention to them. At times, they seem to be rather bureaucratic responses in the sense that universities simply add a course on "learning to learn" or "critical thinking" rather than changing teaching practices.

Degrees of General Education

Our research also allowed us to distinguish several degrees of general education by design. While almost all universities have included at least two or three courses of a more general content in one of the three categories above, most limit entrance to these courses to the first semesters, thus serving as a type of remedial instruction (type 1) but also as an introduction to courses that speak to the institutional mission (type 2), or even as quasi-experimental courses representing emphases currently popular in international education (type 3). Examples of these types of courses are found at the Universidad Nacional Autónoma de México and the Universidad Autónoma Metropolitana, two of the major public universities.

A more advanced level of general education presents a core curriculum common to all students that requires several courses taken in different years. A frequent strategy developed by universities offering this kind of curriculum is to create a special academic entity in charge of the common courses for all majors and to consider these courses as a "horizontal alignment." Thus, all students will need to take "critical thinking" or "sustainable development" during their studies, no matter what their major might be. These courses tend to be separated from the normal course load and are taught by teachers from outside the Faculty, thus sidestepping the traditional Faculty structure. This type of organization is found in both public and private universities, such as the Benemérita Universidad Autónoma de Puebla (BUAP), the Universidad Veracruzana (UV), the Universidad Autónoma de Nuevo León (UANL), and the Instituto Tecnológico de Estudios Superiores de Monterrey (ITESM).

A third variation creates a curricular structure in which several academic units participate within a major, typically within a departmental structure. An example of this type of organization is the undergraduate major in business administration in the Universidad Iberoamericana. The core courses are taught by the Department of Administration, but the Department of Engineering teaches the math courses, and the Departments of Social Sciences or Humanities are responsible for still other courses.

The number of courses of a general character is an important marker of the level of debate about a general versus a specialized curriculum. Given that the undergraduate curriculum in Mexican universities requires a student to take between 40 and 50 courses, the inclusion of two or three general courses has only marginal impact. The requirement of 10 courses points to a more serious commitment to general education.

Based on this criterion of numbers, general education in Mexico remains marginal in the higher education enterprise. The Nacional Autónoma de México follows the traditional model, with only sporadic common courses. The Universidad Autónoma Metropolitana includes general education courses in the first semesters (e.g., "History of Mexico"), but such courses tend to exhaust the general offerings. Other public universities likewise have introduced a few common courses, but these courses tend to represent less than 10% of the curriculum.

Private universities have a broader common core, though with important variations. Small private universities tend to simply copy the curricula from public universities and therefore include only a few common courses. The more consolidated universities, however, have developed their own curricular structure, often inspired either by a religious background or by an international model. A crucial aspect is that they tend to be organized into departments, a structure that allows sharing courses between majors. An example is the *licenciatura* degree in the humanities and social sciences offered by ITESM. Its study plan outlines nine semesters each offering about six courses, making a total of about 54, and covering a huge variety of topics: from management, law, and political science, design, and "Communication with the Media," to philosophy, sociology, anthropology, semiotics, postmodernism, world history, and world literature. However, this degree does not seem to resemble a well thought out core of general education classes that would provide a common instructional and skill foundation. Rather, it seems to be a large accumulation of very miscellaneous courses.

As this survey makes clear, the debate about what higher education should prepare its students for and how it should achieve that goal continues. But given the near absolute autonomy that universities can exercise in this regard, the result is an enormous variety.

General Education by Default

A second aspect to consider in appraising the level and future of general education in Mexico is that some majors might be offering a type of general education "by default," meaning that such majors were never planned as general education with a specially designed curriculum but, in practice, do perform this role. According to Moura Castro and Levy (1997), for example, several majors offer a de facto general education. The characterizing element of these programs is that instructors are "teaching in what are called professions, but whose labor market is saturated or ill-defined" (p. 19). Given this uncertainty about the graduate's employability once he or she has completed the course, considerable creativity may be exercised within traditional disciplines to align them to the labor market.

For example, several supposedly specialized professional majors, such as law, have actually prepared graduates for a broad array of occupations. Many continue to do so. Results from recent alumni tracer studies (Cabrera et al., 2008) show that traditional majors such as law and administration prepare their graduates for jobs ranging from public servants to independent consultants or private sector employees. Some more recent majors, such as psychology, education, economics, and communication, seem to offer similarly broad preparation. As Moura Castro and Levy (1997) have commented, many of these traditional majors do not prepare their students for a specific profession, nor do they offer a specific type of vocational training. Instead, they offer a type of general preparation for a broad sector of jobs.

A second aspect is that these majors do, in fact, incorporate a broader curriculum than might be indicated by their titles. A major in law or administration tends to include not only courses on economics, international law, history, and ethics, but also on accountancy and statistics. In contrast, a major in physics tends to limit itself to physics.

Beyond the Curriculum

Besides the formal curriculum, aspects of a more general education can be discerned in several areas. First is extracurricular activities, an area in which public universities have been traditionally stronger than the private colleges. Since the beginning of the 20th century, Mexican universities have considered that their role is threefold: teaching, research, and outreach. The outreach component goes beyond simply cooperating with outside actors on areas of mutual interest. Rather, it asserts that public universities should develop extracurricular educational and artistic activities with the goal of transmitting culture to students and to society at large.

Consequently, many public universities actively support theaters, cinemas, radio and television stations, publishing houses, concert halls, and museums—all with energetic and broad programs. Studies on youth culture have found that students from public universities actively participate in these activities, whereas students from private universities tend to seek cultural activities outside their institution. We are not aware of any studies examining what students actually learn from these activities, but it seems logical that the existence and range of cultural activities play a crucial role in retention and personal development. Equally logically, the absence of these activities at a university leads to less cultural and social participation (de Garay, 2004). Thus, especially at public universities, students are exposed to some sort of general education outside the classrooms.

A second variety of extracurricular experiences depends on the campus organization. The Universidad de las Américas is the only university that provides on-campus dormitories and housing for both faculty and students, an outgrowth of taking Oxford and Cambridge as its models. But while other universities do not have on-campus housing, they provide such facilities as libraries, meeting rooms, cafeterias, and computer laboratories that are not only centers of knowledge acquisition but also provide locales in which mingling and informal communications are encouraged. Such on-campus facilities particularly characterize public universities since the 1990s; they have moved away from an infrastructure focused exclusively on classrooms.

Most small private institutions differ markedly from this model in presenting more fluid boundaries and less time on campus. They typically resemble a sort of "take-out" education. The teachers tend to be part-time, paid by the hour, and without offices, research facilities, or library carrels. They tend to teach their classes and then leave the school building. Students do the same. No extracurricular activities, libraries, cafeterias, or meeting spaces encourage them to linger.

Something similar occurs in branch campuses: over the last two decades, both public and private institutions have set up small university campuses outside the major cities, with the idea of taking education to the students. These branches have the same curriculum and generally the same faculty (who travel to teach), but the learning environment is clearly minimal. These campuses have little infrastructure, do not sponsor cultural or extracurricular activities, offer only a few majors, and tend to have a limited number of students.

If Pascarella and Terenzini (2005) are correct in arguing that about half of learning takes place outside the classroom through extracurricular activities, then the distinct learning environments offered by different higher education institutions have direct ramifications for the learning experiences of their students. Table 4.1 displays the combination of curricular and extracurricular activities at several universities.

Does Mexico Need General Education?

As our inventory indicates, liberal education as such is nonexistent, and no institutions of higher education explicitly offer liberal arts preparation. However, several institutions have undertaken initiatives to provide courses that are explicitly designed to offer a more general education. Is this trend

TABLE 4.1 The formal and informal learning environment at selected Mexican universities

Institution	Sector	Research	General courses	Courses	Extracurricular activities
Universidad Autónoma Metropolitana	Public	Yes	Yes	Core curriculum in many departments. The Social Science and Humanities Division has common courses in history and society, political and social doctrines, economy, politics and society, academic writing, reading comprehension, and Mexican literature. But other departments have few common courses.	Many
Instituto Politécnico Nacional	Public	Yes	No	No core curriculum, but some common topics: statistics, philosophy of science, and science and society.	Few
Benemérita Universidad Autónoma de Puebla	Public	Yes	Yes	Several common courses: complex thinking skills, use of information and communication technologies, human and social education, foreign language, and innovation and entrepreneurship.	Many
Universidad Autónoma de Nuevo León	Public	Yes	Yes	General courses: information technologies, communication competencies, arts appreciation. Other courses (not common to all majors): English, ethics, society and profession, arts and humanities.	Many

Institution	Type			Description	
Universidad de Guadalajara	Public	Yes	No	Only some common topics: research methodology, statistics, speaking and writing skills, foreign language.	Many
Universidad Tecnológica de Tecámac	Public, technological	No	Yes	Common courses: foreign language, socio-cultural education, speaking and writing skills.	Few
Instituto Tecnológico de Estudios Superiores Monterrey	Private, secular	Yes	Yes	Common courses: English, writing, mathematics, computer use.	Few
Universidad de las Américas	Private, secular	Yes	Yes	Core curriculum: learning approaches, foreign language, writing skills, critical thinking, and interdisciplinary approaches.	Many
Universidad Iberoamericana (Golfo-Centro)	Private, religious	Yes, but limited to humanities	Yes	Reading and speaking, introduction to university thinking, synthesis and assessment workshop, human development in a global world, human coexistence, social service, civil crisis and human future, foreign language.	Many

significant? Would some sort of liberal or general education be desirable, feasible, or even inescapable for Mexican higher education?

Some factors clearly point to a need for a more general type of education, including what might be called a liberal arts program. First, the current model of specialized, rigid, professionally oriented and long-term programs is highly inefficient. National graduation rates are below 50% five years after matriculation, while some majors register graduation rates below 20%. Second, faculty and student mobility is practically impossible. Third, this traditional approach requires a huge number of courses and hours in the classroom, but these requirements are based more on faculty teaching requirements than on student learning goals. Fourth, the introduction of postgraduate programs has produced a paradoxical situation where a long-term first cycle of five or six years to achieve the *licenciatura* is followed by another five or six years of postgraduate cycle, which means that it takes about 12 years to obtain a Ph.D.

At the same time, vocational training, whether offered either by technological universities or by the addition of novel programs at the universities, does not seem to be very successful, as it prepares its graduates for very narrow niches in the labor market (Cabrera et al., 2008).

Given the cumbersomeness and inefficiency of this system, the U.S. model of providing a four-year first cycle of a more general education, shifting more toward specialization in the last two years, would clearly mean an improvement. The U.S. system has four advantages over the traditional European model: it is shorter, provides a broader base from which to specialize, allows for mobility through credit recognition, and is better geared to meeting the needs of a variety of students within a system of mass education (Altbach, 2001).

Further pressure toward reforming Mexican higher education comes from international factors. As Andrés Bernasconi (2008) points out, the traditional Latin American model seems to become increasingly obsolete as globalization and internationalization, together with curricular reform in other parts of the world, urge the advantages of greater efficiency and greater mobility. For example, the North American Free Trade Agreement (NAFTA) between Mexico, the United States, and Canada calls for a free movement of professionals and a mutual recognition of degrees. An increasing number of Mexicans leaving for Canada or the United States nowadays do so with a university degree but encounter problems in having their degrees recognized.

In a similar vein, changes occurring in the European Union after the Bologna agreement pose serious questions. Traditionally, Mexican universities have paid little attention to the United States compared to the attention they have given European higher education. As Europe moves toward something resembling the U.S. model, the Mexican system of six-year professional education is seen as increasingly unwieldy in the face of two international systems that offer more general and flexible four-year undergraduate preparation. In short, Mexican higher education is becoming increasingly incompatible with most of the world. Ironically, it would still be defending the Napoleonic model after even the French have abandoned it.

As two additional difficulties, several Mexican universities are engaged in international academic exchange programs, but their success requires credit recognition between institutions. Last, but not least, some private universities are now foreign owned, adopting curricular models from abroad, and encountering all of the compatibility problems mentioned above.

In the face of these conditions, even setting aside the question of how well the traditional system of Mexican higher education serves its students and the nation, an inescapable question is whether that model of five- or six-year professional majors can remain viable in an environment that is moving toward three- or four-year undergraduate degrees. Nor is the question of efficiency inconsequential. Why should it take six years to educate an engineer in Mexico when it takes four years in other countries? And how valuable is that engineering degree if it cannot be recognized as equivalent in settings outside Mexico?

Despite these undeniable advantages favoring change, educational reform faces several serious obstacles. The first is cultural. The U.S. model of liberal education is unknown in Mexico. Despite the geographical proximity of the two nations, academic exchange has occurred only in the area of postgraduate studies, not at the undergraduate level. No U.S. or international organizations have ever promoted the concept of liberal education in Mexico. Because no one in Mexican academia is familiar with liberal education, it simply does not appear on the agenda of possible alternatives. Furthermore, ideas coming from abroad are always eyed with a certain reserve.

This cultural suspicion also seems to apply to changes occurring in Europe following the Bologna reforms. As José Joaquín Brunner (2008) observes for Latin America, the Bologna process has been followed with interest by some but has been entirely dismissed by most. A similar range of positions can be found among faculty members and administrators in many Mexican universities. Furthermore, public policies have carefully avoided questioning the traditional model because so many influential voices continue to defend the Latin American model (Bernasconi, 2008)

A second factor concerns structural or organizational aspects. The traditional model of Faculties offering specialized and professional licenciaturas has seen little change over time. As documented above, most universities, both public and private, have generated some general courses that are positioned in the first semesters of students' programs; but while this development points to increased attention to a more general education, the countermovement is that nearly all new majors created since the 1990s have been modeled after the existing ones—in short, the creation of a five- or six-year program resulting in a license to practice. These changes seem to have produced increasing specialization, rather than a more general education.

Some private universities have innovated majors that can be completed in three or four years and that offer education of a more general character. However, three factors have hindered these initiatives. First, official recognition by federal, state, or public university authorities invariably requires that qualifying as *licenciatura* demands a certain number of courses and hours. Second, current accreditation processes focus on inputs rather than content or outcomes (de Vries, 2007).

A crucial and complicating factor is that these traditional forms of organization are directly linked to labor conditions and reward systems. Curriculum has traditionally been defined by faculty, not by student needs, with virtually no limitations on institutional autonomy. Academic positions and salaries are determined by teaching loads (i.e., hours spent in the classroom) within each Faculty, which means that changes in curricular content have personal consequences. Reforming the existing majors thus becomes difficult.

A third factor is that students continue to demand the traditional majors. By 2008, more than 80% of students remained concentrated in professionally oriented majors, ranging from administration to engineering, while majors in the sciences and the humanities accounted for less than 5% of enrollments. Efforts to redirect students to other options have been mostly unsuccessful. The attempted reform of introducing enrollment caps on traditional majors in most public universities mainly resulted, not in student interest in less saturated majors, but in the creation of private establishments providing traditional majors that enroll students rejected by the public universities. The creation of new options in the public sector did not change the situation either. The new technological universities account for only 8% of total national enrollment. Likewise, several novel majors created by the public and private universities suffer from a lack of student demand.

The labor market does not seem to demand a new type of graduates either. Although some international organizations and local experts consider that the "knowledge society" is an inevitable development, the Mexican labor market does not seem responsive to these predictions. For the past two decades, government policies have encouraged the creation of many novel "practical" majors that produce workers fitted for emerging niches in the economy. While the Mexican economy has seen a shift from the industrial sector toward the service sector, it does not seem to be accompanied by a need for new types of majors or a more general type of higher education. Paradoxically, alumni tracer studies show that traditional majors remain better geared to the current labor market than many novel options (Cabrera et al., 2008). This finding suggests that the general programs "by default" that give graduates broad preparation for a rapidly changing economy actually present a better strategy.

Finally, external—national or international—pressures for change continue to have only marginal effects. Mexican universities prepare for the local labor market, not for the global economy. Few undergraduate students study abroad and Mexican universities do not seek to attract foreign students. Accreditation criteria are local, based on the traditional model; and the major public and private universities have already received official quality recognition by these accrediting bodies. Public funding is not related to outcomes or results but rather to sustaining the payrolls of the public universities. And while there have been some efforts toward regional collaboration in Latin America, there is nothing similar to the processes currently underway in the European Union that would call for a serious revision of Mexican undergraduate education.

Conclusion

Undeniably, a liberal or general education tradition is absent from Mexican higher education. Although the theme has popped up at several points, it has never made serious headway against the traditional professions that remain the backbone of the Mexican system. It is true that several institutions have included courses of a more general character in their curricula. As universities are free to define their curricula, these courses manifest a huge variety: from remedial classes to topics on the relationship between higher education and society to general competencies. Many of these courses can be seen as adaptations or fads by universities, responding to current international debates. Most of them are promoted by certain sectors of academe but do not seem to be supported by students, employers, or the (traditional) professions. In any case, this type of general education seems to play only a marginal role, representing less than 10% of total course loads.

However, the debate about a general versus a specialized curriculum continues. Within the context of increasing internationalization, Mexican universities are under some pressure to reconsider curricular structures, reduce the number of courses, and look for areas of major convergence with systems in other countries. Whether such pressures will lead to a more general type of higher education remains doubtful, as the current debates and policies focus rather on vocational relevance or the need for postgraduate studies in research universities. By and large, there are no signs that anyone, whether in the public or private sector, is looking for undergraduates with a liberal arts background.

Note

1 Our inventory includes the following institutions: Universidad Autónoma Metropolitana, Benemérita Universidad Autónoma de Puebla, Universidad Autónoma de Nuevo León, Universidad Tecnológica de Tecámac, Universidad Intercultural del Estado de Tabasco, Universidad Autónoma Indígena de México, Instituto Tecnológico de Estudios Superiores Monterrey, Universidad de las Américas, Universidad Iberoamericana, and Centro de Estudios Universitarios Monterrey.

References

Acosta, A. (2000). *Estado, políticas y universidades en un período de transición*. Mexico: Universidad de Guadalajara, Fondo de Cultura Económica.

Altbach, P. G. (2001). The American academic model in comparative perspective. In P. G. Altbach, P. J. Gumport, & D. B. Johnstone (Eds.), *In defense of American higher education* (pp. 11–37). Baltimore, MD: Johns Hopkins University Press.

AACU. American Association of Colleges and Universities. (1998). *Statement on liberal learning*. Retrieved on February 18, 2010, from www.aacu.org/About/statements/liberal_learning.cfm.

Bernasconi, A. (2008). Is there a Latin-American model of the university? *Comparative Education Review, 52*(1), 27–52.

Brunner, J. J. (2008). El proceso de Bolonia en el horizonte latinoamericano: Límites y posibilidades, *Revista de Educación*, número extraordinario, pp. 119–145.

BUAP. Benemérita Universidad Autónoma de Puebla. (2009). *Modelo Universitario Minerva: Documento de integración*. Puebla, México: Benemérita Universidad Autónoma de Puebla.

Cabrera, A., de Vries, W., & Anderson, S. (2008). Job satisfaction among Mexican alumni: A case of incongruence between hunch-based policies and labor market demands. *Higher Education, 56*, 699–722.

Camp, R. A. (1995). *La política en México*. México: Siglo XXI editores.

CEPAL-UNESCO. (1992). *Educación y conocimiento: Eje de transformación productiva con equidad*. Santiago de Chile: CEPAL (Economic Commission for Latin America).

Clark, B. R. (1983). *The higher education system: Academic organization in a cross-national perspective*. Berkeley: University of California Press.

Comas, O. (2003). *Movilidad académica y efectos no previstos de los estímulos académicos: El caso de la UAM [Universidad Autónoma Metropolitana]*. México: Asociación Nacional de Universidades e Instituciones de Educación Superior.

De Garay, A. (2004). *Integración de los jóvenes en el sistema universitario: Prácticas sociales, académicas y de consumo cultural*. Barcelona: Ediciones Pomares.

De Vries, W. (2002). *Federal policies in Mexican higher education*. Alliance for Higher Education Policy Studies. Retrieved on November 13, 2007, from www.nyu.edu/iesp/aiheps/research.html.

De Vries, W. (2007). La acreditación mexicana desde una perspectiva comparativa. *Revista Complutense de Educación, 18*(2), 11–28.

De Vries, W., & Álvarez, G. (2005). Acerca de las políticas: La política y otras complicaciones en la educación superior mexicana. *Revista de Educación Superior, 34*(134), 81–106.

DGEST. Dirección General de Educación Superior Tecnológica. (2010). Retrieved on February 9, 2010, from www.dgest.gob.mx/.

Diario Oficial de la Federación. (2008). *Acuerdo 442*.

Fuentes, O., Gago, A., & Ortega, S. (1991). El sentido de la evaluación institucional: Un debate. *Universidad Futura, 2*(6–7), 3–14.

Gago, A. (1992). Ejes de la reforma: Calidad y pertinencia. *Universidad Futura, 4*(10), 14–33.

Garciadiego, J. (1996). *Rudos contra científicos: La Universidad Nacional durante la Revolución Mexicana*. Mexico: El Colegio de México, Universidad Nacional Autónoma de México.

Gil, M. (2005). El crecimiento de la educación superior privada en México: De lo pretendido a lo paradójico ... ¿o lo inesperado? *Revista de Educación Superior, 34*(133), 9–20.

Latapí, P. (coord.). (1998). *Un siglo de educación en México, tomo 2.* México: Consejo Nacional para la Cultura y las Artes–Fondo de Cultura Económica.

Levy, D. (1986). *Higher education and the state in Latin America: Private challenges to public dominance.* Chicago: University of Chicago Press.

Mexicanos Primero. (2010). *Brechas: Estado de la educación en México en 2010.* México: Mexicanos Primero Visión 2030 A.C. Retrieved on November 17, 2010, from www.mexicanosprimero.org/images/stories/Reporte_Mexicanos_Primero_-_Brechas_2010.pdf.

Moura Castro, C., & Levy, D. (1997). *Higher education in Latin America: A strategy for the IDB.* Washington, DC: Interamerican Development Bank. Also published as IDB (Interamerican Development Bank). (1997). *Higher education in Latin America and the Caribbean: A strategy paper.* Washington, DC: Interamerican Development Bank.

Odorika, I., & Pusser. B. (2007). La máxima casa de estudios: Universidad Nacional Autónoma de México as a state-building university. In P. G. Altbach & J. Balán (Eds.), *World-class worldwide: Transforming research universities in Asia and Latin America* (pp. 189–215). Baltimore, MD: Johns Hopkins University Press.

OECD. Organization for Economic Cooperation and Development. (1997). *Exámenes de las políticas nacionales de educación: México, educación superior.* Paris: Organization for Economic Cooperation and Development.

Pascarella, E. T., & Terenzini, P. T. (2005). *How college affects students: A third decade of research.* San Francisco: Jossey-Bass.

Paz, O. (1985). *The labyrinth of solitude.* New York: Grove Press.

Rodríguez, R. (2002). Continuidad y cambio en las políticas de educación superior. *Revista Mexicana de Investigación Educativa, 7*(14), 133–154.

Schmelkes, S. (1992). *Hacia una mejor calidad de nuestras escuelas.* Mexico: Secretaría de Educación Pública.

SEP. Secretaría de Educación Pública. (2007). *Programa sectorial de educación.* Mexico: Secretaría de Educación Pública.

Throw, M. (1974). Problems in the transition from elite to mass higher education. In *Policies for higher education: General report on the Conference on Future Structures of Post-Secondary Education* (pp. 51–101). Paris: Organization for Economic Cooperation and Development.

Villaseñor, G. (1994). *La universidad pública alternativa.* México: Universidad Nacional Autónoma de México.

World Bank. (1994). *Higher education: Lessons of experience.* Washington, DC: World Bank.

Zorrilla, J. F. (2008). *El bachillerato Mexicano: Un sistema académicamente precario, causas y consecuencias.* México: Universidad Nacional Autónoma de México.

5

PAKISTAN

Liberal Education in Context, Policy, and Practice

Zulfiqar H. Gilani

Introduction

The education sector in Pakistan, including post-secondary education, is bedevilled with a host of fundamental problems (*State of Higher Education in Pakistan*, 2006). As a result, curricular issues are quite low in priority for policy-makers and educationists, especially because education is seen, not primarily as a learning endeavor, but rather as an enterprise of achieving a diploma. In such a scenario, the inclusion of liberal arts in the curricula and the process of liberal learning do not have much meaning. A telling indicator of the low attention to such matters is the almost total absence of research and/or academic analysis and writings, especially for post-secondary education.

Terms like "liberal education" or "liberal arts," as they are usually understood or discussed in the United States, are quite alien to Pakistan's educational discourse. Most educationists assume that the "other" purpose of education is not very important and is, in any case, being adequately met by offerings in the social sciences, religion, or languages. However, there is very little informed discussion or debate even of such subjects, and the content of those subject areas is, by and large, being determined by ideological/political and bureaucratic considerations—not by educationists. When "liberal education" comes up, it is usually misunderstood to mean something vaguely having to do with a particular moral approach or social view or, as Michael Lind (2006) suggests, pertaining to political liberalism or the liberation of the mind. As David Bloom and Henry Rosovsky (2003) have aptly observed about developing countries in general, the curricular focus in both secondary and higher education remains on vocations; and liberal education, if it is considered at all, is believed to be a luxury and not a necessity.

In order to understand the scant attention paid to the important issue of curriculum content, this chapter examines education policy and practice at a number of levels. First is the broad context of the evolution of modern education in Pakistan's general policy and governance systems. The foundations of modern Western education were laid under colonial rule—a socio-political and historical circumstance that gave education in general and post-secondary education in particular a distinctive shape. Essentially, under British rule participation in post-secondary education was highly dependent on socio-economic status. A very few of the local elite would be sent to British universities for higher education and training, while most of those who finished high school—a very small number in itself—would go to local post-secondary colleges. Overall, the British legacy of post-secondary education was marked by centralized bureaucratization.

The centralizing and bureaucratic thrust of post-secondary education continued in Pakistan even after it achieved independence in 1947 and, in fact, seems to have regressed after that point. This setback can be primarily ascribed to impoverished leadership, academic and otherwise, that failed to recognize and address the educational challenges that the newly independent country faced. A complication was confusion and contestation over national identity and direction. Consequently, in Pakistan, education policy and curriculum development has, by and large, remained centralized, bureaucratic, and informed by the seemingly easy route of trying to foster a so-called Islamic national identity, primarily through the Islamization of education and curricula, but with a narrow and opportunistic version of Islam as the prime driver.

This chapter also examines the process of high school curriculum development, its content, and textbooks in subjects like history and social/Pakistan studies. The process of curriculum development is highly centralized and bureaucratic, and offerings at schools and post-secondary institutions engender narrowness, which is counter to the notion of what is commonly understood to be the purpose of liberal education. Schools are the nurseries from which post-secondary students emerge, and school curricula are the foundation of further education, both in terms of curriculum offerings and in the readiness to explore the deeper meanings and purposes of education. Curricular distortions at the school level (and the mindsets that no doubt develop during that stage) carry over to higher levels, thus posing a major challenge.

Pakistan also experiences fundamental structural problems in how studies are organized. The overall arrangement is based on streaming students starting in the eighth grade, and the firewalls between subject areas continue through post-secondary and university education. Exposure to subjects like the humanities, arts, and social sciences is limited and narrow. After high school, those who seek professional diplomas in fields like engineering and medicine or who obtain a bachelor's degree in science, besides studying specialty professional subjects, also study Islamiyat (Islamic studies) and Pakistan studies. However, as it will become clear later, the exposure to Islamiyat and Pakistan studies is not only sparse but the content also suffers from deep flaws. Students who obtain a bachelor's degree in the arts also study only the same two subjects, Islamiyat and Pakistan studies, besides the elected area of interest, such as a language, sociology, or psychology. For the master's degree, the curriculum is focused entirely on the area of specialization. Until about the new millennium, in the vast majority of cases, a bachelor's degree was awarded after two years of post-secondary education, with a master's after two further years of study. Though the time required for obtaining these degrees has been now lengthened, this change has not been accompanied by an appropriate redesign of the curricula (discussed below). As a result, students continue to be exposed only to an increasingly narrow and hyper-specialized curriculum.

The process of curriculum development and change at universities is inefficient and cumbersome because the weak academic governance systems and other systemic flaws present significant hurdles to curricular review, change, and innovation. Attempts to reform the process of curriculum development have been both few and largely unsuccessful. Since 2002, efforts have been made to redesign post-secondary curricula so that they would include a general education. However, that attempt has also failed to have any real impact because of a variety of impediments, including lack of leadership, low buy-in by critical actors, and the unavailability of the requisite human and intellectual resources for implementation.

The problem not only involves the content of the curriculum but is also compounded by the manner in which the curriculum is delivered—an important element in the definition of liberal education. The content needs to be presented in a manner that fosters learning to learn and typically requires a dialogic, interactive, and student-centered pedagogy. Students must have flexibility of choice in the selection of courses and take greater responsibility for their own learning (Goodwin, 2009, p. 3). Their critical abilities can develop only when the relationship between the teacher, the book, and the student facilitate the student's genuine internalization of the narrative. In Pakistan, problems of the curriculum contents are exacerbated by a pedagogical approach in post-secondary education that typically remains teacher and textbook centered, unidirectional, and non-interactive (Gilani, 1996). However, pedagogical approaches are a separate debate that cannot be adequately addressed here.

In light of the conditions that prevail in Pakistan's higher education sector, the approach adopted for this chapter emphasizes applied and pragmatic issues, rather than an academic thrust, and it does not attempt to address theoretical debates on liberal education. Further, this chapter focuses on the curricula and offerings in public institutions, not only because by far the greatest numbers of students attend such institutions, but also because of the dearth of data about private institutions, which vary widely in their purposes, curriculum, and governance. Moreover, it must be kept in mind that there are also some questions about the reliability and validity of data about education in Pakistan. And, finally, it is important to recognize that I am actively engaged in reforming higher education in Pakistan, including a commitment to a liberal education curriculum at the post-secondary level. That practitioner's prism has inevitably colored my approach to this issue.

Evolution and Participation

The introduction of modern higher education forms part of the evolution of the country's overall education system. As already noted, Pakistan inherited its educational system from the British, who introduced modern education in India primarily to train needed staff. Louis Hayes (1987) observes: "The colonial system of education inherited by Pakistan from the British had been designed to produce literate manpower to assist the colonial masters at the lower levels of government and economic administration" (p. 3). British residents and the very few individuals of Indian origin who obtained post-secondary degrees in institutions in Great Britain had a great advantage in obtaining superior government and managerial positions. Overall the primary instruments the British used for colonization were language and education (Rahman, 1996).

Universities in British India were examining bodies till October 1882, when the University of the Punjab in Lahore (now in Pakistan) became the first teaching university. Formally, teaching was included in the functions of universities after the Indian Universities Commission of 1902 recommended this step. However, the commission's overall recommendations were severely criticized by the newly emerging national/political leadership because of concerns about centralization, a perception that some reforms were sinister, and resentment of the alleged bureaucratic attitude of the British (Education: South Asia, n.d.). The fundamentals of higher education policy in India were articulated in a 1917 report by the Sadler Commission, which recommended, among other items, intermediate colleges with two-year courses, followed by a three-year bachelor's degree, and then postgraduate honors courses. However, the overall focus remained on increasing literacy. Providing post-secondary education that developed students' critical abilities did not seem to be a high priority. The recommended model generally continued after Pakistan gained independence in 1947; but within a few years, the bachelor's degree program was reduced to two years.

Because of nationalist and anti-colonial sentiment before independence, there was major disagreement about access to, and acceptance of, the British educational system. The restriction of the new language and education to a handful of elites meant that most of the people of colonial India could not benefit from modern higher education. Furthermore, some Muslims rejected foreign education on social and religious grounds, resulting in increasing marginalization in terms of educational and social development. Modernist reformers like Sir Syed Ahmed Khan advocated the adoption of the new education and successfully established the Aligarh Muslim University in 1920 to bridge that gap for Muslims (Aligarh Muslim University, 2005). This university produced educated Muslims who later provided political leadership for the independence movement and establishment of Pakistan. However, the opposition of traditional religious leaders to adopting British-style education also proved divisive among Muslims in India, especially those from the areas that now comprise Pakistan. As a result, they lagged behind their contemporaries in both education and employment.

At independence in August 1947, Pakistan inherited a rather weak educational infrastructure, as well as a cadre of human resources that were only meagerly trained. At that juncture, Pakistan had only two universities, with a total enrollment of 644, of whom only 56 were women.

The initial years after independence required a concentration on consolidation and exploration. The first constitution, adopted in 1956, recognized the state's obligation to provide education as one of the basic necessities of life. Beginning in 1955, Pakistan adopted a series of five-year plans for economic and educational development. The constitution of 1973 made practically no changes to the original educational policy. Further, the focus remained on literacy and primary education, while post-secondary education continued to follow the template inherited by the British. In general, education policy continued to be highly centralized, hierarchic, and bureaucratic.

Furthermore, modern secondary education and higher education remained accessible only to a few elites, due to socio-economic constraints. Most of the population remained unschooled. This level of participation remained largely unchanged until the late 20th century when the demand for education, including higher education, began to rise rapidly in Pakistan. This demand was doubly driven, first, by the rapid population expansion, and, second, by Pakistan's economy, which increasingly required a skilled and properly trained workforce. Unfortunately, the lack of political leadership and strong governance resulted in a dearth of policy-making and planning for higher education that would meet these social needs.

As in many developing countries, initially Pakistan's government was the sole provider of education. With the increasing demand for education and emergence of new areas and methods of study in higher education, pressures increased for the government to provide greater financial and academic resources, improved access, and reforms that would modernize the governance and management of institutions of higher learning. The traditional bureaucratic machineries, planning, and governance capacities, and the government's weak financial position were not adequate to cope with the changing demands. Consequently, the education sector, like other social sectors, declined perceptibly in Pakistan starting from the late 1970s (Hoodbhoy, 1998).

Beginning slowly in the 1980s, the government began allowing private pro-viders of education, including post-secondary education, to enter the market. Since about 2002, Pakistan has seen a veritable boom in the number and range of higher education providers in response to demographic patterns and demands for higher education. Even so, only a minority of post-secondary stu-dents have access to higher education. Compared to international enrollment rates, enrollments in post-secondary education in Pakistan remain extremely poor. According to Pakistan's Task Force on Higher Education, only 2.6% of the cohort ages 17 through 23 were enrolled in institutions of higher educa-tion. Of this meager number, less than 0.8% attended universities (*Report of the Task Force*, 2002). This low participation rate put Pakistan among the world's worst-performing countries. According to projections for 2008 col-lected in 1998, 6.5% would have earned a high school equivalent, 4.38% would have a B.A./B.Sc. and equivalent, and 1.58% would have an M.A./M.Sc. (Population Census Organization, 2008). Since more current data are not available, it is not clear whether these projections have been met.

Thus, while Pakistan has seen some quantitative expansion in higher edu-cation provision, it has remained quite haphazard, market driven, and mostly without much attention to the curricular content. The nation's higher educa-tion as a whole is hampered by a host of problems, but one major weakness has been inattention to curriculum design, resulting in the omission of content areas that could foster liberal learning.

Using Education to Forge an Islamic Identity

Since independence, Pakistan has been struggling with unifying a culturally and linguistically diverse population by attempting to define a common national identity. This effort has, not surprisingly, been the cause of considerable political conflict and violence. At the policy level, educational curricula have been used in an attempt to overcome the deep confusion about and contestation over national identity and direction. Thus, in Pakistan, education policy has been driven by the political goal of unifying people through a homogenized and pur-portedly Islamic identity. However, national and educational leaders have never attempted to supply a precise definition or clearly articulate what they meant by "Islam" or "Islamic," since it was not possible to do so in a way that all citizens of Pakistan would accept. Therefore, by and large, politicians and/or the ruling elite, rather than religious scholars, decided what was "Islamic." As a result, religion was (and still is) being used for political and opportunistic purposes. Leaders have tended to use a "cherry-picking" strategy in selecting aspects or interpretations of Islam that would insure their political power, calculating that the ordinary citizen would hesitate to criticize anything that is presented in the garb of Islam.

The root of the problem may be related to the confusion over identity, which has resulted in tensions between ethnic/local identities on the one hand

and (an imagined) national one on the other. The founding fathers, especially Mohammed Ali Jinnah, stressed the importance of avoiding the categorization of Pakistan as an ideological state.[1] However, he died soon after independence, while the identity question was still undecided. For a variety of complex political reasons, the theological drift was convenient—an easy extrapolation from the orally articulated and vague "two-nation theory," which argued for a separate country for the Muslims of India due to their religious distinction. It also provided a rhetorical cover for the absence of a credible political program. While this ideological thrust is clearly discernible in Pakistan's educational policy, it seems to have spiked significantly after 1971 when the eastern wing of the country (East Pakistan) seceded, and Bangladesh came into existence. Thereafter, the need to forge an identity based on Islam, primarily through even more Islamized curricula, became especially urgent as the separation of a Muslim majority province (East Pakistan) brought into question the very basis of the country.

Historically, education was the main instrument through which leaders attempted to create a common identity. The nation's first conference on education occurred from November 27 to December 1, 1947. Although Mohammed Ali Jinnah did not refer to Islam or Islamic ideology in his address to that conference (*Proceedings of the Pakistan Educational Conference*, 1947), its proceedings identify three notable points. First, the conference recommended Urdu as the lingua franca and medium of instruction in Pakistan. Urdu was to be taught as a compulsory language in schools, the stage at which it would be introduced in the primary schools being left to the provincial governments. Second, the conference recommended that the basis of education in Pakistan should be inspired by Islamic ideology, emphasizing its characteristics of universal brotherhood, tolerance, and justice. However, these characteristics seem never to have been translated into practice, which showed a contrary trend. Third, religious instruction would be compulsory for Muslim students in schools, and attendance at religious instruction would be compulsory for Muslim students in colleges.

The political employment of education to serve the purpose of national integration is captured in the *Report of the Commission on National Education* (1959). The document outlines two areas of priority: national integration and economic development/modernization. In her analysis of the document, Rubina Saigol (2003) notes:

> Since Pakistan was forged as a new entity in 1947, carved out of India by amalgamating five distinct regions/provinces, each with its own history, culture and local traditions, national integration was a major state imperative. Pakistani identity had to be imagined, elaborated and inscribed on the children's minds. Regional belonging, and sentiments associated with it, had to be diminished if not eliminated. Education was

assigned the task of creating the "good Pakistani citizen" with love for and loyalty to Pakistan. The values of patriotism, duty, obedience, honesty and service were emphasized in the process of forming the good citizen, capable of thinking in national rather than parochial terms.

(p. 41)

The educational policy of the fourth five-year plan period (1970–1975) is consistent with earlier policy. Educational institutions "continue to play an important role in the preservation and inculcation of Islamic values as an instrument of national unity and progress" (Saigol, 2003, p. 165). Religion appears to be the major—in fact, the only—conduit through which educational policy attempts to fashion the concepts of unity and progress.

This ideological emphasis in education continued to increase over time. By 1979 the Islamic thrust had become dominant, when General Zia-ul-Haq, who had declared martial law after overthrowing an elected government in July 1977, articulated an education policy. The broad principles outlined in earlier policies were refined and concretized during this period. By the time the National Education Policy and Education Implementation Programme was announced in 1979, Islamic studies (Islamiyat) and Pakistan studies were made compulsory at all levels from class I in the primary grades through the bachelor's degree, including medicine and engineering (*National Education Policy and Implementation Program*, 1979). The Islamic thrust was most visible in the educational policy that mandated a religious curriculum for 14 years. Furthermore, courses in history, social studies, and Urdu were also largely laden with Islamic materials. In fact, it was state policy to "Islamize" all educational material. A virulent, narrow, and intolerant version of Islam thus permeated the whole of the curriculum (Nayyar & Salim, 2003). At least in educational circles, a vague and undefined "ideology of Pakistan"—by which was meant an Islamic ideology—could not be critically examined.

The country's fifth five-year plan (1978–1983) focused on an "expansionist" approach to educational development. Building schools was a central element in increasing educational participation for the primary school population. Setting literacy goals had the aim of promoting a better-educated public. Similarly, the sixth five-year plan (1984–1989) emphasized enrollment and literacy. However, this plan's curriculum and textbook development section also states: "The objective should be to strengthen faith in Islam and the Pakistani nationhood together with an enlightened approach to life" (Planning Commission, 1983–1988, p. 253).

In 1998, the objectives, policy provisions, and implementation strategy of the National Education Policy outlined both philosophical and curricular tenets that clearly upheld and strengthened the Islamic state (*National Education Policy: 1998–2010*, 1998). Some illustrative quotations from that document follow, with comments where necessary. The document's Section 1.7

explicitly states an ideological basis: "The ideology of Islam forms the genesis of the State of Pakistan. The country cannot survive and advance without placing the entire system of education on sound Islamic foundations" (p. 2). Objective 2.5.1 states that the aim of the policy is "to make the Qur'anic principles and Islamic practices … an integral part of curricula so that the message of the Holy Qur'an could be disseminated in the process of education as well as training" (p. 6). Under "Islamic Education," Objective 3.2.1 states that education and training "should enable the citizens of Pakistan to lead their lives according to the teachings of Islam as laid down in the Qur'an and Sunnah" (p. 12). With regard to curriculum and practice, Policy Provision 3.3.1 mandates: "Teaching the Holy Qur'an with translation shall be introduced from Class VI and will be completed by Class XII." Policy Provision 3.3.2 asserts that "the basic teachings of the Holy Qur'an shall be included in all courses of studies." Implementation Strategy 3.4.1 says that "Islamiyat shall be continued as a compulsory subject from Class 1 to B.A./B.Sc. levels including professional institutions." Implementation Strategy 3.4.2 states that "*Nazira* [Reading] Qur'an shall form an integral part of Islamiyat compulsory for Class I to VIII."

As these statements make clearly apparent, this educational policy not only maintained its Islamic focus but also carefully planned for its continued study throughout a student's education. Chapter 9 of the *National Education Policy: 1998–2010* supports the concept of Islam for higher education but is inconsistent in its language. The policy notes that education should support a system that will "preserve the Islamic values and the cultural identity of the Nation" (p. 65). This terminology suggests that the nation has a single identity, which is based on the fundamental principles of Islam. Objective 9.2 of the document, which focuses on the purpose of higher education, states that it is to be "guided by the Holy Qur'an and the Sunnah through inculcation of Islamic ideology and moral values and preservation of our religious and cultural heritage" (p. 75). This ambiguous wording is unclear in its emphasis.

In summary, starting from the early days of independence, there was an insistence that Islam was to inform the educational offerings. This underlying philosophy reached its zenith during the dictatorship of General Zia-ul-Haq (July 1977 to August 1988), from which time education has been used as a means of indoctrination, with the public education system promoting an official vision of Pakistan as a fundamentalist Islamic society and state. As A. H. Nayyar and A. Salim (2003) note:

> In Pakistan, the education system from the very beginning has been aimed at re-enforcing one particular view of Pakistani nationalism and identity, namely that Pakistan is an Islamic state rather than a country with a majority Muslim population. This came about partly due to the insecurity that the newborn nation was facing, and partly because of the

emphasis on the "two-nation theory" as the basis for Pakistani identity. These combined to produce the need for a singular homogeneous majoritarian Muslim identity that could be sharply differentiated from that of India, even though it meant suppressing the many different shades within Pakistan.

(p. 2)

The deeper problem is that the infusion of Islam in the curricula has been motivated primarily to achieve certain political purposes. That complex and controversial topic lies outside the parameters of this study. But in essence, Pakistan's leaders have used a particular version of Islam that serves certain vested political interests to legitimize themselves and to suppress criticism, as they recognized that, with an overwhelmingly Muslim population, questioning or opposing the "Islamization" of education would be close to impossible.

High School Curricula, Textbooks, and Learning

Besides being framed in the above policy context, the process of curriculum development for schools is highly centralized. For all practical purposes, final authority for school curricula lies in the Curriculum Wing of the Federal Ministry of Education. The Federal Ministry of Education formulates the education policy, and its Curriculum Wing then develops national curricula that reflect that policy. Provincial Textbook Boards, each of which has its own standing list of designated authors, then prepare textbooks according to the Curriculum Wing's guidelines.

The guidelines are interpreted, mostly in arbitrary ways, by the provincial education bureaucracy, which generates the details that turn policy into practice. The Curriculum Wing is shielded from oversight by several layers of the Federal Ministry of Education's bureaucracy, which has resulted in significant continuities among the many national curricula over the past several decades. Very often the federal education ministers are unfamiliar with and uninterested in the details of previous education planning documents or with the process of policy-making within the ministry. Therefore, they are unable to oversee matters or intervene effectively.

The Provincial Textbook Boards have a monopoly on the books to be used in public schools in their respective province, which allows them to act as ideological gatekeepers, ensuring that only material that they see as ideologically acceptable reaches the classroom. The boards choose authors who willingly conform to and even strengthen the ideological thrust of schoolbooks. The monopoly of the textbook boards gives rise to corruption in various forms, including the creation of cartels of textbook writers. The books are mostly badly written and printed, but students and teachers have no alternative but to use them.

In grades 11 and 12, besides Islamiyat, the "soft" subjects taught include social/Pakistan studies, Urdu, and English. Non-Muslim students take civics instead of Islamiyat. In general, the four above-mentioned subjects are heavily laden with narrow, exclusionary, and over-idealized Islamic content. It is in these disciplines that students are supposedly exposed to issues of tolerance, identity, and civic values that shape their worldview. The study of these subjects in some form or other begins in the first primary class. Islamiyat and Pakistan studies continue through the bachelor's degree, including in professional fields like medicine and engineering. Thus, there is a progressive build up, as well as considerable redundancy and over-learning.

As an illustration, the textbook of Pakistan studies for grades 11 and 12 reveals that students learn a distorted history. The guidelines to writers instruct them that the topic of Pakistan studies essentially emerges from the "Pakistan Movement" and "Pakistan Ideology" and includes items such as the Islamization of all institutions of society toward achieving the goal of an Islamic society. The guidelines aim to make the student realize the importance of the revival of Islamic society in the changing world context, and the importance of Pakistan as a step toward the establishment of an Islamic society in the modern world. Other items included in the guidelines are knowledge of the ideology of Pakistan, an understanding of the British and Hindu attitudes toward the creation of Pakistan, and knowledge and appreciation of the Islamic provisions of the constitution of Pakistan (Nayyar & Salim, 2003).

The textbooks prepared following these guidelines have been found to be historically biased, likely contributing to a narrow understanding of the struggle that led to the creation of Pakistan and the founding principles that form the basis for citizenship. Professor Ayesha Jalal (1995), a Tufts University historian, has aptly pointed out that history has been rewritten from an Islamic point of view and refined to a bureaucratic art, which is furthered by a state-controlled curriculum and a captive market for history textbooks. She points to the deeper implications of these policies by noting that the lessons learned in school serve as the basis of a certain kind of psychological approach to national ideology.

In a similar vein, Professor Tariq Rahman of Quaid-i-Azam University, Islamabad, notes some important shortcomings of history textbooks currently in use in Pakistan: they ignore the non-Muslim part of Pakistan, condemn the contribution(s) of Hindu culture, and portray Hindus and the British as evil and the Muslims as righteous. Thus, the textbooks make no mention of the fact that Muslims killed Hindus and Sikhs at the time of partition in 1947. Also notable is the portrayal of India as the source of all problems in Pakistan and the Hindu as the "hated other." These texts also present the country's founding fathers, Mohammed Ali Jinnah and the poet Mohammed Iqbal, as orthodox Muslims but suppress aspects of their lives that do not conform to that image. In short, the overall thrust of Pakistan's history textbooks is to reinforce Islamic ideological nationalism and militarization (Rahman, 1995).

As this analysis illustrates, the state has adopted a narrow and biased approach toward curricula and subjects that form the student's worldview. Although some criticism has been voiced of this approach, it has been weakening over time. So far the decision-makers have not considered it politically advantageous to remedy the situation, though some have talked about it. More importantly, anecdotal evidence strongly points to the fact that almost all send their own children to private schools, which, in most cases, use the Cambridge or other Western curricula and have high fees. But the vast majority of parents of school-going children cannot afford to send them anywhere but to the government-run public schools.

Another important example involves Madrassah (religious school) education, which has attracted increasing international attention. Such institutions are seen as fostering rising extremism in Pakistan. Although statistics are not available, credible anecdotal evidence suggests that only a very small minority of children attend such schools. In a relatively recent television discussion on a private channel in Pakistan, the figure cited was 4.2% (Hasan, 2009). Notwithstanding the contribution of such schools to intolerance and extremism in Pakistan, a more serious concern is that the curricula of the public schools also foster such attitudes. Therefore, if the purpose is to address the source of undesirable worldviews, it would be much more fruitful to revisit the offerings in government-run schools where the vast majority of children are receiving their education.

Post-Secondary Offerings

The specific challenge for policy-makers and institutions of higher learning in Pakistan is a lack of clarity about the purpose of education, which in turn impacts curricula and their development. Not much thought seems to have gone into harmonizing and coordinating the purpose of education and curricular offerings with the wider socio-cultural and historical needs of society or with prevailing institutional and governance patterns. From my observations and experience of higher education policy, little consideration is given to the quality of learning in secondary schools, the limited access to higher education, the relevance and utility to Pakistan's current needs, institutional frameworks, policy considerations, the labor market that the university serves, the quality of university faculty, available financial and infrastructural resources, and the pedagogical methods being used.

Meanwhile institutions of higher learning have had to increasingly cater to the rising demand in disciplines that have better prospects in the local or, to a greater extent, global, job market, with management, medicine, and information technology being among the most popular. The rapid emergence of private providers has further strengthened that trend, since they are strongly motivated by financial considerations to offer subjects that will attract students. Because students naturally anticipate pecuniary benefits from their educational investment, further pressures toward selective and narrow curricula result.

More importantly, except for some private providers, post-secondary offerings have manifested considerable inertia with regard to change and innovation. Despite demographic changes and shifts in the labor market, university programs and curricula remain stagnant, creating an ever-widening gap with programs internationally. Even in areas that have seen change, they have been haphazard, opportunistic, and driven by myopic and mostly non-academic considerations. As a result, although Pakistani degrees were acceptable in most other countries until the late 1970s, at present Pakistani graduates are finding entrance to international programs or job markets increasingly difficult.

Pakistan has seen an ongoing tension between the dominant majority who consider employment to be the main purpose of higher education and the relative few who also see it as a means of producing good citizens, critical thinkers, and individuals who have learned how to learn. There has been some recognition, though quite hazy, that higher education in Pakistan suffers from not being well rounded. However, this concern remains a minor disquiet, and there are no indications of any serious policy shift to remedy the situation. Thus, the "other" purpose of higher education, which the liberal arts curriculum traditionally addresses, is considered "not useful" (i.e., not economically beneficial).

Structural Problems and Streaming

The situation is further compounded by the structural problems with regards to the curricula, teaching, and examinations of post-secondary students, as well as rigid streaming.

In line with global norms, higher education in Pakistan refers to all levels of education above higher secondary, which is equivalent to 12 years of schooling. After the first 10 years of education, students proceed either to a higher secondary school or to a college for the 11th and 12th years. On completion, students obtain an intermediate degree with a science or an arts focus. Exceptions include the very limited number of children receiving external school certificates—typically from British universities, equivalent to the General Certificate of Education and General Certificate of Secondary Education, or an American school, equivalent to junior high and high school. After grade 12, students may continue their post-secondary education in a college, obtaining a bachelor of arts or science degree after two years of study. After this degree, a student may pursue a master's degree, which is offered mostly at universities and at only some colleges and which requires an additional two years of study. Those who have the requisite qualifications for admission join professional studies like engineering or medicine after grade 12 with a science focus.

A structural constraint on higher education in Pakistan is the arbitrary bifurcation of colleges and universities. Colleges in Pakistan are peculiarly positioned, providing education which, in international terms, is the equivalent to years 11 and 12 at the secondary level and also years 13 and 14 at the post-secondary level (*Linkage of Colleges and University Education*, 2005). While colleges enroll a large majority of post-secondary students, universities determine the post-secondary offerings. All colleges are affiliated with a university and must adopt the university's curriculum, have its students examined by the affiliating university, and award the university's degrees. By and large, universities do not offer bachelor's programs, although college degrees are awarded by the affiliating university. Though the college curricula are designed and developed at the university, the college teacher has very little influence on the curriculum. They also are, by policy, excluded from marking the exams of their own students, though they may invigilate.

Most of the college teachers also teach grades 11 and 12, raising a host of pedagogical issues that cannot be discussed here. Further, only minimal infrastructure and learning resources are available in the colleges. As a result, students purportedly engaged in undergraduate studies are, in terms of teachers and learning resources and environment, attending a high school.

Because of the early start of streaming, by the time students reach post-secondary education, their exposure and options are narrowed considerably. Streaming starts after grade 8, when a student goes into the arts or sciences stream. After grade 10, an arts student can choose from a number of subjects in the social sciences, languages, and the like. The science student, in contrast, must choose either the natural sciences and mathematics, or the biological sciences. In short, after grade 8, students are divided into two broad groups; and after grade 10, the science group is further sub-divided into two, ending up with three groups in grades 11 and 12. The curriculum is designed on the firewall principle, so that it is almost impossible for a student from one stream to switch to another. Furthermore, until grade 12 only the languages (Urdu and English), Islamiyat (or civics for non-Muslim students), and Pakistan studies/ social studies are common across the various streams. For the science streams, languages, Islamiyat/civics, and Pakistan/social studies are the only non-science subjects available in grades 11 and 12.

Table 5.1 displays the numbers of students streamed into the different subject areas for 12th-year examinations in 2005–2007.

By the time students commence post-secondary study, their curricular path has been narrowed and over-determined. English is compulsory for everyone, and only two other non-specialty or general subjects are offered: Islamiyat and Pakistan studies. For science students during the next two years (years 13 and

TABLE 5.1 Number of students sitting for high school (grade 12) examinations, 2005–2007

Year	Arts	Pre-medical	Pre-engineering	Total
2005	56,1004	12,7211	109,251	797,466
2006	53,4558	135,746	102,488	772,592
2007	55,2713	143,867	114,901	811,281

Source: Federal Bureau of Statistics (2009).

14), at which point they obtain their bachelor's degree, no non-science subjects are permitted except for Islamiyat and Pakistan studies. Students pursuing a bachelor of arts degree may select two electives from a menu of social sciences and languages on entry. However, they cannot change those electives after the initial selection.

To obtain a master's degree currently, students have few options besides seeking admission to a university or to one of the few colleges that offer a master's degree. Pakistan has both general and professional universities in the public sector, the former being more numerous. Professional institutions include engineering, agriculture, and medicine, all three focused in terms of specialization and curricula (Isani & Virk, 2003). The only non-specialty subjects taught at professional universities are Islamiyat and Pakistan studies.

The general public universities have departments and faculties covering most of the traditional areas of study in the arts and the social and natural sciences. Students enrolled in a university science department have no exposure to subjects outside their area of specialization. Even those who join an arts or a social science department are exposed to subjects only in their own specialty. Professional studies like law and education likewise offer no subjects outside those areas. In short, the university curricula are over-specialized, allowing no exposure to other areas of study.

The Curriculum Development Process in Universities

While curriculum problems abound, in this section I focus primarily on problems that are systemic in nature.[2] The process of post-secondary curriculum development is somewhat ambiguous, since both the federal Higher Education Commission and the individual university have overlapping authority and responsibility. However, given the hierarchical nature of Pakistani culture, the Higher Education Commission usually dominates. Until 2002, post-secondary curriculum development and revision was the domain of the national-level University Grants Commission, a task that was assigned to its replacement entity, the Higher Education Commission. Since that time, the Higher Education Commission has been responsible for the development and revision of curriculum at the graduate and postgraduate levels. Its website currently specifies curricula for about 142 subjects.

The Higher Education Commission develops the curriculum for universities through a curriculum committee for each subject area. Commission bureaucrats select individuals to serve on each curriculum committee, which develops and finalizes the curriculum. That "approved" curriculum is then conveyed to the universities for adoption, at which point the weaknesses of this centralized approach to academic governance become more apparent. In theory, universities are autonomous in terms of the development, approval, and adoption of curricula. However, the pressure to adopt the centrally developed curriculum is great, as the Higher Education Commission controls funding for public sector universities. A commission representative sits on both the Academic Council and Syndicate (equivalent to the governing board of a university) of every public university, which is the final authority for curriculum approval. Therefore, in most cases, the conveyed curricula are rubber-stamped by the various university bodies and thus go through a process of pseudo-legitimization.

Within universities the process of curriculum development also remains bureaucratic and requires many steps. Any changes in a course must be processed by the board of studies of the concerned department, the board of the Faculty concerned, the Academic Council, and finally the Syndicate. On average a change in a course takes one to two years. The unnecessary duplication and bureaucracy are complicated by the systemic flaws within these structures, dominated as they generally are by politics. Interestingly the same bodies process the establishment of new programs or the winding down of old ones, although closing programs are rather rare occurrences and usually take place only on instructions from the Higher Education Commission.

The underlying problem is that while, in theory, curriculum development and change are the faculty's responsibility, in practice there is no incentive for the faculty to effect such changes. In fact, if anything, the opposite is true. Change would not only entail work in its own right but would also require reading new materials and preparing new lessons. The educational system provides no compulsion to perform additional work and definitely no institutional reward for doing so. Therefore, in practice many departments have very dated curricula, and professors continue to teach what they were taught when they were students. For example, as of 1997, the curriculum and courses of the Institute of Education and Research at the University of Peshawar had not been changed since 1979. Consequently, the required texts and readings were also quite dated. A process of change was initiated by its director and dean, who invited faculty to respond with suggestions. Unfortunately, such suggestions were extremely meager, and the faculty also manifested considerable resistance. As a second example at the same university, in 2001 when the vice chancellor noted that the offerings in most departments were quite dated, he issued written instructions to review the curricula and courses as beginning a process of change. In both instances, the faculty were largely averse to the possibility of change, and their resistance was motivated by the fact that making such changes would mean more work for them.

In short, taken as a whole, the faculty at Pakistan's universities is weak academically, and there is a great dearth of academic leadership. These conditions are compounded by the cumbersome, inefficient, and politicized academic governance systems in universities. Governance is itself a major hurdle in curriculum development, improvement, or innovation. As a result, curricula as well as course contents are stagnant, narrow, dated, and irrelevant. It would take this chapter too far afield to detail problems of course offerings and contents, but it is surely not surprising to find them also lacking in many respects.

Reform Proposals and Travails

Inspired by the World Bank report on Higher Education in Developing Countries, the government of Pakistan set up a Task Force for the Improvement of Higher Education in 2001. The Task Force's report recommended radical reforms, including in the curricula (*Report of the Task Force*, 2002). Two strong recommendations were doing away with early specialization in primary and secondary schools, and including general education courses in post-secondary education that would equip students with the skills for critical and moral reasoning, effective communication, and self-directed life-long learning. This report correctly concluded that introducing the general education system would entail creating a core curriculum, which would prevent the premature narrow focusing in disciplines and which would motivate students to become familiar with a core body of knowledge. It also recommended that, for international comparability, universities should award a bachelor's degree after 16 years of study rather than the prevailing requirement of 14 years.

The recommendations of the Task Force were approved in 2002, soon after the publication of the report. Unfortunately, the recommended curricular reforms attracted little attention. More importantly, the proposed curriculum reform was totally misunderstood and ended up muddying the waters even further. For reasons that need not be dwelled on here, the most superficial aspect of the recommendation became the Higher Education Commission's center of attention, and a source of debate and disquiet in the academic community and students—the proposed awarding of a bachelor's degree after 16 years of study. The more crucial issue of exposing all students, regardless of speciality, to a mix of core subjects was completely sidelined.

The Higher Education Commission instructed all public universities to introduce four-year undergraduate programs but placed no emphasis on redesigning the curricula or including general education as a crucial component. The faculty and administration of most universities also remained largely unaware of the recommendation's real purpose and took the Higher Education

Commission demand literally. The result was the announcement of four-year undergraduate degrees by many universities, accompanying existing two-year programs, while the design and content of the degree remained focused on the single discipline. A quick glance at most (although not all) of the public sector offerings for four-year degrees confirms that they have lumped the two years of existing bachelor's content with two years of master's content to produce what is still a hyper-specialized, largely myopic, and broadly ignorant graduate.

While overall confusion about changing the scheme of studies prevailed, an exercise was undertaken to conceptualize a contextually relevant integrated curriculum, first between 2001 and 2003, at the University of Peshawar, a public-sector university, and then in 2004 at Foundation University, Islamabad, a private institution. The model developed was rooted in indigenous realities and could form the basis for post-secondary studies that achieve the same broad purpose as that of liberal education. A flexible and grounded approach was adopted, somewhat in the spirit noted by Dan Edelstein (2010), of Stanford University, who observes that top U.S. universities like Chicago, Harvard, and Stanford, still require a core curriculum, but now allow students to make their own choices from a selection of classes.

The two-pronged principle that guided the integrated curriculum was to ensure that students have a wider and general exposure to academic topics outside their area of specialization, as well as greater depth of understanding in their main area of study. The purpose was to provide a broad-based education within which the specialized courses would become more effective and socially relevant. The four-year integrated undergraduate program would also provide greater flexibility and choice to the student. As envisaged, during the first two semesters students would have a list of topics on offer, from which they could choose any three elective subjects. This program would provide an opportunity of exploration for one academic year; therefore, they could make a decision about a major in their third semester that would be more in line with their aptitudes and abilities. In addition, regardless of the chosen major, breadth of knowledge would be ensured by offering minors.[3] Students would have the opportunity for a flexible selection of courses from among the minors, which would be relevant to the major but not from within it. For example, a psychology major would be able to choose minor courses in sociology, philosophy, etc., from a list of minors relevant to psychology. This pattern of studying related subjects would hold for all majors, ensuring considerable breadth of knowledge, while also maintaining focus or depth in the major.

Most importantly every student would study some core compulsory subjects like English, mathematics, or philosophy. The concept of compulsory core subjects was analogous to the idea of a liberal education. In the proposed scheme of studies, courses in the major area would constitute 51% of the total exposure, core subjects 23%, minors 16%, and electives 10%. In other words, about half of the students' studies would be in areas other than the major.

As this innovative program was a work in progress, there was room for further refinement and improvement in the overall design, especially after feedback from the field. Regarding core courses, after considerable research and consultation, a short list was developed that included English, mathematics, basic science, philosophy, behavioral studies, history and culture, development studies, environment, and computers. Again, the determination of what to include in core courses was open to modification and change and would be best left to the internal decision of each institution. However, due to the education policy in place in Pakistan, Islamiyat and Pakistan studies were necessary inclusions.

The start of the debate and the opening of the conversation that was triggered by the World Bank's report on higher education in developing countries gained momentum through the work and activities of the Task Force and by a Steering Committee set up by the president of Pakistan to develop an implementation plan for the recommendations of the Task Force. One of the outcomes was the development of the curriculum design mentioned above. However, the proposed reforms floundered at the implementation stage for the reasons already discussed: lack of appropriate academic leadership, weak faculty and other human resources, the centralizing impact of the Higher Education Commission, structural and systemic weaknesses in the education system as a whole, the general lack of understanding of the need for change among political leaders, and a lack of a will and adequate buy-in to implement such changes.

Concluding Reflections

The problem Pakistan faces regarding curricula is embedded in the overall crisis of its public education system, which not only seems perpetual but also seems to worsen with time. The almost broken public education system is, in turn, part of the wider crisis of state and society in Pakistan. In that context, education has not been a high national priority, and little attention or thoughtful reflection have been devoted to education policy in general and curricula in particular.

Due to a weakness in educational human resource available at independence, until the late 20th century, the main focus in education was to raise the nation's literacy levels. Almost all other aspects were ignored. More importantly, policy-making seemed to have been done hastily, taking the relatively easy route of Islamizing the curricula as a mechanism for forging a homogeneous national identity. The new rulers of Pakistan took a page from their previous colonial masters and used language (Urdu) and education to achieve that purpose. Over time, that approach has become deeper and wider.

Starting in the early 1980s, the government permitted private schools and institutions of higher learning to operate in Pakistan. These private institutions joined a number of Christian fee-paying private schools, largely operated by missionaries, which were mostly holdovers from colonial times. Ironically, this happened at the same time when the Islamization of education was most zealously pursued as state policy. Consequently, anyone who could afford it—which included, as far as I am aware, all higher state functionaries and decision-makers—sent their children to private schools, the better of which used Cambridge or Oxford curricula. As a result, a sort of educational apartheid emerged, with the majority of children attending public schools and a minority of the elites' children attending private ones. Therefore, interest declined in the curricula, offerings, and textbooks at public schools because they had no direct implications for the children of those who were in a position to make and implement decisions.

Still deeper problems of attitudes and pedagogical approach are interlinked with the curricula. In Pakistan, education is primarily a diploma-earning exercise rather than a learning endeavor. The primary emphasis is on completing the courses and passing the examinations. Thus, the education process is textbook, teacher, and exam centered. The memorization of received information starts in the primary grades and continues through university. This educational approach presents a bifurcated model of those who have knowledge (the teachers and the books) and those who are ignorant and need to receive it. The teacher is usually quite unaware of the process of producing knowledge and conveys information uncritically to the pupil. As a consequence, knowledge is imbibed without curiosity or questioning; the pupil's natural reflective and critical capacities are systematically sidelined. In fact, questioning or critical examination are often penalized. As a result, the cognitive and learning capacities and attitudes of a student in the Pakistani system are at considerable risk of being warped. Knowledge is perceived as disconnected from reality, human action, and real life. And last but definitely not least, students internalize an attitude of passivity. They experience themselves as recipients, not as potential producers of knowledge. In the wider hierarchical culture of authoritarianism, institutions of learning are also authoritarian and contribute to its perpetuation. Although this topic has yet to receive the attention of researchers, anecdotal evidence suggests that students' alienation and helplessness have increased over time. While such effects are functions of a complex set of historical, political, and socio-economic conditions, I believe that the curricula and pedagogical approaches have contributed significantly to these feelings.

Given this context, the possibility of introducing liberal post-secondary education in Pakistan seems extremely unlikely. A number of deep and fundamental changes must occur across the spectrum of secondary and post-secondary education. The focus will have to shift from numbers to less tangible matters like student learning. Notwithstanding these challenges, however, the necessity of pursuing that path is urgent. As U.S. higher education researcher Philip G. Altbach (2008) aptly notes:

The humanities and social sciences are not only an essential part of an idea of a university; they are at the core of understanding contemporary society. History, sociology, philosophy, and other disciplines interpret today's key challenges. The university, as the central institution providing careful analysis and interpretation of society, requires the soft sciences as never before.

(p. 6)

Exposure to a liberal education is particularly urgent in Pakistan where years of their neglect, compounded by the compulsory study of a narrow version of Islam for political ends, have produced intolerance and extremism that are eating at the vitals of its society. More importantly, with the prevailing curricula, Pakistani undergraduates are obtaining degrees, but their learning abilities are inadequately developed and they are ill prepared for the job market or to meet the complex challenges of modern life.

Notes

1 An examination of the relatively few speeches of Mohammed Ali Jinnah reveals an absence of references to any ideology, Islamic or otherwise.
2 Much of what follows in this section is based on my personal knowledge and observation during my professional career of working in and with universities as a faculty member, dean, and vice chancellor, and as a higher education policy analyst.
3 Although the terminology used is the same as in international practice, the specific connotations may be slightly different. However, semantics do not have any bearing on the concepts.

References

Aligarh Muslim University. (2005). Retrieved on August 29, 2009, from www.indianmuslims.info/history_of_muslims_in_india/aligarh_muslim_university.html.

Altbach, P. G. (2008, Summer). The humanities and social sciences in Asia: Endangered species? *International Higher Education*, No. 52, pp. 4–6.

Bloom, D. E., & Rosovsky, H. (2003, Winter). Why developing countries should not neglect liberal education. *Liberal Education*. Retrieved on April 9, 2010, from www.aacu.org/liberaleducation/le-wi03/le-wi03feature2.cfm.

Edelstein, D. (2010, March 30). The third way in liberal education. *Inside Higher Education*. Retrieved on April 9, 2010, from www.insidehighered.com/views/2010/03/30/edelstein.

Education: South Asia. (n.d.). *Britannica online encyclopaedia*. Retrieved on April 25, 2010, from www.britannica.com/EBchecked/topic/179408/education/47706/South-Asia.

Federal Bureau of Statistics. (2009). *Pakistan statistical year book, 2009*. Retrieved on April 25, 2010, from www.statpak.gov.pk/depts/fbs/publications/yearbook2009/yearbook2009.html.

Gilani, Z. (1996). Authoritarian thinking: Implications for education. *Journal of Humanities and Social Sciences*, 4(2), 1–16.

Goodwin, K. (2009, April 6). *Liberal education beyond the U.S.: A paradox*. Unpublished manuscript.

Hasan, M. (2009, August 15). Statement on Geo TV: "Chauraha" (town square), a discussion program.

Hayes, L. D. (1987). *The crisis of education in Pakistan*. Lahore, Pakistan: Vanguard Publications.

Hoodbhoy, P. (Ed.). (1998). *Education and the state: Fifty years of Pakistan*. Karachi, Pakistan: Oxford University Press.

Isani, U. A. G., & Virk, M. L. (2003). *Higher education in Pakistan: A historical and futuristic perspective*. Islamabad, Pakistan: National Book Foundation.

Jalal, A. (1995). Conjuring Pakistan: History as official imagining. *International Journal of Middle East Studies, 27*(1), 73–89.

Lind, M. (2006, Autumn). Why the liberal arts still matter. *Wilson Quarterly, 30*(4), 52–58.

Linkage of Colleges and University Education: Policy Brief. (2005). Islamabad, Pakistan: Centre for Higher Education Transformation.

National Education Policy: 1998–2010. (1998). Islamabad, Pakistan: Government of Pakistan, Ministry of Education.

National Education Policy and Implementation Programme. (1979). Islamabad, Pakistan: Government of Pakistan, Ministry of Education.

Nayyar, A. H., & Salim, A. (2003). *The subtle subversion: The state of curricula and textbooks in Pakistan*. Islamabad, Pakistan: Sustainable Development Policy Institute.

Planning Commission, Government of Pakistan. (1983–1988.) *The sixth five year plan*. Chapter 18: "Education: A vital investment in human resources development," pp. 388–389.

Population Census Organization. (2008). Retrieved on April 25, 2010, from www. statpak.gov.pk/depts/pco/statistics/pop_education/pop_education_sex.html.

Proceedings of the Pakistan Educational Conference. (1947). Islamabad, Pakistan: Government of Pakistan.

Rahman, T. (1995). *Language-teaching and world view in Urdu medium schools*. Islamabad, Pakistan: SDPI Research Papers Series.

Rahman, T. (1996). *Language and politics in Pakistan*. Karachi, Pakistan: Oxford University Press.

Report of the Commission on National Education. (1959). Islamabad, Pakistan: Government of Pakistan, Ministry of Education.

Report of the Task Force on the Improvement of Higher Education in Pakistan: Challenges and opportunities. (2002, April). Islamabad, Pakistan: Pakistan Ministry of Education.

Saigol, R. (2003). *Becoming a modern nation: Educational discourse in the early years of Ayub Khan (1958–1964)*. Islamabad, Pakistan: Council of Social Sciences, Pakistan.

State of higher education in Pakistan, 2005: Quality. (2006, May). Islamabad, Pakistan: Centre for Higher Education Transformation.

6

POLAND

The Place of Liberal Education in Post-Soviet Higher Education

Ewa Kowalski

The National Higher Education Landscape

The political and economic transformation toward democracy and the market economy on which Poland embarked in 1989, followed by the country's integration with the European Union in 2004, created a need for an educational system that resonates with the new socio-political, economic, and technological context. With the demand for skilled professionals rapidly rising throughout the 1990s, top priority was given to the reform of higher education, seen by the political and economic sectors as critical to the success of Poland's democratic and economic transformation.

The passage of a new law on higher education in 1990, further amended in 2005 (Law on Higher Education, 2005), brought a number of far-reaching changes in the structure, organization, funding, and governance patterns in Poland's tertiary system, thus marking its departure from the socialist legacy toward greater democratization and diversification (Sorensen, 1997). The impact of the new law is reflected in changes such as the de-politicization and de-ideologization of teaching and learning in higher education institutions. These changes are critical to revitalizing their vibrant intellectual culture and restoring the importance of the arts, humanities, and social sciences in their curricula. Its impact is also evident in greater diversification of the funding structure, which allows institutions to obtain funds through research grants and from sources outside the state budget (e.g., donations, tuition fees) (MSHE, 2009a). Despite these changes, the subsidies provided by the state continue to be the most important source of funding for public institutions today.

Concurrent with the above changes, the structural transformation of Poland's higher education was initiated in the 1990s, reflecting major political and economic changes and trends at the national, regional, and global levels. The impact of these changes is evident in, among other areas, the emergence of a strong private (non-state) higher education system alongside the public (state) sector and, consequently, in a rapid expansion and massification of a once highly elitist Polish academic system. In addition, most public and private institutions (except for medical and some agricultural universities) introduced a new three-cycle degree structure with the purpose of preparing a more educationally and professionally diverse workforce. As a result, a uniform five-year master's (*magister*) level course was replaced with a degree system comprising the bachelor's level (*licencjat/inżynier*) and master's level (*magister*) courses ("3+2" or "4+2"), followed by three-/four-year doctoral studies (*doktorat*) (Dąbrowa-Szefler & Jabłecka-Prysłopska, 2006). After Poland joined the Bologna Process in 1999, the new degree structure was further aligned with the requirements of the Bologna's three-cycle system (undergraduate, graduate, doctoral), in which each level corresponds to a common European Credit Transfer System, with the purpose of preparing students for the world of work.

Despite substantial changes in the landscape of Poland's higher education in recent decades, the institutional structure of higher education has not changed in a significant way and remains, as was the case during the socialist period, fragmented along vocational lines. Based on the Soviet model adopted in the 1950s, a number of faculties were removed from universities and reestablished in separate, vocationally oriented institutions, including academies (*akademie*), institutes (*instytuty*), polytechnics (*politechniki*), and higher vocational schools (*wyższe szkoły zawodowe*). These institutions were placed under the supervision of central government ministries to reinforce professional aspects of their disciplines. For example, medical academies are supervised by the Ministry of Health (Sorensen, 1997). This move also resulted in the separation of the humanities and technology/science tracks. In addition, all institutions were internally fragmented and compartmentalized by narrow specializations created within the disciplines to limit the scope of academic research and activity and to deemphasize interdisciplinary focus (Axer, 2007; Sorensen, 1997).

Today Polish higher education institutions continue to offer education under the jurisdiction of the Ministry of Science and Higher Education (MSHE) and other pertinent ministries, and the institutional network remains dominated by vocational institutions and narrow specializations. At present, the Polish higher education system comprises 94 public, five denominational, and 250 new private institutions, as well as a large number of colleges (e.g., teacher training colleges), operating in partnership with universities and providing basic professional education (MSHE, 2009a). Among these institutions, 35 new higher vocational schools have been established since 1997 with the purpose of diversifying forms of study at the tertiary level and offering a wide spectrum of practical skills-based specializations specific to particular

professions and labor market needs (MSHE, 2009a). The vocational orientation of the recently expanded institutional network can be seen as an indication that higher education is embracing and adjusting to the policy discourse
of "practical" vocationalism and the pragmatization of learning.

The European Dimension of Poland's Higher Education Policy

Closely related to the developments at the national level are changes at the
regional level. Motivated primarily by the aspiration to "catch up" with
Europe, Poland joined the Bologna Process in 1999 and has since largely
adopted its standards with the expectation of bringing prestige and a more
cosmopolitan character to its higher education system, becoming a full-fledged
member of the European academic community, and generating funding for the
development of its underfunded institutions and research programs (Kowalski,
2004; KRASP, 2009a). The overarching goal of the Bologna Process is to
establish a common European higher education area, based on a unified and
compatible European set of standards, procedures, and guidelines for credit
(European Credit Transfer System) and degree (Diploma Supplement) recognition; quality assurance; and a three-cycle degree system. Through this unified
framework, its proponents seek "to enhance the employability and mobility of
citizens and to increase the international competitiveness of European higher
education" (*Bologna Declaration*, 2000).

Paradoxically for Polish higher education, which has, in recent decades,
been striving to overcome its socialist heritage and to develop its own identity,
integrity, and autonomy, the adoption of the Bologna discourse and standards—as well as the political symbolism and self-legitimization associated with
the process—appear to have come at a high price. Not only has this initiative
encouraged greater rigidity and standardization of the Polish academic system,
but it has done so within the broader framework of the regional convergence
of European higher education policy and structures, a process that bears certain
similarities to the trends that characterized the higher education systems of
Poland and other Eastern European countries prior to 1989.

The increased standardization and rigidity that have resulted from implementing the Bologna reforms have caused resistance among some members of
the Polish academic community. As explained by the Polish Rectors Conference (KRASP, 2009a), opinions in this debate by Polish academics are sharply
divided and focus primarily on the tensions between the traditional norms and
values of higher education and the norms and values resulting from the
Bologna reform. On the one hand, Polish faculty associate the Bologna Process
symbolically with "a return to the medieval roots" and the ideals of academic
unity and autonomy across European higher education (Tygielski, 2007, p. 55).
Thus, substantial consensus exists today on core aspects of the Bologna Process,
especially on the importance of increasing student mobility, recognizing

qualifications, increasing employability, and sustaining inter-institutional cooperation (KRASP, 2009a). At the same time, however, the return to Poland's reintegration into Europe and the aspiration of building an open European higher education space is taking place in the new geo-economic, political, and institutional context of the European Union—and thus within the boundaries of the new converging system of standards, ideologies, norms, and values of the European university that, in many ways, challenge the local traditions of higher education and decision-making autonomy about how to achieve these goals.

Institutional Autonomy, Academic Freedom, and Governance

At the institutional level, the reform efforts focused on redefining the pre-1989 relationship between the state and institutions of higher education. This relationship had, during the 42 years of socialist rule, been characterized by a high degree of state intervention and monopolistic control, exercised through the Ministry of National Education (*Ministerstwo Edukacji Narodowej*/MEN) and other pertinent ministries, that were responsible for the general organization, management, and supervision of academic institutions and their activities (Sorensen, 1997). During that time, all decisions regarding educational goals, academic curricula and fields/lines of study, written course materials and exams, admission quotas, and the hiring and appointments of faculty and key academic positions were made at the ministry level and in line with the needs and goals of the Socialist Party and the centrally planned economy (Dąbrowa-Szefler & Jabłecka-Prysłopska, 2006).

The 1990 law brought changes in the exercise of authority, allowing for the substantial devolution of the decision-making authority from the Ministry of National Education to higher education institutions and their representative elected bodies. While these changes have had a great impact on increasing institutional autonomy, academic freedom, and self-governance in higher education, the extent to which institutions are allowed to truly exercise these rights in all areas of their activity continues to be subject to restrictions imposed by the Ministry of National Education (KRASP, 2009a). On the one hand, institutions and faculty have been granted a high degree of autonomy over such internal affairs as (a) the election of representative bodies (e.g., rectors, Senate, faculty/*kolegia* councils), (b) internal organization, (c) expenditures, (d) the writing and enacting of their own statutes, (e) some aspects of program and curriculum development (e.g., design of syllabi, admission standards), (f) the selection of research areas and topics, (g) cooperation with foreign institutions, and (h) the hiring and promotion of faculty (Law on Higher Education, 2005). In a similar vein, the power of elective collegial bodies (i.e., KRASP, the General Council for Higher Education/*Rada Główna Szkolnictwa Wyższego*, and the State Accreditation Committee/*Państwowa*

Komisja Akredytacyjna) has been augmented, allowing them to influence decisions on higher education matters such as program/curriculum development (Sorensen, 1997).

On the other hand, however, the Ministry of National Education has retained the capacity to interfere with some internal areas of academic activity such as program development through its use of funding and other regulatory mechanisms like audits and evaluations (Szapiro, 2007; Tygielski, 2007). For example, faculty today have the authority to propose the study lines they wish to offer and courses within them; however, the Ministry of National Education mandates the overarching curricular framework within which these programs and courses must be designed and developed. In consequence, the Ministry of National Education determines the graduate profile of degree requirements and required qualifications for all fields/lines of study (Law on Higher Education, 2005). In order to minimize the extent of state interference in internal academic affairs, institutions tend to implement curricular changes primarily within existing programs that the Ministry of National Education has previously approved.

Current Debates and Developments in Higher Education

It can be concluded that, although the trend in recent decades has been toward greater autonomy for higher education, that autonomy nevertheless is accompanied by the restraints imposed by state-defined boundaries. Research conducted in Poland demonstrates that, while numerous voices within the academic community have contested the extensive state controls over higher education, there has been little collective effort among its members to challenge these powers and to present an alternative reform agenda (Kieniewicz, 2007; KRASP, 2009a; Szapiro, 2007; Tygielski, 2007).

In 2009, the Polish Rectors Conference presented a comprehensive two-part document called *Strategy* (KRASP, 2009a, 2009b), which can be seen as a step in this direction, as it aims to redefine the present state–academia relationship and reformation process. The document, which was created in consultation with the Polish academic community, seeks, among other purposes, to increase academic self-governance and to move higher education beyond its present narrow responsibility to the nation's economic development toward a more balanced vision—one that embraces the public responsibility and social mission of higher education for the local, national, European, and global communities in which it is embedded. Importantly, the document also adopts the overarching framework of the Bologna Process within which to pursue these goals. Because the concepts of higher education's autonomy, self-regulation, and higher social function also underpin the discourse of the Bologna Process initiatives (e.g., Bergen Communiqué, 2005), the adoption of this reform also means accepting its economically oriented policy discourse within which these notions are introduced and interpreted, along with its framework of academic standards and regulatory mechanisms (e.g., quality assurance) used to monitor institutions and curricula (Karseth, 2006). In this regard, the demands of the Bologna Process appear to limit rather than promote academic self-governance. Thus, this reform fosters a restrictive policy environment, similar to the one being contested today at the national level.

General Education in Secondary Schools

Structure and Changes to the Post-Primary System after 1989

In 1989, Poland inherited a secondary education system designed to serve the goals and demands of the socialist state and its centralized economy. As these goals and demands lost their relevance following Poland's political and economic transformation, efforts were undertaken to reform its education system in ways that were consistent with the principles and values of the new political and economic context. The changes introduced in the early 1990s, the first phase of the reform process, focused on democratizing the education system and resulting in an increased diversity of school choice (e.g., private, public, denominational) and the de-ideologization of school curricula (Jung-Miklaszewska, 2003). The second phase of the reform, launched in the late 1990s, was marked by substantial structural changes, including the adoption of a diversified secondary education model that now consists of lower (*gymnasium/gimnazjum*) and upper secondary school, with the latter schools further differentiated along a continuum of specialization. At one end of the continuum is the lyceum (*liceum*) with an exclusively academic curriculum, and at the other end of the spectrum is the specialized technical-track school (*technikum*). Secondary schools (*specialized lyceum/liceum profilowane*), lying in the middle of the continuum, combine elements of the two types of schools. In addition, there are basic vocational schools (*szkoła zawodowa*) that offer specialized vocational training for lower secondary school graduates who wish to proceed directly to the workplace (Jung-Miklaszewska, 2003). An extensive curriculum revision in 2008, which complemented these structural and organizational changes, aligned the national curriculum and school textbooks for various subjects with the European Union standards (MEN, 2009). These reform efforts have focused primarily on increasing academic rigor through the curriculum in all types of schools and creating opportunities for more equitable education for all students than was the case during the socialist period (Jung-Miklaszewska, 2003).

Changes in Upper Secondary School Curricula

Efforts to diversify the curriculum are also evident in the shift from a subject-based encyclopedic model, supported prior to 1989, toward a more interdisciplinary and individualized model organized around six major learning areas (modules) and centered on the student's needs and interests. Each module comprises course offerings designed for different secondary school levels and different education tracks, including (a) language arts (Polish, foreign, ethnic/minority, and regional languages; literature), (b) mathematics and technical studies (mathematics, technical studies, technology, information studies), (c) history and society (history, social/civic studies, fundamentals of entrepreneurship, family studies, philosophy, choice-based studies in religion or ethics), (d) natural sciences (environmental studies, geography, physics and astronomy, chemistry, biology), (e) arts (music, fine arts, history of music, history of fine arts, culture studies, Latin, antiquity studies), and (f) physical education and military training (MEN, 2009).

School Curricula According to Education Track

The examination of the new curriculum demonstrates a shift toward a more unified general education curriculum in all types of schools, aimed at an all-around development of students, regardless of whether they proceed to higher education or enter the labor market upon graduation. Thus, all upper secondary institutions and all education tracks today share the same core academic curriculum, including the same course offerings, curricular content, and instructional time allocated to their provision (MEN, 2009). At the same time, these institutions differ substantially with respect to the orientation of their compulsory specialization and with the level of exposure they provide to the arts, humanities, and social sciences. Students attending general education secondary schools are required to take an academic specialization, which involves participation in three or four extended academic subjects of their choice, including additional exposure to the arts, humanities, and social sciences component. In the case of vocationally oriented upper secondary schools (specialized lyceums, technical schools), academic specialization is not available at all, and students are required to participate in a professional component consistent with their area of specialization, such as fine arts or nursing (Jung-Miklaszewska, 2003). Consequently, the level of exposure to the arts, humanities, and social sciences component is also lower than in general upper secondary schools.

It is also worth noting that some course offerings such as Latin and philosophy, which are crucial for students seeking admission to highly esteemed fields like medicine and law, are offered exclusively as part of the academic specialization in general upper secondary schools. Given that admission to higher education institutions is based on a competitive exam system, early aca-demic specialization and additional exposure to the academic curriculum favor students in general upper secondary schools over their peers in other secondary school types, thus substantially enhancing their chances of being admitted to and succeeding in a prestigious higher education program and institution.

Toward a More Liberal Curriculum and Instructional Model

In order to prepare highly motivated and critical-thinking students for higher education, the revised curriculum shifts its emphasis from the factual and structured teaching/learning approach fostered during the socialist period toward a more exploratory, learner-centered, and problem-based instructional model. While the new curriculum establishes a clear philosophy and a set of overarching goals consistent with the guiding principles of this model, there appears to be some tension between these goals and the strategies selected to achieve them. For example, the examination of the learning objectives for all upper secondary schools demonstrates the prevalence of verbs that deempha-size the creative dimension of student work and encourage readily assessable activities such as reproducing and recounting information. These include terms like "characterizing," "describing," and "defining," rather than verbs such as "analyzing," "formulating," "comparing," and "constructing" (MEN, 2009). These patterns indicate that, while the course design and curricular content have undergone substantial changes in recent years, the learning processes and strategies through which to enhance the development of critical thinking skills across all types of education tracks have not as yet been sufficiently addressed.

However, unlike during the socialist period, Polish teachers today are free to modify the curriculum by selecting textbooks that best suit their teaching needs and by expanding instructional goals, objectives, and strategies beyond those required by the core curriculum in order to best address the learning needs of their students. The extent to which teachers exercise this authority and the extent to which students experience learner-centered education in the classroom differ across schools and depend largely on the teacher's and the school's teaching philosophy, knowledge, and instructional expertise; their commitment to learner-centered education; and how closely they conform to the demands of the required curriculum (Behar, Pajares, & George, 1996). These outcomes are also closely related to the quality of instruction that instructors experience in teacher preparation programs. According to KRASP (2009a), teachers today receive an education that encourages a more creative implementation of the curriculum. However, given that the Polish education system continues to rely heavily on oral and written testing for assessing stu-dents' progress, including as selection criteria for admission to higher educa-tion, learner-centered education that encourages a critical and analytical learning environment may not as yet be a regular experience for students in all types of secondary schools and education tracks.

Curricular Formation and Role of the Liberal Arts in Higher Education

The liberal arts tradition in Poland dates back to 1364 when *Studium Generale*, today known as the Jagiellonian University (*Uniwersytet Jagieloński*), was established in Kraków (Cracow), modeled after its university counterparts in Bologna and Paris. In 1367, the year in which the university opened its doors to the first group of students, the liberal arts faculty was created alongside its other two faculties of medicine and law. The curriculum structure of the medieval university reflected a hierarchical order of the medieval society in which the liberal arts held the humblest position and theology (religion) the highest (Jagiellonian University). Consequently, the liberal arts became the basic course of study and the cornerstone of the curriculum and thus the center of the institution, as all university students were required to begin their studies and university professors their careers at the liberal arts faculty before they could continue at one of the other faculties.

During the 14th and 15th centuries, the liberal arts programs flourished at the Jagiellonian University, becoming sites for intellectual exchange, dialogue, discovery, and learning for many renowned scholars—one of whom was Nicholas Copernicus—and their disciplines. The liberal arts thus contributed to the development of a rich and vibrant intellectual culture characterizing the institution (Jagiellonian University, 2010; Tygielski, 2007). The tradition of liberal arts initiated at the Jagiellonian University has, over the centuries, become a powerful source of inspiration for Polish higher education and society, even during epochs when the liberal arts themselves were questioned and deemed less important. For example, during the socialist period, such liberal arts ideals as intellectual freedom, critical inquiry, and responsibility for service and leadership provided what Jan Lutyński (1990) calls a philosophical and ethical compass for Poland's higher education, and persisted as an attitude of intellectual resilience and personal freedom that inspired civic action and Poland's democratic transformation in 1989.

The Arts, Humanities, and Social Studies during the Socialist Period

Over the four decades of the socialist period, the role of liberal arts education was severely diminished. Political authorities considered liberal arts education risky because of the emphasis it put on inquiry, questioning, and understanding (Heyneman, 1998). As a consequence, Poland's higher education system was redesigned structurally and philosophically to meet the needs of the socialist economy, society, and ideology—a direction that took it away from the liberal tradition. At the structural level, an emphasis was placed on linking higher education closely to the economic sector by expanding technical and vocational institutions, programs, and courses designed to prepare a vocationally proficient workforce. Marxist/Leninist doctrine was imposed to the exclusion of all other ideologies in an effort to instill the socialist values of conformity and obedience (Heyneman, 1998; Lewowicki, 1997). Accordingly, academic courses demonstrated completeness of knowledge within disciplines, with an emphasis on the transmission and acquisition of ready-made knowledge, which in turn discouraged critical inquiry and exploratory learning (Lewowicki, 1997). Likewise, a system of written and oral exams focused on ensuring the mastery of factual knowledge. While state control over higher education institutions remained strict throughout the socialist period, the level of ideological and political conformity that faculty and students were required to display waxed and waned during that time, occasionally creating space for an "unofficial" curriculum and for more critical narratives to emerge in the classroom (Sorensen, 1997).

Still, socialist educational policy had a detrimental impact on the state of the arts, humanities, and social sciences in all types of tertiary education. In the case of vocationally oriented institutions, characterized by an expanded vocational curriculum and a primary focus on the quantitative and mathematical, the demand for courses in the humanities and social sciences remained low. This low level of interest can be attributed to a strong perception among a large portion of Polish students that the arts, humanities, and social sciences were too ideologized, politicized, and structured—hence, not likely to advance their personal and professional development. Similar effects and low prestige levels were associated with the humanities and social sciences as university disciplines, except for English philology or German philology. Thus, a large percentage of Polish youth associated universities and pedagogical institutes with lower-status professions such as teaching. The popularity of vocationally oriented institutions resulted over time in increased government funding for these institutions with a corresponding shift of resources away from universities.

Despite these unfavorable circumstances, the humanities often provided a niche for scholars with dissident views, allowing critical and progressive thought to exist (Axer, 2007). For many of these scholars, the collapse of the socialist regime and the democratic transformation of 1989 created a window of opportunity for transforming Poland's higher education in ways that were consistent with the values of a democratic society, as well as for revitalizing the arts, humanities, and social sciences in the public sphere.

Current Curriculum Discourses and Debates in Poland

Since the 1990s, Poland's higher education has operated under challenging social, political, and economic circumstances as the policy, industry, and public expectations continue to emphasize the responsibility of institutions to be increasingly efficient, entrepreneurial, and responsive to the country's changing economic needs, while at the same time fostering democratic values, innovation, and high-quality teaching. Amid these challenging conditions, numerous debates about the role of Poland's higher education in the new political and economic context have emerged, and different stakeholders have raised curriculum questions at the institutional, national, and international levels. These debates and questions, which often represent contesting and conflicting perspectives, have evolved and shifted over the past two decades as a result of changes in Poland's political and economic contexts, shaped by the processes of democratization, Europeanization, and globalization.

The prevailing view that emerged, primarily driven by concerns in the business and public sectors in the 1990s, was that higher education should be instrumental in achieving individual economic success and national economic growth. Thus, the discourse of practical market-oriented vocational preparation of students for the knowledge economy gained increasing prominence as being best suited to achieving these goals (Kowalski, 2004). The professional and educational aspirations and expectations that shape individuals' philosophies have, in recent decades, been reinforced by this rhetoric, increasingly pressuring them to pursue practical job-specific training relevant to the needs of the economic sector. Correspondingly, higher education institutions have experienced pressure to provide such education (Kowalski, 2004).

Because of the undeniable importance of national rebuilding, a similar discourse of market-oriented professional education was also adopted at the national policy level. Although the overarching policy goals are broadly defined in terms of preparing students for their roles as professionals and citizens in a democratic society (Law on Higher Education, 2005, Art. 13), the most important is the preparation of a highly skilled workforce. Today each of the two-cycle levels of undergraduate and graduate courses is aligned with these goals. According to the Law on Higher Education (2005, Art. 2), the aim of the undergraduate study cycle is to produce a vocationally proficient person equipped with foundational job skills· and specific knowledge. The second cycle aims to provide students with specialist knowledge in their area of specialization.

This professional orientation is further reflected in the guidelines of the National Qualifications Framework (*Krajowe Ramy Kwalifikacji*), developed centrally for all programs of study by Poland's Ministry of Science and Higher Education, and aligned with the requirements of the Bologna Process (Bologna Process, n.d.; MSHE, 2009c). The qualifications guidelines emphasize the acquisition of specified professionally relevant knowledge, transferable skills, competencies, and credentials that are deemed prerequisites to the individual's professional mobility or to entering a particular profession in the European Union labor market. Today, all public higher education institutions in Poland are required to develop professionally oriented courses within the above curricular framework.

These national policy trends give rise to several issues. First is the prevailing utilitarian view of education, whereby institutions are seen as providers of profession-specific training to students, reducing higher education to a strictly economic function as producers of a trained workforce. Second, this vocational policy discourse creates the impression that there is no place or need in Poland's higher education for approaches that go beyond this utilitarian view of education to encourage a free pursuit of knowledge, exploration, and inquiry as part of student preparation. Also undermined at the policy level are the issues of preparing students for democracy and a consideration of the broader social role that higher education plays in the process of such preparation.

Because of these political and economic pressures, Polish higher education has, in recent decades, become a terrain for marketization and commercialization agendas. These approaches have also shaped debate within the academic community on the role and place of higher education in post-1989 Poland. Several major curriculum points of discussion have emerged. On the one hand, numerous voices are in favor of the professional model of higher education. They are found especially in professionally oriented institutions that emphasize the importance of giving students practical preparation for the labor market. On the other hand, a disciplinary discourse has emerged among faculty members who contest the professional education model as a continuation of the socialist-era vocational model. Instead, they argue for a curriculum with a strong academic focus (Kowalski, 2004). Out of this debate, an argument in favor of liberal arts education also emerged in the early 1990s, advocating the development of a broadly educated person and professional.

The debate has also been shaped by factors such as the rapidly decreasing state funding for tertiary institutions in the 1990s, which in turn made these institutions increasingly dependent on other sources of income and which compelled scholars to seek additional employment (Kwiek, 2005, 2002; Sorensen, 1997). According to KRASP (2009a), these factors had a substantial impact on the emergence of a more convergent model of higher education and the adoption by both universities and professionally oriented institutions of a more central curricular discourse, whereby universities have supported the emphasis on the practical aspect of the curriculum and professionally oriented institutions on the curriculum's academic dimension. In both types of institutions, this trend has resulted in the adoption of a market-oriented professional curriculum, evident in an increase of fee-paying course offerings in highly marketable programs such as accounting, business, and marketing. According to

KRASP (2009a), this trend has resulted not only in institutions increasingly accommodating their program offerings to the immediate market demands, but also in a decreasing institutional distinctiveness, integrity, and programmatic diversity across Poland's higher education. The net result is increased uniformity and vocationalization. As noted by Tomasz Szapiro (2007), the impact of these trends has also become evident in the decreasing quality and growing narrowness of education that comes from the market-oriented, vocational, and homogenizing curriculum.

As some Polish scholars have pointed out, these market-oriented trends have, in recent decades, produced "a culture of accommodation" in higher education, evident in its departure from traditional academic values and social roles (Kieniewicz, 2007; Szapiro, 2007; Wilczek, 2010). Further, as indicated by the same scholars, faculty members have accommodated themselves in large part to the market-driven demands and ideologies. Recent scholarship on Polish higher education demonstrates efforts by Polish faculty to challenge these trends and redefine curriculum discourse in ways that balance the social, cultural, and economic goals and needs that are all part of the realities of a democratic society (Axer, 2007; Szapiro, 2007; Wąsowicz, 2007). Proponents of this strategy, many of whom are part of the liberal arts movement, seek to move away from the prevailing overspecialization that trains students as experts in a narrow field. Instead, they propose a curriculum that provides broad-based academic preparation, allowing students to be better human beings, better citizens, and thus better professionals (Axer, 2007; Wąsowicz, 2007; Wilczek, 2010).

In the past decade, this vigorous debate on curriculum has been challenged by the goals of the Bologna Process and its policy of restructuring curricula. The result is the addition of a new supra-national layer to national policy. Although the reforms emanating from the Bologna Process have thus far been primarily structural and have not officially addressed changes in the degree content or methodologies for its delivery, they have nevertheless shaped and influenced curriculum decision-making in Polish higher education. Its impact is evidenced, for example, in the growing modulizing of the curriculum, the implementation of the European Credit Transfer System, and the emphasis on the development of specific professionally oriented competencies (MSHE, 2009c). According to Bologna proponents, these uniform standards allow students greater flexibility of choice and mobility within European higher education systems and labor markets (Bologna Process, n.d.).

In contrast, opponents of the Bologna Process and its direction argue that the ways selected to achieve these goals—aligning higher education curricula with the outcome-oriented Bologna model—are leading to the greater standardization, rigidity, and convergence of higher education curricula across European universities (Karseth, 2006; Tomusk, 2007). The same scholars argue that this approach not only limits opportunities for the use of critical and

reflective approaches in the classroom by reducing learning to the development of readily assessable competencies, but also impoverishes diversity of
learning experiences across European institutions. In post-Soviet contexts such
as Poland, the adoption of the Bologna policy discourse and goals can be seen
as representing continuity with the socialist model rather than as a change in
patterns and trends of curricular/policy transformation. In short, it can be seen
as a return to the old problems and old dilemmas under a new guise.

Rising in response to the developments triggered by the Bologna Process
has been an alternative vision of student preparation at the undergraduate
level. Promoted by the consortium of European Colleges of Liberal Arts and
Sciences (ECOLAS), this vision places education within the context of the
liberal arts and sciences tradition and connects cognitive, societal, economic,
and civic dimensions as part of student preparation (ECOLAS, n.d.). As
explained by Professor Piotr Wilczek, director of the Collegium of Inter-
Faculty/Interdisciplinary Individual Studies in the Humanities (MISH) in
Poland and a member of ECOLAS, the value of such programs lies primarily
in their emphasis on academic formation or *Bildung* as a foundation for the
professional preparation of students at the graduate level. As he further
explains, this kind of program organization also allows maintaining programmatic variety across European higher education systems and institutions, while
at the same time supporting a unified focus on the cognitive and social dimensions of student learning (Wilczek, 2009). In post-Communist higher education systems, such as Poland's, efforts undertaken by ECOLAS play an
especially important role in redefining and shifting the purpose of undergraduate education away from the strictly vocational orientation that has prevailed
in the system for the past few decades.

The Arts, Humanities, and Social Sciences in Institutional Offerings

Given recent developments in the national and regional contexts, three main
questions arise: (a) What has been seen as the place of the arts, humanities,
and social sciences in Poland's higher education curricula today? (b) How has
that role changed following the democratic transformation of 1989? (c) To
what extent has liberal arts education been embraced and integrated into
higher education curricula as part of students' professional preparation across
all types of institutions?

With the exception of art-oriented institutions, offerings in the arts,
humanities, and social sciences in professionally oriented institutions (e.g.,
polytechnics, and schools of economics) are curricularly marginal and institutionally peripheral. As a result, now as during the socialist period, vocational
course offerings constitute a substantial portion of the core and specialized curriculum at both undergraduate and graduate levels. In contrast, courses in the

arts, humanities, and social sciences tend to be reduced to a handful of offerings such as obligatory language courses (MSHE, 2009c). In the case of agricultural universities, for example, departments can choose between offering courses in the arts, humanities, and social sciences or in economics; this choice tends to favor economics. In institutions in which arts, humanities, and social sciences courses are offered as part of the compulsory general education curriculum (e.g., engineering and economics), a tendency toward the professionalization of the arts, humanities, and social sciences courses and a parallel fragmentation of knowledge is evident. For example, courses in ethics, sociology, and psychology tend to focus on professionally relevant aspects of these disciplines and to deal with issues from a strictly organizational perspective in an attempt to develop students' professional competence in such areas as, for example, business ethics or the psychology of management.

In contrast, Polish universities, which include a number of denominational (primarily Catholic) institutions, have traditionally offered a wide range of arts, humanities, and social sciences courses as part of their programs. The distribution of these courses differs across the various disciplines and departments, with the natural and physical sciences (e.g., chemistry, biology, physics) being the most limited. In contrast, philology, law, political science, journalism, sociology, and teacher education offer the widest range of such courses (MSHE, 2009c). However, as in professionally oriented institutions, the scope and focus of general education courses offered at Polish universities tend to focus on professional perspectives and, hence, lack a balance between the humanities and sciences.

Paradoxically, a similar trend toward the separation of the humanities and sciences is evident in interdisciplinary programs and fields of study that have been established since 1989 to reduce the narrowness of student preparation that results from this professional specialization and discipline-based approach. Three examples of such programs are interdisciplinary studies in mathematics and natural sciences, the humanities, and pedagogy. Despite this intent, interdisciplinary programs still tend to be organized around narrowly based groups of disciplines rather than programs that bring together sciences and humanities (MSHE, 2009c). This approach reduces the role of the arts, humanities, and social sciences to a tool for developing professional competence. Furthermore, it continues to encourage the perception that the humanities operate separately from the sciences and thus have little relevance to students' professional preparation.

Teaching Methodologies

Recent research has found that the trend toward more liberal teaching approaches and learning environments in all types of institutions and programs can be traced in an increased emphasis on small group settings, project work, group discussions, and debate. Still, the need for improved teaching continues to present a significant challenge to higher education institutions (Kowalski, 2004). One barrier to better teaching is the still strong tradition of teaching that focuses primarily on knowledge and skills transfer. The legacy of such teaching is especially evident in the area of student assessment, which continues to rely primarily on testing and face-to-face and/or written exams. Aimed at verifying the student's mastery of course content, these assessment methods tend to stifle deep learning, reflection, critical thinking, and analysis that lie at the heart of liberal teaching and learning (Kowalski, 2004).

Enrollment Patterns by Field of Study

As documented by Poland's Central Statistical Office (GUS, 2006) and Ministry of Science and Higher Education (MSHE, 2009b), post-1989 enrollment patterns in higher education reflect strongly the changing labor market trends and emerging career prospects. In the 2005–2006 school year, the largest proportion of students—25.7%—was enrolled in the newly created or restructured majors of economics, business administration, and management. Enrollment in these fields had grown by more than 70% since 1990–1991 (see Table 6.1). During the same period, the percentage of students enrolled in the once highly popular and competitive field of engineering plummeted by more than 50% (GUS, 2006; MSHE, 2009b). In other professionally oriented institutions, schools of medicine saw enrollment increases of 70%, while technology and computer studies rose by 60% between 2002–2003 and 2005–2006 (MSHE, 2009b). These data indicate that, while enrollment distributions have shifted in professional institutions following Poland's economic transformation, the demand for a highly specialized education remains high.

TABLE 6.1 Higher education enrollment in Poland

Field of study	Proportion of students (%)		
	1990–1991	2002–2003	2005–2006
Economics, business administration, and management	15	28.7	25.7
Engineering/technical fields	17	9.80	7.9
Medical studies	10	2.9	4.7
Technological and computer fields of study/ information technology	n.a.	3.1	5.3
Social studies (e.g., psychology, sociology)	4	13.2	13.5
Teacher education	14	12.6	12.8
Arts/fine arts	2	1.0	1.1
Humanities	n.a.	7.9	8

Source: GUS (2006).

In contrast, fields of study characteristic of universities continue to be less popular, even though enrollment rates in some fields have increased significantly. Two examples are a growing demand for foreign language teachers, psychologists, and sociologists. The latter areas are relevant to the business, health care, and government sectors. Between 1990–1991 and 2005–2006, enrollment in the social sciences more than tripled, while remaining relatively stable for teacher education programs, and enrollment in arts and fine arts (1.1% in 2005–2006) and the humanities (8.0% in 2005–2006) has also continued to be low. These two disciplines continue, as was the case during the socialist period, to be associated with lower-paying jobs and less prestigious careers than the more specialized field; hence, Polish youth see them as less attractive career choices (MSHE, 2009b).

Current Liberal Arts Programs

Reclaiming the Liberal Arts Tradition

The findings presented in this chapter thus far demonstrate a trend toward overspecialization in Poland's higher education and the lack of broad-based general education programs beyond secondary-level education. Partially filling this gap are the liberal arts programs established by Professor Jerzy Axer at the University of Warsaw in 1992 with the purpose of providing an alternative form of preparation of students. Today similar liberal arts programs are offered at nine leading Polish universities[1] and provide instruction that is embedded in the classical tradition of education as the cultivation of critical and independent thinkers. According to some Polish scholars associated with the liberal arts movement (Axer, 2007; Wąsowicz, 2007), the long-term neglect of the social, civic, and moral aspects of student development, both during the socialist period and as a result of current trends in education, has resulted in a narrow and impoverished form of higher education as a place for career preparation. According to Piotr Wąsowicz (2007), the impact of these trends is also evident in what he calls the erosion of morals and values that characterizes today's Polish society. The results are that social and civic virtues and the concept of a common good are seen as having little value or resonance with the accompanying result that they tend to be subjected to economic priorities.

Given the current socio-economic and policy trends toward the pragmatization of values and the continued vocationalization of higher education, this liberal arts movement represents efforts by some Polish faculty to transcend the boundaries and constraints that these policies impose on academic institutions and to create a space for an alternative curriculum and a differing set of values, ideals, and worldviews (Axer, 2000, 2002, 2007). The liberal arts movement challenges the narrowness of education that comes from the instrumentalist perspective on the purpose of higher education and the traditional disciplinary framework. Instead, it seeks to reframe the current public discussions about civic life in general and higher education specifically (Axer, 2002, 2007). The subversive contexts of this movement are not limited solely to their programmatic and curricular initiatives but demonstrate a more broadly based sense of social agency aimed at rebuilding academic and national communities in a spirit of commitment to the liberal ideals of freedom, dialogue, informed citizenship, and service. Springing from a foundation of an alternative understanding of and attitude toward how to approach the world through education, the movement seeks to encourage the academic community and students to see the present, often restrictive, policy environment and socioeconomic trends as an opportunity to challenge and transcend these constraints, rather than conform to them.

Transcending Boundaries and Borders

The liberal arts movement, which began as a grassroots academic initiative at the Center for Studies on the Classical Tradition in Poland and East-Central Europe (OBTA) in 1992, has grown over the past two decades into a network of broad activities supporting liberal arts education, research, scholarship, and outreach initiatives, all grouped under the overarching term Artes Liberales. During this time, the Artes Liberales movement has become a force for change at the institutional, national, and regional levels. Initially a small interdisciplinary program, it has over time grown to include: (a) the Collegium of Inter-Faculty/Interdisciplinary Individual Studies in the Humanities (MISH) established in 1993, (b) the Artes Liberales Academy, an inter-university system of MISH colleges at nine Polish universities (1994), (c) the Collegium Artes Liberales (College of Liberal Arts and Sciences/CLASs), which offers an honors program, and (d) the East-Central European School in the Humanities (MSH) (1996), which crosses geographical borders to provide a collaborative platform for interdisciplinary doctoral studies for students from Ukraine, Lithuania, Belarus, Poland, and Russia. Modeled after the Polish program founded by the Collegium of Inter-Faculty/Interdisciplinary Individual Studies in the Humanities, similar programs have also been established at universities across the region: in Lviv in 2002, in Grodno in 2003, and in Minsk in 2004. At this writing, similar programs are being established in Kyiv in the Ukraine and in Vilnius and Kovno in Lithuania. At the institutional level, the MISH program and its general education curriculum have been used as a model for the development of a new experimental interdisciplinary undergraduate education program (Wilczek, 2009).

In 2008, the Institute for Interdisciplinary Studies Artes Liberales (IBI AL) was created to further expand the range of activities undertaken by the Artes Liberales movement. This institute's activities include outreach initiatives to schools and teachers, scholarly collaborations with European and North

American universities, humanities scholarship, and the dissemination of that scholarship through publishing, conferences, and seminars. Particularly note-worthy among these initiatives are professional development seminars for ele-mentary and secondary schoolteachers, acknowledging the important role they play in revitalizing the long-neglected partnerships between universities (theory) and schools (practice) and in challenging the existing discipline-based model of teacher preparation. According to Axer (2000), for schools to produce well-rounded, critical, and thoughtful students, teacher preparation programs need to ensure that teachers receive a strong liberal arts background and are well versed in liberal arts ideals, principles, and practices within their content areas, including instructional theory and its practical application. As he further explains, the teacher's ability to create learning environments that instill curiosity and an open mind in students is crucial to the improvement of teaching in Polish schools. Such an improvement will also impact universities as students move through the lower levels of the national education system and enter higher education.

The Place of the Liberal Arts in Higher Education

Despite recent policy changes, the liberal arts continue to be excluded from national higher education policies and denied their place as a legitimate element in the preparation of all students. At present, liberal arts education is offered exclusively through programs sponsored by the MISH and the CLASs. These programs, in the two decades since their founding, have created their own unique niche in the Polish higher education system. As part of this dis-tinctive status, the liberal arts programs comply with some national and Euro-pean standards, while at the same time they operate independently—outside the jurisdiction of the Ministry of National Education. Since the liberal arts do not have the status of a degree program recognized by the Ministry of National Education, they can only be taken in conjunction with a degree program that offers specialized education, such as law, journalism, or economics.

Like all other daytime university programs offered at public institutions, liberal arts programs are tuition free. Unlike these programs, however, liberal arts programs are privately funded. The U.S.-based Christian Johnson Endeavor Foundation is their principal funder. As Wilczek explains (2009), this financial independence, though imposing constraints in some areas gives the programs wide decision-making autonomy in the area of curriculum devel-opment, which in turn allows the faculty the freedom to develop their own courses and students their own individualized study programs. In conformity with the Bologna Process's European Credit Transfer System, students earn the required credits but based on the program's own system of internal student evaluation criteria. Administrative decisions, such as the recruitment of students, are made through shared governance by the Council of Deans representing all departments that participate in the programs. Faculty members who teach in these programs are seconded from other university-based departments and represent a broad range of disciplines, research interests, and expertise to ensure broad-based education.

Education in the Collegium of Inter-Faculty/Interdisciplinary Individual Studies in the Humanities (MISH) and the College of Liberal Arts and Sciences (CLASs)

According to Piotr Wilczek (2009), both the MISH and CLASs programs are designed as models of alternative preparation for highly motivated, gifted, and self-directed students with broad interests in the humanities. Admission to these programs is limited and based strictly on academic merit. Therefore, a substantial number of MISH students are winners of national Olympiads in areas such as the humanities and mathematics, as well as graduates of general education secondary schools (lyceums). MISH students can select from a variety of courses offered at any two or three participating departments at their own institution or at any other MISH collegium in Poland (see Table 6.2). Graduates of the two-year MISH program receive a diploma supplement with a degree in their major field of specialization (e.g., in psychology) and a second (non-degree) liberal arts specialization.

On the methodological level, all programs are based on the classical model of the mentor–student relationship which, according to Axer (2002), allows for greater attention to the needs of academically gifted students. As further explained by Axer (2000), the mentor–student program differs from other university-based programs because it shifts the emphasis away from the learning outcome to the learning process and thus redefines the student's role from that of a passive recipient of knowledge to that of an active participant. The role of the teacher also shifts from that of a supervisor to a guide and advisor in the learning process. Likewise, the classroom environment and setting have been redefined to support and be enhanced by the use of student-centered learning strategies. Thus, all classes are organized into small groups averaging about 10 students to maximize their opportunities to develop the habits of analysis and reflection and the attributes of reason and critical engagement. The focus on the learning process is also reflected in the use of evaluation strategies which, in contrast to more standardized outcome-based evaluation methods (e.g., tests, face-to-face exams) employed broadly across other programs, are based on a wide range of student work, including research papers, project work, presentations, and participation in classroom discussions and debates (Wilczek, 2009).

TABLE 6.2 Popularity of departments among students in the Collegium of Inter-Faculty/Interdisciplinary Individual Studies in the Humanities (MISH) (in %)

Departments participating in MISH	2004–2005	2005–2006	2006–2007	2007–2008	2008–2009	MISH diplomas issued
History	38.08	38.34	32.98	32.55	27.32	85
Polish studies	36.53	37.05	38.52	35.16	36.34	126
Psychology	26.17	25.65	25.33	19.79	21.65	94
Philosophy and sociology	59.84	51.55	55.94	52.34	51.80	152
Applied social sciences and resocialization	16.58	23.83	20.58	15.89	10.57	51
Neophilology	16.58	13.21	16.09	18.23	16.75	63
Institute for Oriental Studies	5.96	5.44	8.97	8.07	10.31	6
Geography and regional studies	0.52	1.81	1.58	2.6	2.84	1
Journalism and political science	25.91	26.17	29.55	25.52	28.35	54
Pedagogy	0.52	1.81	0.53	1.56	0.77	n.a.
Law and administration	22.28	22.54	28.76	29.17	30.67	47
Economic sciences	5.18	6.48	5.8	7.03	5.41	8
Institute of American and European Studies	3.11	3.37	2.64	2.6	2.32	n.a.
Institute for Interdisciplinary Studies—Artes Liberales	2.33	3.37	6.07	7.29	13.14	n.a.
OBTA*/MISH	54.66	50.78	43.8	33.07	28.61	n.a.
Other departments and units at University of Warsaw	6.74	5.70	1.32	0.78	5.16	n.a.
Polish Academy of Sciences	2.07	2.07	1.6	0.52	1.55	n.a.
Other institutions	7.77	8.81	6.86	8.07	7.22	n.a.

Source: adapted from MISH (n.d.).

Notes
* OBTA: Studies on the Classical Tradition in Poland and East-Central Europe.

Challenges of the Liberal Arts Programs

Based on these characteristics, it seems clear that, while the liberal arts programs functioning under the rubrics of the MISH and CLASs challenge and transcend many external organizational and systemic boundaries and barriers, they are also faced with a challenge of overcoming their own internally created barriers. One of these barriers is the programs' small enrollment capacity and their highly selective admission criteria, which in countries such as Poland tend to be associated with added prestige and elitism. These factors, combined with the fact that the liberal arts programs are offered exclusively as a second non-degree major or minor, favor students who are academically oriented, locally based, and able to afford the additional costs (e.g., supplies/living costs) associated with such participation. Wilczek indicates (2009) that these financial constraints are detrimental to the liberal arts programs' ability to attract and support gifted students from non-urban areas and less privileged socio-economic backgrounds. Given the lack of state incentives for gifted students and the programs' own limited financial resources, access to the liberal arts education and, consequently to more prestigious professional opportunities, appear biased in favor of students from relatively privileged socio-economic backgrounds from urban areas.

Another constraint is that the emphasis in the liberal arts programs is placed primarily on the individual development of students, while excluding community-oriented learning. Axer (2000) and Wilczek (2009) agree that the programs have not as yet been very successful in finding ways to link the individual and collective dimensions of the student's development and create the program environment that embodies and develops among students a sense of community, collaboration, and collective responsibility to the larger society of which they are a part.

Student Enrollment in the Liberal Arts

The MISH (n.d.) data demonstrate the increasing popularity of the liberal arts programs in Poland and the growing student enrollment that has increased from fewer than 50 in 1993–1994 to 500 in 2009–2010. This significant increase in enrollment reflects a growing interest in this type of education and signals that perception about the humanities among students is gradually changing. On the one hand, according to Wilczek (2009), this increase can be attributed to MISH's reputation as a provider of high-quality alternative education and thus as a prestigious place for students with distinctive learning needs.

On the other hand, this renewed interest in the liberal arts education demonstrates a need for a more balanced approach in higher education—an approach that recognizes the private value of learning and the importance of both intrinsic and instrumental benefits of the humanities as part of students' preparation. Wilczek (2009) explains that, although students increasingly see the liberal arts as "an interesting field of study and begin to see their value, they also believe that these programs should be done in combination with a more 'pragmatic' and practical specialization demanded in the job market." Thus, the liberal arts programs tend to be seen by youth primarily as an add-on to "pragmatic" professional preparation, rather than as a foundation for it.

Conclusion

Unlike Poland's political and economic systems, the country's higher education system has not undergone a radical transformation, following the country's transition from socialism to political democracy and market economy in 1989. Though the economic and political contexts have undergone a fundamental change since 1989, the national development priorities have not altered substantially and continue to be aligned primarily with the economic goals. As a result, social and civic development have been given little attention and continue to be subsumed to the economic priorities. Similar trends can be identified in relation to higher education.

While the creation of a new higher education landscape that is better placed to address the changing socio-political and economic conditions became a necessity in the early 1990s, the national reform efforts have often been fragmented in their purpose and direction. Although higher education structures and curricula have been modified in response to the national and regional (Bologna Process) needs, the purpose of higher education and its role in a democracy have been lost during the reform process. The lack of attention to these issues has preserved rather than challenged the legacy of socialist policies and practices—specifically in their emphasis on the economic function of higher education. As a result, the concept of vocational education, a key aspect of the socialist education model, has been redefined in terms of the market rhetoric and has been renamed "professional education" to differentiate it from its socialist predecessor.

At the institutional level, policy changes have resulted in increased academic autonomy and a healthy development of the core values of tolerance, dialogue, and diversity among Polish academics (Wąsowicz, 2007). At the same time, according to Wąsowicz (2007), the academic community has not been very successful in spreading these ideals to the public space by preparing students for democratic participation or by its own participation in the public sphere, as economic and professional goals took precedence in higher education after 1989. At present, the external (national/Bologna policy) and internal (institutional) environments are aligned along these goals, which in turn substantially restricts the possibility of the liberal arts education at Polish higher education institutions. The "pragmatic" view of the purpose of education, which underlies the present policy and practice, is reflected in the emphasis on early specialization and vocationalization at both undergraduate and graduate levels. These values manifest themselves most strongly in the focus on the professional preparation of students through the development of "specialized" and "applicable" knowledge and "practical" skills. Within this framework, liberal arts education is seen as incompatible—and thus irrelevant—because it does not provide a foundation of what is considered as "useful" practical knowledge, skills, and abilities for professional preparation. Thus, liberal arts education is considered more as an alternative to professional specialization at the policy level or as an add-on to students, rather than as a foundation for specialization. As such, it continues to be excluded from the national curriculum. If it were not for funding from external, often foreign, donors, faculties participating in the program, and competitive state teaching and research grants, the liberal arts programs, according to Wilczek (2009), would not be represented in Poland's higher education system today.

Paradoxically, however, the same national curriculum guidelines for different fields of study consistently emphasize the importance of developing "critical skills," "higher order and applied problem-solving abilities," "ethical judgment," "interpersonal and communication skills" in the Polish and foreign languages, "independent thinking," and "active engagement and teamwork," all of which are the domain of liberal arts education (MSHE, 2009c). This characterization of skills and abilities by the national qualifications framework demonstrates that liberal arts education is not only compatible with its own objectives of the professional preparation of students but, more importantly, has the potential to prepare them beyond the scope of the strictly professional training model that currently prevails. The narrow focus on discipline-related aspects of the arts, humanities, and social sciences by policy-makers and higher education institutions, combined with the long-standing neglect of liberal arts education, has resulted in an impoverished version of "practical" education that has not only affected the quality of students' job preparation but has, in essence, failed to put their professional preparation into the broader context of students' social responsibility, critical understanding of the world, and commitment to the public good.

Given the national curriculum's characterization of desired skills and abilities, a logical question is how graduates with a liberal arts background are seen in the workplace today. As Wilczek (2009) explains, graduates from liberal arts programs have been in high demand and are markedly successful in businesses and governmental institutions, not only because of their professional skills, but also because of the coherence of their preparation and their flexibility in working effectively with people from different disciplines, backgrounds, and beliefs. Thus, these graduates appear be improving social perceptions of the applicability and benefits of liberal arts education for the workplace and in the broader contexts of social and economic development. In other words, they can be seen as gradually redefining the role and place of the humanities and social sciences in the workplace and society. The demand for graduates with a liberal arts background further demonstrates a growing need for professionals with a broader vision and understanding of the world. These abilities are in great demand in the increasingly diverse and globalizing workplace, even though this need and the public benefits of having students with such preparation may not have been openly acknowledged or identified by the business sector, governmental institutions, and policy-makers.

Given the present policy emphasis on the specialization and vocationalization of education and the dichotomous relationship between liberal arts education and the professional preparation of students, the academic community can play a unique role, not only in challenging and redefining this relationship, but also in redefining the role and purpose of higher education in relation to the goals and needs of social—and not merely economic—development (Wilczek, 2010). Meeting this challenge cannot occur without the commitment of higher education institutions and its members. Such a commitment requires them to actively challenge and redefine current assumptions about higher education's purposes, priorities, and values—and the academic practices in which these purposes are manifested—in ways that are consistent with the social and economic goals, in both policy and practice (Axer, 2007). Without addressing these issues, Polish higher education will continue to ignore its social purpose and responsibility, and the liberal arts will continue to be marginalized. By fostering commitment to social purpose, institutions can reposition and reestablish themselves as creators of change in the academic and national life, rather than merely following the dictates of top-down policies and external trends (Axer, 2007).

While many institutions have adopted ways to integrate the humanities and social sciences into their own programs and courses, differences exist in how and to what extent they have embraced these disciplines as part of student undergraduate education. These differences further reflect how these institutions position themselves in relation to the national curricular framework and the disciplines of the liberal arts. In the case of numerous institutions, these efforts have often been selective and have shifted the focus in the study of the humanities and social sciences away from social discourse and toward more professionally related considerations. Efforts to teach the liberal arts have often succumbed to a more instrumental than exploratory approach, falling back into the traditional role of developing student "know-how." Examples of institutions committed to teaching liberally are still rare. Among these noteworthy institutions are some public universities and church-related institutions, including the University of Lublin. Many of these institutions are a place where professionally oriented education has been redefined and taught in a "different" way from widespread practices by laying an emphasis on understanding professional practice in relation to the ethical, human, social, and civic dimensions and contexts of the individual's decisions and choices.

The emphasis on professional specialization at the policy and practice levels, and specifically the professional discourse at the curriculum level, is closely linked to the professionally oriented priorities and strategies of the Bologna Process, particularly in the European Credit Transfer System. Accordingly, the Bologna Process primarily emphasizes the professional preparation of students at the undergraduate level and the development of specialized knowledge, skills, competencies, and abilities relevant to the needs of the European Union labor markets. This focus not only signals an increasing standardization of higher education and greater conformity in the skills and competencies defined in European professions, but also reduces higher education to skills and competency development (Tomusk, 2007).

Today, only nine Polish universities support liberal arts education. The liberal arts programs remain relatively small and are considered elitist, not only because they serve a select group of students, but also because the purpose of education—which shifted during the socialist period away from preparing students to become critical and independent thinkers and toward professional skills acquisition—has not thus far been sufficiently challenged and redefined at the policy and practice levels. In today's vocationally oriented education sector, liberal arts programs tend to be associated by students—and increasingly by employers—with a sense of achievement and elitism that translates in turn into increased professional status.

Despite their relatively modest representation, the liberal arts programs have nevertheless become a source of innovation, inspiring curricular experimentation and change at their home and other higher education institutions, both locally and regionally. Over the past decade, they have established themselves as programs of high-quality education. They have shown significant and sustained impact in the broader education community, gradually redefining teaching, teacher education, and school practice. While crossing boundaries and barriers on many different levels and in many different areas appears to be an underlying theme of the liberal arts programs and initiatives, one important impact that the Artes Liberales movement has had is on reinvigorating the academic community itself and in changing its perceptions of the goals and role of the university in the academic and national life. In 2010–2011, an amended law on higher education is expected to be introduced in Poland. Under its provisions, existing overarching curricular frameworks will be deregulated, giving some "best performing institutions" increased autonomy in the area of program development and financing (MSHE, 2010, p. 4). While all institutions will be required to develop programs within the boundaries of the Bologna framework, this change will nevertheless create greater opportunities for innovation and new solutions in Polish higher education, allowing the academic community to have greater ownership of educational decision-making and to become agents of educational change.

Note

1 These institutions are Warsaw University, Katowice University, Toruń University, Kraków University, Catholic University in Lublin, Collegium Europaeum Gnesnense/Poznań University, Wrocław University, Lublin University, and Szczecin University.

References

Axer, J. (2000, November 18–19). Komandosi edukacji [Education Commandos]. *Gazeta Wyborcza.*

Axer, J. (2002). Liberal arts: Liberated from what? *Polish Market*, 6, 36–37.

Axer, J. (2007). On civic virtue and the university. In *Autonomia uniwerystetu: Jej przyjaciele i wrogowie* (pp. 143–148). Warszawa: Fundacja Instytut Artes Liberales.

Behar, L. S., Pajares, F., & George, P. S. (1996). The effect of teachers' beliefs on students' academic performance during curriculum innovation. *High School Journal*, 79, 324–332.

Bergen Communiqué. (2005, May 19–20). *The European higher education area: Achieving the goals.* Bergen: Ministers Responsible for Higher Education. Retrieved on July 2, 2010, from www.ond.vlaanderen.be/hogeronderwijs/bologna/documents/MDC/050520_Bergen_Communique1.pdf.

Bologna Declaration on the European Space for Higher Education: An explanation. (2000). Retrieved on June 25, 2010, from http://ec.europa.eu/education/policies/educ/bologna/bologna.pdf.

Bologna Process. (n.d.). *The official Bologna Process website.* Retrieved on July 13, 2009, from www.ond.vlaanderen.be/hogeronderwijs/bologna/about/index.htm.

Dąbrowa-Szefler, M., & Jabłecka-Prysłopska, J. (2006). *[The] OECD [Organization for Economic and Cooperative Development] thematic review of tertiary education: Country background report for Poland.* Retrieved on July 16, 2009, from www.eng.nauka.gov.pl/_gAllery/30/69/3069/OECD_Tertiary_Review_CBR_Poland.pdf.

ECOLAS. European Colleges of Liberal Arts and Sciences. (n.d.). *Building [a] liberal arts program.* Retrieved on February 10, 2010, from www.ecolas.eu/content/organization.php.

GUS. Central Statistical Office. (2006). *Szkoły wyższe i ich finanse w 2005r* [Tertiary institutions and their finances in 2005]. Retrieved on July 22, 2009, from www.nauka.gov.pl/mn/_gAllery/18/66/18662/publikacja.pdf.

Heyneman, S. P. (1998). *From the party/state to multi-ethnic democracy: Education and its influence on social cohesion in the Europe and Central Asia region.* Florence, Italy: International Child Development Center, United Nations Children's Fund.

Jagiellonian University. (2010). *The past and the present.* Retrieved on February 23, 2010, from www.uj.edu.pl/dispatch.jsp?item=uniwersytet/historia/historiatxt.jsp&lang=en.

Jung-Miklaszewska, J. (2003). *The education system in Poland.* Bureau for Academic Recognition and International Exchange (BUWiWM). Retrieved on July 16, 2009, from www.buwiwm.edu.pl/publ/edu/System.pdf.

Karseth, B. (2006). Curriculum restructuring in higher education after the Bologna Process: A new pedagogical regime? *Revista Española de Educación Comparada*, 12, 255–284.

Kieniewicz, J. (2007). Poszukiwanie prawdy i przestrzeń dialogu [Searching for the truth and the space of the dialogue]. In *Autonomia uniwerystetu: Jej przyjaciele i wrogowie* (pp. 61–63). Warszawa: Fundacja Instytut Artes Liberales.

Kowalski, E. (2004). *Changing teaching in Polish higher education in the new political and economic climate: A case study of perspectives of Polish university teachers*. Ph.D. thesis, Ontario Institute for Studies in Education, University of Toronto.

KRASP. (2009a). *Tom I: Strategia rozwoju szkolnictwa wyższego 2010–2020. Projekt środowiskowy* [Higher Education development strategy 2010–2020: Proposal]. Retrieved on February 23, 2010, from www.krasp.org.pl/news/Strategia_I.pdf.

KRASP. (2009b). *Tom II: Polskie szkolnictwo wyższe. Stan, uwarunkowania i perspektywy* [Poland's higher education]. Retrieved on February 23, 2010, from www.krasp.org.pl/news/Strategia_II.pdf.

Kwiek, M. (2002). Academe in transition: Transformations in the Polish academic profession. In P. G. Altbach (Ed.), *The decline of the guru: The academic profession in developing and middle-income countries* (pp. 281–305). Boston: Boston College, Center for International Higher Education.

Kwiek, M. (2005). *Poland: A higher education policy review*. Retrieved on July 13, 2009, from www.cpp.amu.edu.pl/pdf/HE_policy_Poland.doc.

Law on Higher Education, Act of July 27, 2005. (2005). Warsaw: Ministry of National Education. Retrieved on July 13, 2009, from www.cepes.ro/hed/policy/legislation/pdf/Poland.pdf.

Lewowicki, T. (1997). *Przemiany oświaty: Szkice o ideach i praktyce edukacyjnej* [Changes in education]. Warszawa: żak.

Lutyński, J. (1990). *Nauka i polskie problemy: Komentarz socjologa.* [Education and Polish problems: A sociologist's commentary]. Warszawa: Państwowy Instytut Wydawniczy.

MEN. Ministry of National Education. (2009). Reforma Programowa [National Curriculum Reform]. Retrieved on July 30, 2009, from www.reformaprogramowa.men.gov.pl/dla-nauczycieli/.

MISH. Interdisciplinary Institute for Studies in Humanities. (n.d.). Dane statystyczne [Statistical data]. Retrieved on August 22, 2009, from www.mish.uw.edu.pl/node/5.

MSHE. Ministry of Science and Higher Education. (2009a). *Higher education.* Retrieved on June 25, 2009, from www.eng.nauka.gov.pl/ms/index.jsp?place=Menu06&news_cat_id=28&layout=2.

MSHE. Ministry of Science and Higher Education. (2009b). *Informacja o wynikach rekrutacji na studia na rok akademicki 20082009 w uczelniach nadzorowanych przez Ministra Nauki i Szkolnictwa Wyższego oraz uczelniach niepublicznych* [Recruitment/admission data]. Retrieved on June 25, 2009, from www.nauka.gov.pl/mn/_gAllery/49/50/49501/Informacja_o_wynikach_rekrutacji_2008–2009.pdf.

MSHE. Ministry of Science and Higher Education. (2009c). *Szkolnictwo wyższe: Krajowe ramy kwalifikacji* [Higher education: The national qualifications framework]. Retrieved on July 25, 2009, from www.bip.nauka.gov.pl/bipmein/index.jsp?place=Lead07&news_cat_id=117&news_id=982&layout=1&page=text.

MSHE. Ministry of Science and Higher Education. (2010). *Założenia do nowelizacji ustawy: Prawo o szkolnictwie wyższym oraz ustawy o stopniach naukowych i tytule naukowym oraz o stopniach i tytule w zakresie sztuki* [Amendments to the Law on Higher Education]. Retrieved on April 12, 2010, from www.bip.nauka.gov.pl/_gAllery/73/10/731020091030_EEE_zalozenia_po_RM.pdf.

Sorensen, K. (1997). *Polish higher education en route to the market: Institutional change and autonomy at two economics academies.* Stockholm: Institute of International Education.

Szapiro, T. (2007). *Autonomia uczelni i jej relacje z biznesem: Uczelnia zaczarowana* [The autonomy of the university and its relation to the world of business: The university under a spell]. In *Autonomia uniwerystetu: Jej przyjaciele i wrogowie* (pp. 37–48). Warszawa: Fundacja Instytut Artes Liberales.

Tomusk, V. (2007). Bologna Process: For the men of integrity, for the women of letters. In *Autonomia uniwerystetu: Jej przyjaciele i wrogowie* (pp. 65–80). Warszawa: Fundacja Instytut Artes Liberales.

Tygielski, W. (2007). Czy współczesny uniwersytet zasługuje na autonomię? [Does the contemporary university deserve autonomy?]. In *Autonomia uniwerystetu: Jej przyjaciele i wrogowie* (pp. 49–59). Warszawa: Fundacja Instytut Artes Liberales.

Wąsowicz, M. (2007). Cnoty republikańskie a uniwersytet [Republican virtues and university] Dyskusja panelowa. In *Autonomia uniwerystetu: Jej przyjaciele i wrogowie* (pp. 149–152). Warszawa: Fundacja Instytut Artes Liberales.

Wilczek, P. (2009, July 3). Director of the Collegium of Inter-Faculty/Interdisciplinary Individual Studies in the Humanities (MISH). Telephone interview.

Wilczek, P. (2010). Uniwersytet: Innowacyjność i tożsamość [University: Innovation and identity]. In Z. Kadłubek (Ed.), *Universit150as nova: Innowacyjny uniwersytet* (pp. 53–65). Katowice: Podhalańska Agencja Reklamowo-Artystyczna "PARA."

7

RUSSIA

Against the Tide, Liberal Arts Establishes a Foothold in Post-Soviet Russia

Jonathan Becker, Andrei Kortunov, and Philip Fedchin

Liberal arts education currently plays a relatively minor role within the Russian system of higher education. Indeed, a Google search under "liberal education" (*liberalnoe obrazovnie*) in Russia reveals relatively few hits, the most prominent of which is a Russian translation of one of the author's articles, "What a Liberal Arts Education Is … and Is Not."

The thin footprint of liberal arts education in Russia, however, does not mean that it plays no role or that it has no future. Indeed, given the multiple transitions and challenges that the Russian system of higher education is facing, there are many reasons to believe that it will play an increasingly prominent role over the next decade.

In this chapter, we explore the presence and prospects of liberal arts education in Russia. For our purposes, a modern liberal arts education can be defined as

> a system of higher education designed to foster in students the desire and capacity to learn, think critically, and communicate proficiently, and to prepare them to function as engaged citizens. It is distinguished by a flexible curriculum that allows for student choice and demands breadth, as well as depth, of study, and by a student-centered pedagogy that is interactive and requires students to engage directly with critical texts within and outside of the classroom.
>
> (Becker, 2004)

In other words, liberal arts education suggests a comprehensive package of activities, or a system that is curricular, pedagogical, administrative, and student dependent.

The chapter will explore current structures and pedagogic practices and the impact of Soviet legacies, the role of liberal arts education in Russian secondary schools and higher education, with a special focus on Smolny Institute/College, Russia's first liberal arts institution, and then reflect upon the future prospects of liberal arts education in Russia.

Russian Higher Education: Legacies and Structural and Pedagogic Challenges

Russia poses a challenging environment for liberal arts education due to the dual legacies of Tsarist Russia and the Soviet Union, which have created structural challenges and pedagogic approaches that inhibit and, in some cases, run contrary to approaches found in liberal arts systems. Today, as in Soviet and Tsarist times, the state remains the driving force behind higher education in Russia. Even with the greater autonomy of the post-Soviet period, universities remain wedded to the state, which remains "the ultimate funder, supporter, client, and source of legitimacy" (Kortunov, 2009, p. 4).

Both the number of students attending higher education institutions and the total number of higher education institutions have grown dramatically in the post-Soviet period, with many adults pursuing requalification, particularly in the areas of business and management. In 1995, Russia's 762 higher education institutions had 2.8 million students; the number of institutions reached a high point of 1,423 by the end of 2008 and, by June 2009, had dropped to 1,325, teaching 7.5 million students (Ot redaktsii, 2010). While private institutions have seen substantial growth, they account for a relatively small fraction of total students taught in higher education. In 2008, private institutions accounted for nearly half (685 of 1,423) of all higher education institutions, but they taught only about 17% of students (Vainio, 2009).

A significant number of institutional reductions occurred in private higher education due to economic pressures. Private institutions tend to focus on fields that do not require substantial investment in infrastructure and equipment, addressing fields like business, law, economics, computer science, and modern languages. While a few, such as the European University of St. Petersburg, have distinguished themselves, many serve as little more than diploma mills.

The economic structure makes huge demands on the professoriate. Most professors hold positions at multiple institutions and thus have incredibly high teaching loads and relatively little time for class preparation or research. Teaching methods, whether in private or state institutions, have, if anything, worsened under the pressure of current economic conditions. As Artemy Magun (2010), a Professor of Philosophy and Politics at St. Petersburg State University, has argued,

Although the structure of study programs has largely remained the same, the general social atmosphere, low salaries and even lower scholarship have created a new culture: students do not feel forced to attend class and instructors have no motivation to evaluate them rigorously.

Such continuity with old Soviet practices should not be surprising, since most university faculty and administrative staff who currently hold senior positions in the Russian education system received their own training and initial job experience in the former Soviet Union. Many of today's senior government officials and education leaders maintain the old Soviet-era conviction that the country's education system is the best in the world and therefore requires no borrowing from foreign practices and models or revision of standards and procedures. The discussion over whether Russia should join the Bologna Process revealed the presence of a strong "preservationist" lobby in Russian higher education, and observers predicted that the country's integration into the global educational space would be a long and precarious process (Lyubimov, March 2010).

However, the post-Soviet period has already left its own imprint on the Russian educational system. Over the last 20 years, Russia has witnessed a select number of bold and innovative experiments aimed at reinventing old public institutions and even launching new ones. A new cohort of ambitious and forward-thinking rectors has emerged. A large number of Russian universities—and not only an exclusive group of elitist higher education institutions from Moscow and Saint Petersburg—have been able to develop research partnerships, faculty exchanges, and even dual-degree programs with their peers in North America and Western Europe. Many Russians have studied abroad and are gradually bringing new methods of teaching to the Russian higher education system.

However, problems remain. For many institutions of higher education, the natural answer to the chaos of the 1990s has been to sacrifice the principle of university democracy and to return to very centralized and authoritarian management practices (Magun, 2010). If Russian leaders choose to use modifiers like "managed" and "sovereign" to describe the country's democracy, the same can be said of its institutions of higher education (Anderson, 2007).

Many higher education institutions rushed to exploit new market opportunities, inflating their stature and losing positions in areas of their natural comparative advantages. New institutions, sprouting like mushrooms, have tended to place a huge emphasis on business and management; and quality has not been a particular concern. Lev Lyubimov (March 2010), Deputy Academic Director of Moscow's Higher School of Economics, in decrying the "unprofessionalism" of teachers and graduates, looked at the massive growth of institutions producing economists and lawyers and asked ironically, "Where did all the professors come from?" Corruption in higher education had been present during Soviet times as well, but it became much more explicit in the 1990s, an unfortunate concomitant of the new Russian economy and the growing autonomy of higher education institutions (Danilova, 2007).

Russia's economic boom (2000–2008) and the large amounts of public funding flowing into the higher education system also had a controversial impact. Due to oil revenues and the overall economic recovery, the financial situation in higher education improved considerably; many higher education institutions were able to make significant investments in their physical infrastructure, including libraries, university labs, and dormitories. Faculty salaries increased markedly, allowing universities to recruit younger faculty and improve the quality of postgraduate students, although professors holding multiple jobs remains the norm.

At the same time, the increased inflow of public funds slowed down reforms in Russian higher education by reducing institutional incentives to change. A large number of university managers concluded that their main function was to lobby for additional governmental subsidies, not to raise the efficiency of their own institutions. Though the Ministry of Education and Science tried to link new funding with innovation and system changes, in most cases this link was superficial or purely formal; and to the extent that change occurred, it often has been focused on graduate education and on a relatively narrow range of fields. The attempt to consolidate the sector by reducing the number of higher education institutions has largely failed, facing too many legal, technical, and even political obstacles.

Likewise, attempts to integrate research and teaching by building stronger ties between universities and the Russian Academy of Sciences had only modest results. The Academy of Sciences receives most of the research dollars, while higher education institutions tend to be "assigned mainly the role of training future professionals." In spite of the growth of higher education institutions as important centers of research, they receive "only around 6% of the total volume of internal expenditure on research and development" (Vainio, 2009, p. 64).

Among key strategic decisions made by the state affecting higher education during the 21st century's first decade, three are likely to have the most significant impact on the system's future. First is the introduction of the "consolidated exams" designed to replace both the graduation exams for high schools and the entrance exams for universities. All students are required to take Russian language and mathematics, but they then can choose exam subjects from among chemistry, physics, literature, information and communication technology, geography, history, social studies, biology, and foreign languages (English, German, French, and Spanish) (Vainio, 2009, p. 73). A person who scores a certain number of points on the consolidated examination can enter a university without any additional tests. One goal of these examinations is to promote educational mobility—to give high-achieving students from low-income families or remote areas the opportunity to enroll in the best national universities.

The second critical goal is to fight corruption in the university system at its most dangerous point: university admissions. The consolidated exam was first introduced in select regions of the Russian Federation in 2001 and was applied to the entire country in 2009. It is not yet clear whether this new mechanism will help to achieve the stated goals, but such an innovation significantly changes how universities recruit their students.

The third controversial decision is the shift from the old Soviet-type "specialist" degree system, which was normally granted after five or six years of study, to the new, two-level degree system (bachelor's and master's). The shift became inevitable once Russia joined the Bologna Process in 2003, but it was only in academic year 2009–2010 that most Russian universities were forced to adopt the new system as their standard practice for incoming students. The shift should have a profound impact on the whole system of higher education in the country, and, as discussed in greater detail below, could have a significant impact on the potential for liberal arts education in Russia.

These changes will not, however, address some of the most important challenges facing Russian higher education: demographics. If Russian higher education institutions experienced huge growth in the 1990s and can now relatively easily absorb the million annual graduates from Russian secondary schools, they will face a huge competitive challenge in the next few years when the demographic crisis, which originated in the hard times of the 1990s, reduces the number of graduates to close to 600,000. Compounding difficulties is the fact that Russian universities are no longer internationally competitive, drawing only 1.5% of their students from abroad compared with up to 12% in Soviet times (Malykhin, 2009). Therefore, the competition for students is becoming more and more intense. Moreover, it is hard to imagine that public spending on higher education will increase significantly in the near future. Other social needs—such as public health and social services—are likely to gain political priority over education.

Given the breadth of needs of so many higher education institutions and the various economic challenges facing the country, government leaders face some difficult choices. The current policy seems to be that of selectively choosing winners that will, it is hoped, serve as "agents of change" in the education system at large and address the educational priorities of innovation and modernization, the two current mantras in higher education.

In 2009–2010, the Ministry of Education and Science launched three new federal programs in higher education that give a clear indication of the government's overall approach. First, the ministry selected a cohort of 14 national research universities in 2009, adding another 15 in 2010. These schools received not only substantial additional funding (which nearly doubled some budgets), but also a degree of autonomy that goes far beyond that granted to "regular" higher education institutions. The assumption is that these national research universities will both become test grounds for developing new, innovative methods of research and teaching and, perhaps more importantly, act as interfaces between education and private businesses. The overwhelming majority of these newly established national research universities were selected from specialized technical schools rather than from so-called classical universities that have a significant emphasis on social science and humanities. As Igor Remorenko (2008), Director of the Department of State Politics in Education at the Russian Ministry of Education and Science, said, "National research universities should be oriented towards the needs of breakthrough technology development."

The second large-scale initiative was launching the "federal universities" network to complement the national research universities. The first two federal universities (the Southern Federal University and the Siberian Federal University) were institutionalized in about 2007, but the Ministry of Education and Science selected another five sites in 2009, thus creating a nation-wide network. In general, these new institutions were created by consolidating major higher education schools in a given city (or even a region), forming a university that is more robust than their individual component schools. Like national research universities, they are supposed to become centers of excellence in research and teaching. However, federal universities have the broader mission to interact with regional systems of general education, assist service institutes, promote civil society, and serve as hubs for regional cultural and intellectual life. It remains unclear how these institutions will cope with these multiple tasks, but the Russian government is committed to expanding this network further (Medvedev, 2009; Ministry of Education and Science, 2010).

Finally, the Ministry of Education and Science has made special provisions for St. Petersburg State University and Moscow State University, Russia's oldest and leading universities, granting them not only substantial funding but also significant control over their own curricula and policies. As the Minister of Education and Science, Andrei Fursenko (2009), put it, "The foundation of the system—the two overall declared leaders—are St. Petersburg and Moscow Universities."

There are implications to the choice to create a clear hierarchy of institutions. If the future of these three cohorts of higher education institutions can be considered secure for at least the near- to mid-term, the basic question remains: what is going to happen to the rest of the Russian higher education system? After all, the status of national research universities and federal universities will extend to no more than 50 schools altogether. More than 1,000 existing higher education institutions are likely to be left out in the cold with no chances of receiving preferred treatment from the federal authorities and are thus left severely disadvantaged.

Liberal Education in Secondary Education

The post-Soviet era has seen a great struggle in secondary education. Despite some interesting experiments, particularly in big cities, the economic hardships in the late 1980s and 1990s and a concomitant lack of state funding have created tremendous difficulties, particularly in Russia's regions. As a report by the Higher School of Economics (2010) puts it,

> For more than ten years the needs of the secondary school and tertiary education institutions have been underfinanced by more than two-thirds, with the expected result of uncompetitive salaries for the teachers, depreciation of the equipment, and obsolete character of the teaching materials.

Russian secondary educators face a broad range of problems. Educational expert Elena Kazakova (2010), a professor at St. Petersburg State University and a former private school principal, points to an acute shortage of qualified teachers, a generally low level in teacher professional development programs, and management difficulties resulting from the growing bureaucratic limitations. As a result, school development models are forced upon schools from the top. Kazakova echoes a 2008 report prepared by the Commission on Issues of National Intellectal Potential of the Public Chamber of the Russian Federation, whose main recommendations were to broaden the involvement of civil society in developing the educational system and to substantially increase teachers' salaries (Public Chamber of the Russian Federation, 2008). Unfortunately, despite general acknowledgment of the need for changes, the government has created new standards on the primary and university levels only and has thus far failed to address secondary education (grades 10 and 11) or to significantly raise teachers' salaries.

At the same time, the post-Soviet era has seen the emergence of a number of opportunities in the sphere of secondary education. In contrast to the Soviet period, secondary schools in the 1990s were given much more freedom to define curricula and overall educational approaches. These opportunities led to diverse experiments based on new conceptions of education. Anna Zinder (2010), a teacher at Anichkov Lyceum, an elite St. Petersburg high school established in the early 1990s, stated:

> In Soviet times there existed a planned economy, which had as its parallel in the school the standard curriculum; all schools had the same programs and textbooks. After the collapse of the USSR the opportunity arose for the teachers to correct or to change these standard programs, and there were many new schools, created from below, not from the top, by the teachers themselves who were really interested in teaching children in a better way.

Some experimental schools established specific practices rooted in principles of liberal arts education, including offering more advanced multidisciplinary curricula, introducing at least a limited number of electives, and relying much more substantially on syllabi developed by the school's teachers rather than on standard textbooks. Such personalized curricular and pedagogical approaches presuppose much more interactive and conscientious teaching. Unfortunately, these experiments took place mainly in major cities like Moscow and St. Petersburg or in large regional centers. They rarely extended to small towns or rural areas.

As far as school curricula and student choice are concerned, Soviet-era secondary choice was limited. Besides regular high schools, students could choose from a select number of pre-vocational schools, so-called math schools with advanced programs in math and science, and specialized language schools which offered advanced programs in one or two languages. This idea of relatively early professionalization was questioned in the early 1990s, resulting in a significant decline of pre-vocational education and the emergence of some experimental schools with multidisciplinary curricula. However, in the last decade, the former tradition has reemerged in the new classification of high schools into four major types: (a) comprehensive schools; (b) specialized schools with advanced programs in specific subjects, such as languages, or in narrow fields like physics and chemistry or philology; (c) lyceums, or specialized schools with advanced programs in math and natural sciences; and (d) gymnasiums, or specialized schools offering advanced programs in languages, social sciences, and the humanities. In 2008–2009 there were 28,555 comprehensive schools, 4,223 specialized schools, 1,407 gymnasiums, 1,021 lyceums, and 117 military schools.

The comprehensive schools have a more diverse curriculum but are not particularly distinguished in their teaching and in the general quality of their education. The reforms have stultified some of the experiments associated with multidisciplinarity that were taking place in the lyceums and gymnasiums. For example, some gymnasiums offering programs in the humanities and sciences were forced to deemphasize math and science and focus exclusively on the humanities or be forced to convert to comprehensive school status which would have resulted in receiving far fewer resources. The changes have represented a shift back toward hyper-specialization that threatens multidisciplinary liberal arts curricula, which strike a balance between different disciplinary spheres.

Student electives receive little emphasis in secondary schools. Currently, electives comprise about 25% of the curriculum of comprehensive schools, a reduction from 50% in the 1990s. However, financing arrangements substantially limit the scope of choice, and many schools use this option to introduce additional advanced courses that are simply extensions of the required standard school subjects instead of new areas of inquiry. As far as the gymnasiums and lyceums are concerned, reform attempts that introduced a significant number of electives in the 1990s failed. Institutions that tried, for example, to expand student choice abandoned their plans, citing the challenges that choosing courses presented for students, the structural difficulties associated with Russia's two-year (grades 10 and 11) approach to high school, financial limitations, and the need to prepare students for new countrywide university entrance exams. As Sergey Buryachko (2010), Principal of St. Petersburg Classical Gymnasium, put it, "The experiment failed at our school and countrywide." The result is that student choice and liberal arts educational models in secondary schools have diminished, rather than expanded, since the 1990s.

In spite of the post-Soviet challenges, the Russian system of secondary education still produces some reasonable results. According to the Public Chamber (2008) report, the country is still "the world leader in educational participation at different levels of education." Fifty-five percent of Russians have a vocational or higher education degree—twice as high as the OECD average: the figures are higher for the current generation of university age youth, exceeding 60% (Public Chamber of the Russian Federation, 2008, p. 15). Unfortunately, these statistics, though commendable, do not translate to education quality.

Liberal Education in Higher Education

Russian higher education is not designed to be friendly to the liberal arts. This characteristic is paradoxical, given the difficulties experienced in secondary education, where a once-proud system is faltering under the weight of economic difficulties. Students entering higher education are, in general, less well prepared than in Soviet times and often have a narrower scope of knowledge. A number of factors limit the capacity of liberal arts education to gain strength within the Russian system of higher education.

Stated Goals

The Russian government, which remains the most important driver of change in the higher educational sphere (Howlett, 2009), espouses goals that seem to support liberal arts education models but that, more often than not, fail to do so. On the one hand, higher education is seen as a critical component of the government's most sought-after goals of promoting "innovation" and "modernization," watchwords found in any major Russian discussion of higher education reform. For example, Andrei Fursenko (2009), the Minister of Education and Science, asserted that an innovative economy presupposes "the ability to quickly and flexibly react to changing conditions" and that "learning throughout the course of life is becoming not a desirable, but rather a necessary condition." Igor Remorenko (2008), Director of the Department of State Politics in Education, Ministry of Education and Science, could have been a proselytizer for liberal arts education when he stated: "Education needs to formulate in citizens … creative talents, the ability to solve problems, skills of participating in complexly organized project-oriented work, [and] the ability to orient oneself in the conditions of quickly changing technology." But, in reality, there are conceptual, structural, attitudinal, and behavioral challenges that have and will likely continue to limit the scope of liberal arts education in Russia.

Challenges to the Liberal Arts

Conceptually, the notion of liberal learning suffers from two critical deficits in Russia. First, concepts underlying liberal arts education—including breadth of study, students' choice of major during their academic career, and interdisciplinarity—face a challenge from a narrow interpretation of the role of higher education in modernization and innovation. Too often when Russian leaders speak of the need to innovate and modernize, they are referring to higher education in a very narrow sense—focusing on education's potential to develop specific breakthroughs in science and technology that can be harnessed in the business sphere. In some ways, this emphasis harkens back to the Soviet period when the regime devoted tremendous resources to the expansion of higher education but, for political and ideological reasons, preferred to support technical schools instead of classical universities (Kortunov, 2009, p. 1).

Education reform often appears to be a mechanistic, top-down affair. For example, Minister Fursenko (2009) has declared that "many young people, at twelve, fifteen and even twenty years of age can't choose for themselves a sphere for self-realization" and thus need the "correct signal" from society. Touching on the common interpretation of modernization, he continued,

> I think that, in the near future, young people will express a considerably larger interest in exact sciences and technical specialties, that is, in those programs which are a priority for the Russian economy, and that thus possess strong prospects.

As a consequence, it appears that the educational reform efforts that are emerging from an emphasis on innovation and modernization are likely to result in a narrowing rather than a broadening of curricula and a greater emphasis on science and technology at the expense of the humanities and social sciences. Thus, in the first competition to identify so-called national research universities, which would then receive extra government funding, 11 of the 12 institutions chosen specialized in the natural sciences and only one focused on social sciences (Balzer, 2010, p. 5). Remorenko (2008) made it clear that the 29 new national research universities "should be oriented toward the needs of breakthrough technology development."

If there are major areas outside science and technology in which the government is placing its resources, it is in the spheres of business and management. Huge financial support has been given to the Skolkovo Innovation Center outside Moscow, which will include a to-be-determined number of higher educational institutions but with a focus primarily, if not exclusively, on science, technology, and business.

A second conceptual challenge to the expansion of liberal arts education is that "liberal" is itself problematic because of the connotations associated with political parties that take anti-authoritarian and free market approaches. Even if one strips away the more narrow political meaning, the broader notion of liberalism finds less traction in a country where the leadership espouses "managed" democracy and where broad enthusiasm for citizen engagement in political processes is limited (Anderson, 2007).

The structural challenges to liberal arts education in Russia emerge in part from the close connections between the system of higher education and the state (Howlett, 2009). At the same time, the state, from Tsarist times to the present, has traditionally been suspicious of universities and their potential as sources of dissent (Kortunov, 2009, p. 11). Internal university structures are influenced by their close links with the state: "Since universities were founded and financed by the state," comments Kortunov (2009), "they inherited a lot of particular features of 'standard' state bureaucracies: hierarchy, lack of transparency, high degree of corruption, red tape, and so on" (p. 11).

As throughout much of Europe, Russian universities have been divided into Faculties (*fakultety*), which, while not independent from the central university administration, operate with a tremendous degree of autonomy and are largely independent from one another. (We capitalize "Faculty" in reference to administrative units and lower-case it in reference to teaching staff.) Each Faculty has traditionally been headed by a powerful dean who oversees finances, the curriculum, and academic appointments. An interesting development is that, in 2009 and 2010, the Rector of St. Petersburg State University, Nikolai Kropachev, instituted a series of reforms that will fundamentally weaken the role of long-standing deans, many of whom have moved into the rectorate. The result is a strengthening of the central university administration, which stands above the Faculties and which gives greater emphasis to the academic programs that fall beneath them.

The academic and institutional narrowness of the Faculties also inhibits the breadth of liberal arts education. Faculties are subject-specific, similar to those in higher education institutions in continental Europe. They are more analogous, at least in subject matter, to academic departments in the United States. They tend to jealously guard their subjects, creating barriers to interdisciplinarity and often manifesting a hostile predisposition toward disciplinary experimentation encouraged by the liberal arts. Moreover, it is extremely difficult for students to take courses in more than one Faculty.

An additional structural challenge to liberal arts education that is rooted in its Humboldt and Soviet origins is preference for five-year "specialist" degrees. As of 2007, more than 85% of bachelor graduates continued to pursue a specialist degree (Vainio, 2009, p. 68), with 10% pursuing six-year master's degrees and only 2–5% entering the labor market. While the Ministry of Education and Science has pushed for a four-year/two-year format of baccalaureate/master's degrees and has made this change systemwide for those matriculating in academic year 2010–2011, it has been discussed since the early 2000s. Yet universities have been slow to adopt this proposal. It is therefore not yet clear whether a distinct B.A./M.A. structure will emerge or if a new six-year B.A./M.A. model will replace the old five-year standard. Governmental financing schemes are likely to be determinative in this area.

The structural challenges to liberal arts education in Russia are compounded by attitudinal challenges. Both the higher educational establishment and the labor market (and thus students' parents) look down on the four-year baccalaureate, viewing it as an "incomplete higher education" (Kortunov, 2009, p. 11). The liberal arts B.A. faces the dual challenge of being both a baccalaureate *and* being less focused on a disciplinary subject as students in traditional Faculties. Students who choose this path can then face the challenge of achieving acceptance into M.A. programs where the breadth of students' liberal arts education might not be seen as compensating for the lack of depth provided by the traditional approaches maintained by most university Faculties. Can a student whose baccalaureate program of study consists of a diverse liberal arts curriculum as well as a concentration (or major) in sociology compete for a graduate school place with someone who has taken an academic program with a narrow focus on sociology in the Faculty of Sociology? While U.S. experience has suggested that even liberal arts graduates who major in the natural sciences and engineering are competitive—and may even enjoy an advantage (Cech, 1999, p. 213) on the graduate level—it may take some time for Russia to accept the dual challenge of a baccalaureate, which is poorly understood, and a liberal arts degree, which by definition has a wider focus than most academic programs. In the meantime, unlike in Soviet times, students and their families now often have to pay for their education; understandably, they may well balk at such an uncertain future.

Finally, the spread of liberal arts education faces a behavioral challenge in that universities have been hotbeds of corruption. It is difficult to espouse values of citizenship and engagement effectively given the miasma of corruption that can infect almost every part of the academic process from admissions (the most profitable area for pay-offs) to side payments for higher grades. As Harley Balzer (2010) has stated, "Corruption is among the most damaging institutional weaknesses in Russian education" (p. 15). Indeed, a four-year study conducted by the Russian NGO Information Science for Democracy between 2001 and 2005 asserted that higher education institutions accounted for $580 million of a total of $3 billion in black market bribery in the country (World University News, 2008). Balzer (2010) points out that, while the data were "contested vehemently when first published," they are now "confirmed by Russian officials" (p. 15). While many steps have been taken to limit the impact of corruption, including standardized tests, it would be naive to believe that universities are now free of corruption. Moreover, corruption extends to the classroom, where students often do not consider cheating as anything more than collective work and helping friends. The notion of individual Russian students doing their own work is just not the same as in countries with a longer liberal arts tradition.

Liberal Arts Education in Russia Today

The core elements that constitute liberal arts education are largely missing from, or have a minimal presence in, higher education in Russia. If we look at the critical areas—innovative curricula that require students to take courses across a range of specialties; students' choice of a major after entering the university; interactive, student-centered teaching; and an emphasis on broad student development to create active citizens—the impediments above, along with the Soviet legacy, have largely crippled efforts at educational transformation. However, these challenges have not stopped the incursion of liberal arts models into Russia, and some structures can serve as the basis for expanding liberal arts education in the future.

Curricula

If the goal of liberal arts education is to expose students to a broad canon of thought in the arts, humanities, social sciences, natural sciences, and mathematics before or at the same time that they are moving into specialization in a single field of study, this model has clearly not gained significant traction in Russia. As stated above, the structure of universities has led to the stove-piping of disciplines. Students are admitted into not only all-powerful Faculties but into tightly circumscribed programs within the Faculties that are overseen by *kafedres* (chairs). These programs are based on standards that typically place a strong emphasis on disciplinary rigor but little focus on interdisciplinarity. Inter-Faculty programs are extremely rare, as are interdisciplinary programs. Reform efforts to create more flexibility within academic programs and to reduce the number of state-defined standards from its current number of 500+ have run into tremendous obstacles from universities that are set in their ways (Lyubimov, June 2010).

Russian programs do maintain some tinge of liberal arts education in the form of breadth. Students are often required to take courses in neighboring disciplines, and their academic programs also contain requirements that students take courses outside their primary discipline. Most academic programs maintain some remnant of the Soviet system in which students were required to take Soviet history, Marxist philosophy, and a foreign language, as well as physical culture. Some universities have also added more far-ranging requirements. For example, students studying history at St. Petersburg State University also take courses in economics, mathematics and informatics, and conceptions of contemporary natural science. Similarly, students studying biology must take courses in history, sociology, economics, and philosophy. However, because students usually take more than 10 classes each semester and the non-specialty classes are spread over the semesters, they represent a small fraction of the curriculum and occur after a student has chosen his or her major. As a result, students take the vast majority of courses in their specific area of specialization and "general education" has a minimal imprint on the system.

As far as student choice is concerned, Russian curricula often contain a limited number of "elective" classes. However, there are often only a few electives from which to choose, and the courses are usually selected from within the chairs, which has intellectual and financial interests in limiting the list to the student's chosen field. Paradoxically, the post-Soviet period, in which Faculties have had greater autonomy, has seen the development of an even more intense fortress mentality; the small glimmers of the general education baby are being tossed out with the Marxist-Leninist bathwater. Some have noted a paradox: now that universities and departments are more flexible and freer, they want to reduce, not expand, general education requirements.

On the positive side, the study of the social studies and humanities, which are essential to the liberal arts, remains vigorous in Russia today. Ministry of Education and Science statistics about full-time matriculants in state institutions report that more than 116,000 of the 667,000 are enrolled in the humanities (broadly interpreted to include not just philosophy, history, philology, and religion, but also social sciences such as political studies, international affairs, and psychology), with another 9,000 in the social sciences (primarily sociology) and nearly 17,000 in culture and art, compared with 166,000 in economics and management, and 14,000 in natural sciences (Moscow State University of Instrument Engineering and Computer Sciences, 2008, p. 436; Russian Ministry of Education and Science, 2009).

In the Soviet period, many of the subjects that constitute important elements of a modern liberal arts education, like politics, sociology, and anthropology, barely existed. This condition prevailed in part due to the ideological orthodoxy of Marxist-Leninism, which guided all facets of Soviet public life. On the other hand, while the social sciences have found their way into universities in a robust way, the past certainly has hindered their development. In the Soviet period, many classics of Western thought were prohibited, and the fields were overwhelmed by Marxist-Leninist orthodoxy. Often these subjects continue to be taught by the same faculty as in Soviet times, and teaching pedagogy remains largely unaffected by trends in the rest of the world (Lyubimov, March 2010; Magun, 2010).

During the Soviet period, the arts, both performing and visual, were absent from university structures, being situated almost exclusively within conservatories and specialty schools. They are now beginning to appear in the universities. Indeed, in early 2010 the legendary conductor Valery Gergiev was named dean of the Faculty of Arts at St. Petersburg State University. However, the arts still remain largely absent or isolated on the periphery of most Russian higher education institutions. Conversely, the natural sciences, which constitute an important part of a modern liberal arts education, remain vibrant but are strictly segregated from other parts of the curriculum. The Russian interpretation of modernization and innovation does not lend itself to interdisciplinary approaches that combine the study of the natural sciences, humanities, and social sciences, let alone the arts.

Teaching/Pedagogy

As far as student-centered pedagogical approaches associated with liberal arts education are concerned, changes in the post-Soviet system tend to be more episodic than systematic. They are also very closely associated with individuals who might have been exposed to alternative teaching methods in Europe or North America, rather than as a part of an overall strategy. In spite of economic difficulties, state universities have taken energetic measures to maintain their faculty in spite of economic tribulations. It may be true, as Artemy Magun (2010) has argued, that orthodox Marxist-Leninists "in several cases became orthodox liberals and then orthodox nationalists," but their teaching style certainly remained the same.

Overwhelmingly, the teaching approach of the Soviet and post-Soviet eras is marked by an emphasis on rote learning. Students are in class an enormous number of hours, often taking eight, nine, or 10 courses per semester. Moreover, the traditional syllabus contains a list of readings for a semester but does not provide assigned readings for specific classes, making discussion difficult and placing the teacher in a position of unassailed authority. Resources are lacking. Readings are not readily available, nor are advanced electronic reserve systems operational. Thus, out-of-class work is usually not emphasized. Lectures, which are plentiful, are purely that: professors, often using notes written decades before, literally "read their lecture." The evaluation of students tends to be based on one or two oral exams, rather than through continuous assessment; and memorization and rote learning are generally rewarded.

Faculty spend so much time in the classroom (often working two or three jobs to make ends meet) that they simply do not have time to provide either the quality feedback on written work that is necessary for quality liberal learning or to maintain the type of research agendas that will form synergies with their teaching and allow them to remain current in their disciplines or develop their teaching (Lyubimov, April 2010). Indeed, the Rector of Russia's Higher School of Economics, Yaroslav Kuzminov, has called the dearth of university-level researchers "simply terrifying" and estimates that only 16% of Russia's 625,000 university teachers are engaged in research (quoted in Holdsworth, 2009). As a consequence of such practices, class attendance is largely considered optional, with students relying on outdated textbooks and notes passed down from others to succeed on their oral exams. As Andrei Kortunov (2009) summed up the situation: "The archaic (Soviet) teaching methods, where a student has to memorize large amounts of data and where an oral exam stands for a midterm or final paper, have not changed in any radical way over the last twenty years" (p. 7).

Smolny College

In spite of the many impediments and challenges, the spirit of experimentation that existed in the wake of the collapse of Communism extended to the areas of liberal arts education. The clearest manifestation of liberal arts education is Smolny College (in Russian, Smolny Institute), which is a dual-degree program offered jointly by St. Petersburg State University and Bard College in Annandale-on-Hudson, New York. St. Petersburg State University is Russia's oldest university and is the former employer of Russia's two most recent presidents, Vladimir Putin and Dimitri Medvedev. Bard College, which has just celebrated its 150th year, is an American liberal arts college with a reputation for innovation.

Smolny emerged from discussions between a Russian academic administrator and a Bard College history professor who had led trips of Bard students to Russia. A group of Russian academics who ran a seminar series on the critique of the social sciences became interested in the project. To give an idea of the role of liberal arts education in Russia, Susan Gillespie (2009), Bard's Vice President for Special Global Initiatives, said: "When they first met with visiting Bard faculty members to discuss the idea of a liberal arts program, the Russian language did not have a word for liberal education." She observes that Russian faculty were interested in reforming their disciplines, imagining interdisciplinary programs, and "creating academic programs characterized by greater democracy for both teachers and students" (p. 510). They often harkened back to Russian educational structures of the late 19th and early 20th centuries in schools and universities that demonstrated a spirit of academic exploration, particularly in the humanities, including the eponymous Smolny Institute, a young women's school founded by Catherine the Great.

The modern Smolny Institute accepted its first matriculated students in the fall of 1999, becoming a semi-autonomous institute within St. Petersburg State

University's Philology Faculty. At that point, the program was not formally accredited by the Russian Ministry of Education and Science, although Bard was prepared to provide U.S. accreditation for its part of what all hoped would be a dual-degree program in which students would receive degrees simultaneously from Bard and St. Petersburg State. Russian recognition came in April 1999 when the Russian Ministry of Education and Science granted experimental degree-granting status under the title "Arts and Humanitarian Sciences." Five years later, the "experimental" modifier disappeared, and Smolny's curriculum became a state standard that could be adopted by other Russian institutions.

According to Tatyana Eduardovna Petrova (2009), a former Ministry of Education and Science official, Smolny benefited greatly from an emphasis on the arts and desired to bring the arts from the academy into the university. It is no coincidence that the term "Arts and Humanitarian Sciences" is used for the authorized degree rather than "liberal arts," which, as stated above, is suffused with negative political connotations. However, interest in Smolny did not simply derive from its inclusion of the arts. The Russian Ministry of Education and Science was also interested in the development of progressive teaching methods, interdisciplinarity, and student choice (Petrova, 2009). Other advocates of Smolny, such as Russian Finance and Deputy Prime Minister Alexei Kudrin, who served for several years on Smolny's Board of Overseers, have cited the value of a broad, interdisciplinary education in a changing social and educational environment (Barry, 2011; Tsigankova, 2010).

Smolny has adopted a four-year program that meets the standards of the Russian Ministry of Education and Science and Bard College. It features the core elements of the liberal arts curriculum: student choice in courses and major; distribution requirements that ensure breadth by requiring that students take courses across the curriculum from the visual and performing arts to the social sciences and to the natural sciences; and academic concentrations—in the arts, social sciences, natural sciences, and the humanities—that allow for depth. It has small classes to facilitate discussion, syllabus requirements that mandate assigned class readings for each class session, continuous assessment, and special programs, including "writing and thinking" and a great-books-style first-year seminar, both of which emphasize writing and the careful reading of significant texts. Smolny has academic programs in the fine arts and architecture, film and video, music and theater, literature, philosophy, history of civilizations, sociology and anthropology, political science, international affairs and human rights, economics, the history and culture of Islam, cognitive systems, and complex systems in nature and society. Smolny also encourages faculty research and recognizes the link between research and teaching. It is developing the concept of intellectual life outside the classroom, with public talks and student clubs and activities. Smolny now graduates approximately 100 undergraduates each year, with all students receiving both U.S. and Russian degrees.

One does not want to idealize the situation at Smolny. It faces many challenges. Structurally, the very title of its degree, Arts and Humanitarian Sciences, implies limits in terms of curricular breadth, particularly in the natural sciences. While Smolny has managed to develop offerings in that area, the process of developing a full curriculum or providing the necessary facilities has been fraught with difficulties.

More poignant challenges have come from the faculty and students. While Smolny has had the luxury of attracting faculty members from across St. Petersburg and from many faculties of St. Petersburg State University, the reception of interactive teaching methods, student-centered learning, and continuous assessment has been uneven. Many faculty, who taught for decades using lectures as the standard form of instruction, have found adjusting to interactive methods challenging. Smolny limits the value of oral exams, a practice in Russia that contributes to rote learning and corruption; but faculty, who are often holding two or three jobs, do not always provide the feedback on written and other work that the liberal arts system demands. Having readings readily accessible—a necessary factor for class discussion—has received varied administrative support, although greater emphasis on electronic access to readings and the general growth in computer and Internet access have helped ameliorate some of the problems. However challenging some of the external environmental issues at Smolny have been, its ability to command resources has greatly benefited both its position in such a prominent university and its access to philanthropic support via its special relationship with Bard College.

Another major challenge for Smolny has come from students. On the one hand, many students interpreted Smolny's "liberal" approach to mean "anything goes" and have resisted distribution requirements and program specifications. On the other hand, many have brought with them expectations shaped in other faculties and thus are lax about attendance and preparation for class participation. Many would rather serve as passive recipients of knowledge. They have also illustrated a problem that bedevils Russian higher education: a proclivity toward plagiarism and other forms of academic dishonesty, at least by the standards of classical liberal arts institutions. Smolny also faces the challenges of attracting students, due both to Russia's declining demographic numbers and the concomitant emphasis of students and parents on market-oriented and professional education. Many parents and potential students think in terms of professions, and it can be difficult to convince them that liberal arts education is important for their future.

In spite of its challenges, Smolny remains the only institution in Russia that aspires to the full curriculum, pedagogy, and student expectations characteristic of the liberal arts system. Its status grew even more in the spring of 2011 when it made the transition from one of several hundred academic programs into the university's 22nd faculty, with the title Faculty of Free Arts and Sciences, a name that neatly dodges the stigma of the term "liberal." Equally important, the new dean, whose title is partly honorific, but whose appointment has immense symbolic substance, is Finance Minister and Deputy Premier Alexei Kudrin, who is committed to expanding the liberal arts in Russia (Barry, 2011). Given who is involved and where this experiment is taking place, these changes might lead liberal arts reform in Russia to become more systematic instead of episodic.

Other Experiments in Liberal Arts Education

Russia has had a number of other educational experiments that can fall under the rubric of liberal arts education. While most of them have adopted pedagogic or curricular elements associated with liberal arts education, few have employed the full package that constitutes liberal arts as a system of education.

Several Russian institutions operate under the same state standard, or curricular profile, as Smolny's "Arts and Humanities," including the Academy of Russian Ballet, A. Y. Vangovoi (St. Petersburg); Belogrodskii State Institute of Culture and Arts; Voronezh State University; Ekatrinaburg Academy of Contemporary Art; the Institute of Free Arts and Sciences (Moscow); Karsnodarsk State University of Culture and Art; Kuban State University (Krasnodar); the International University of Nature, Society, and Man "Dubna" (Moscow); Moscow Islamic University; Russian State University Immanuel Kant (Kaliningrad); Russian Friendship University (Moscow); Tul'skii State Pedagogical University L. N. Tokstoi; and South Federal University (Rostov-on-Don).

These institutions are similar to Smolny in breadth of curriculum, flexibility (including interdisciplinarity) and freedom of choice. However, there are limits to their aspirations, curricular breadth, and pedagogical innovations. For example, Belogrodskii State Institute of Culture and Arts requires students to study in disciplines as diverse as history, politics, economics, philosophy, and math, but lacks the performing arts and natural sciences as academic concentrations. As far as teaching is concerned, few have had the resources to attract faculty who can devote the time and energy to develop student-centered teaching methods. Liberal arts education poses a complex funding challenge, because student-centered learning means investing significant resources in faculty and staff at a time of stringent university budgets and providing funds for activities that are not easily classified within the Russian educational system. The lack of an external partner has meant fewer resources. Again, Smolny is an exception, receiving significant funding, particularly in its early days, from joint applications with Bard.

Perhaps most importantly, in translating expectations of liberal arts as a system of education, these institutions have lacked an external body demanding that educational approaches meet academic standards. Smolny has had to meet standards required by Bard's faculty and accreditors, the Regents of the State of New York and the Middle States Commission on Higher Education, as well as those of the Russian Ministry of Education and Science. It is true that Smolny is operated differently from Bard College, as it is a joint project between St. Petersburg State and Bard. It takes into account Russian traditions and realities. However, the fact that there is an external source requiring educational standards for an approach that is alien to recent Russian tradition is important in terms of determining outcomes.

Still, a number of institutions demonstrate significant proclivities toward liberal arts education and have motivated faculty members. The Higher School of Economics, which has a base in Moscow and branches in St. Petersburg, Perm, and Nizhni-Novgorod, has distinguished itself by emphasizing educational reform and attracting an international and internationally trained faculty who are accustomed to more student-centered teaching. Other progressive institutions include the Russian State Humanities University in Moscow, the New School of Economics in Moscow, Kaliningrad State University, and the European University of St. Petersburg (graduate studies only). In each instance, the institutions have attracted interesting and progressive faculty and have created programs that have elements of interdisciplinarity. However, the curricula remain too narrow for the full liberal arts package (they omit the natural sciences and the performing arts), make fewer demands in terms of distribution requirements, and do not fully integrate interactive teaching into institutional standards.

Future Prospects for Liberal Education

The evolution of the Russian higher education system over the next decades will continue to be a painful and contradictory process. The current political and economic situations impose serious constraints on what can be accomplished in the near future. Intense and often cloaked bureaucratic struggles, rampant corruption, nepotism, populist temptations of federal and regional leaders, immense institutional inertia, a profound deficit of skilled and experienced education managers—all these factors will continue to negatively affect the pace and the direction of modernization efforts so strongly espoused by the government. However, the current higher education system cannot be sustained. It no longer reflects basic social and economic needs of the country and, if it remains unchanged, will impede modernization efforts.

The Russian system of higher education, already experiencing difficulties in the post-Soviet transition, will face even greater challenges in the future. The demographic crisis is likely to exacerbate the already emerging financial challenges for higher education institutions, which are used to generous government support. Having fewer students will redound negatively on faculty. One estimate suggests that "from 2011 to 2015, 100,000 vocational school and university teachers—about 25% of their total—may be out of work because of reductions in the number of applicants" (Tovkailo, 2010).

The future for most Russian higher education institutions contains many uncertainties, challenges, and direct threats. Not everybody will make it through the next 10 years; the odds are that we will see considerably fewer Russian universities in 2020 than in 2010. Survival strategies will vary from region to region, from school to school. However, one thing appears evident— a successful survival and development strategy should be based on a much deeper integration in the regional and local social and economic life than is now the case.

A new situation is emerging in Russia. With the exception of the currently emerging private sector in higher education, all of them continue to look to the federal government as the key to their survival. Even while higher education institutions seek increased autonomy from the federal Ministry of Education and Science, they also struggle continuously for budgets, recognition, guidance, and protection from the ministry. At this stage, for the first time in the history of Russian higher education, a shift in the power balance is evident. The federal government wants to focus its resources on a limited number of "advanced" schools, while pushing the rest of the institutions toward more active collaboration with regional and municipal authorities (which have traditionally funded secondary schools but not higher education) and encouraging stronger relations with non-state actors, that can gradually evolve as major stakeholders in particular higher education institutions. Part of this new direction is that, at the end of the first decade of the new millennium, the Ministry of Education and Science is making significant efforts to push for new legislation that would encourage the private sector to endow universities, Faculties, and programs. Needless to say, there are still many legal and administrative obstacles impeding the regionalization of Russian higher education; for example, regional governments cannot directly subsidize higher education institutions that report to the federal ministry, but the overall trend is evident.

Can Russian universities survive in this environment? One might predict that "non-privileged" schools will ultimately split into two big groups. The first, larger group will try to survive by offering highly applicable baccalaureate courses that will fill the vacuum in vocational training left by the collapsed system of Soviet-style technical colleges. No doubt these universities will merge with the remnants of the vocational schools in particular fields. These schools are also likely to develop stronger ties to large- and mid-size businesses active in their respective regions, positioning themselves as natural hubs for outsourcing corporate training and retraining programs. However, they will be competing against national research universities for applied corporate research funding. Still, they may forge strategic alliances with national research universities by supplying graduate students and ambitious faculty.

The second group is more likely to capitalize on the comparative advantage of the liberal arts approach. It would be an overstatement to argue that we will see the emergence of numerous U.S.-type liberal arts colleges, but such liberal arts elements as diverse curricula, emphasis on comprehensive education, interactive teaching methods, communication skills, and interdisciplinary approaches may become the major comparative advantage for many schools. If the first group of schools is likely to focus on engineering, natural sciences, agriculture, and the like, the second group will try to emphasize the humanities and social sciences and may even successfully combine them with the study of natural sciences. Depending on how the system of federal universities evolves, these schools can be partially integrated into the system, serving as junior partners for larger and more affluent federal universities. This group is also likely to provide the bulk of cadres to regional and local administrations, civil society institutions, and local media.

Finally, should secondary school reform emerge and Russian high schools move away from current teaching methods, graduates of the second group of schools might seek employment in secondary schools, including progressive gymnasiums and lyceums, where they will be in a position to compete successfully with graduates from more traditional pedagogical colleges.

The social dimension will be of particular importance to this second group. They can claim a unique place in the Russian education system only if they become deeply rooted in community life through programs of student internships with local institutions, faculty and student volunteerism, and joint ventures with NGOs and community schools. Community involvement should become part of the core curriculum, not an optional feature, which it appears to be in most Russian higher education institutions today.

There are other opportunities for the growth of liberal arts education in Russia. The substantial number of institutions that have adopted the new state standard in the Arts and Humanities degree developed by Smolny Institute of St. Petersburg State University and its American colleagues at Bard College suggests that at least the desire for a diverse curricula has resonance across many Russian institutions. In fact, the curriculum is even broader than the name implies, because this degree also includes natural sciences and mathematics. Smolny's presence at St. Petersburg State for the past 14 years and the ongoing discussion of expanding its liberal arts to Moscow State University is also extremely important, not simply because they are Russia's educational leaders, but also because they have the unique right to shape their own curricula and thus can further develop the Russian version of the liberal arts concept. The transformation of Smolny into a full-fledged Faculty at St. Petersburg State University, with a vice premier as its dean, could have an even greater long-term impact.

In the future, these efforts may well be aided by critical changes in the Russian environment. First, as the new B.A./M.A. supplants the five-year "specialist" degree, there may be greater opportunities for experimentation on the baccalaureate level and greater specialization at the master's level. Second is the hope that many faculty have been exposed to teaching methods typical of liberal arts education. As Smolny College's director, Valeri Monakhov said, the liberal arts "creates a space of creativity for our teachers ... to create something new," an engagement that leaves them "inspired" (quoted in Gillespie, 2009, p. 511). Finally, there is a hope among students. Students are now customers who invest heavily in their education; they naturally have become more demanding in terms of the quality of services they get for their money. In a number of cases, students have expressed discontent over their faculty's lack of professionalism, the university infrastructure, and the corruption in university management. Many have also seen that they can be exposed to curricula in which they play an active role in guiding their future and in which they are treated as participants in a process of education, instead of empty vessels to be filled with facts. As Russian education is increasingly influenced by market realities, students will play an increasing role in determining outcomes and the fate of liberal arts education in Russia.

References

Anderson, P. (2007, January 25). Russia's managed democracy. *London Review of Books*. Retrieved on January 30, 2011, from www.lrb.co.uk/v29/n02/perry-anderson/russias-managed-democracy.

Balzer, H. (2010, June). Learning to innovate? Education and knowledge-based economies in Russia and China. *Pro et Contra*, pp. 52–71.

Barry, E. (2011, June 27). Long-serving finance minister calls for reforms to bolster Russia's Powers. *New York Times*. Retrieved on July 31, 2011, from www.nytimes.com/2011/06/28/world/europe/28russiahtml?scp=2&kudrin&st=cse.

Becker, J. (2004). What a liberal arts education is and ... is not. Retrieved on June 20, 2010, from http://iile.bard.edu/research/.

Buryachko, S. (2010). Interview by Philip Fedchin. Audio recording.

Cech, T. R. (1999, Winter). Science at liberal arts colleges: A better education? *Daedalus*, *128*(1), 195–216.

Danilova, M. (2007, February 2). Russia to fight corruption in education. *Washington Post*. Retrieved on May 25, 2010, from www.washingtonpost.com/wp-dyn/content/article/2007/02/02/AR2007020200835.html.

Fursenko, A. (2009, October 23). Obrazovanie dolzhnoodti v nogu co vremenem. Retrieved on May 25, 2010, from http://mon.gov.ru/ruk/ministr/int/6436/.

Gillespie, S. (2009). Deep partnerships: Bard as a global citizen. In R. Lewin (Ed.), *Handbook of practice and research in study abroad: Higher education and the quest for global citizenship* (pp. 506–526). New York: Routledge.

Higher School of Economics. (2010). Russian education system. Retrieved on May 25, 2010, from http://hse.ru/lingua/en/rus-ed.html.

Holdsworth, N. (2009, January 11). Russia: Rector calls for sweeping reforms. *University World News*. Retrieved on May 25, 2010, from www.universityworldnews.com/article.php?story=20090108185640118.

Howlett, S. (2009). Europe and Russian higher education: The historical perspective. Unpublished paper, Budapest.

Kazakova, E. (2010, May). Interview by Philip Fedchin. Audio recording.

Kortunov, A. (2009). Russian higher education. *Social Research, 76*(1), 1–22.

Lyubimov, L. (2010, March 3). Obrazovanie: Strana neprofessionalov. *Vedomosti*. Retrieved on May 25, 2010, from www.vedomosti.ru/newspaper/article/2010/03/11/ 227747.

Lyubimov, L. (2010, April 9). Rossiiskie vuzy: Pravil'no poschitali. *Vedomosti*. Retrieved on May 25, 2010, from www.vedomosti.ru/newspaper/article/2010/04/09/ 230878.

Lyubimov, L. (2010, June 28). Dushevedenie: Kompromiss za chuzhoi schyot. *Vedomosti*. Retrieved on June 30, 2010, from www.vedomosti.ru/newspaper/article/2010/06/ 28/238735.

Magun, A. (2010, June). Higher education in post-Soviet Russia and the global crisis of the university. Retrieved on June 16, 2010, from http://isacna.wordpress.com/ 2010/06/04/higher-education-in-post-soviet-russia-and-the-global-crisis-of-the-university/.

Malykhin, M. (2009, July 28). Rossiiskie vuzy zhdut pritok inostrannykh studetov. *Vedomosti*. Retrieved on May 25, 2010, from www.vedomosti.ru/newsline/print/ 2009/07/28/809718.

Medvedev, D. (2009, 3 July). Retrieved on May 25, 2010, from http://news.kremlin.ru/ news/4701.

Ministry of Education and Science. (2010, April 2). Federalnye universitety. Retrieved on May 25, 2010, from http://mon.gov.ru/pro/pnpo/fed/.

Moscow State University of Instrument Engineering and Computer Sciences. (2008). Obrazovanie v Rossii–2008: Statisticheskii byulleten.

Ot redaktsii: Nadbavka za znaniya. (2010, May 20). *Vedomosti*. Retrieved on May 25, 2010, from www.vedomosti.ru/newspaper/article/2010/05/20/234905.

Petrova, T. E. (2009, October 21). Interview by Philip Fedchin. Audio recording.

Public Chamber of the Russian Federation. (2008). *Education and society: Is Russia willing to invest in its future?* Retrieved on May 25, 2010, from www.hse.ru/data/ 846/546/1228/report.pdf.

Remorenko, I. (2008, July 18). Model "Rossiiskoe obrazovanie–2020" sozdaetsya v interesakh potrebitelei obrazovatel'nykh uslug. Retrieved on May 25, 2010, from http://mon.gov.ru/ruk/dir/remorenko/int/4793/.

Russian Ministry of Education and Science. (2009, October 30). Retrieved on May 25, 2010, from www.edu.ru/db-mon/mo/Data/d_09/m337.html.

Tovkailo, M. (2010, June 11). Teachers out of work. *Moscow Times*. Retrieved on January 30, 2011, from www.themoscowtimes.com/vedomosti/article/teachers-out-of-work/408160.html.

Tsigankova, M. (2010, September 2). Ministr Finansov stanet dekanom. Retrieved on January 29, 2011, from www.fontanka.ru/2010/09/02/120/.

Vainio, S. (2009). *Quality handbook of higher education in Finland and Russia*. Turku, Finland: University of Turku. Retrieved on January 29, 2011, from www.utu.fi/en/ university/quality/russia/handbook.pdf.

World University News. (2008, March 16). Retrieved on January 30, 2011, from www. universityworldnews.com/article.php?story=20080314085103365.

Zinder, A. (2010, April). Interview by Philip Fedchin. Audio recording.

8

SOUTH AFRICA

Reimagining Liberal Learning in a Post-Apartheid Curriculum

Michael Cross and Fatima Adam

The challenge for educators of the greater focus on the person is to articulate and foreground

> the qualities that enable young people to act responsibly, autonomously and with respect for other persons in a world where new and unpredictable problems are arising, where the past is not in many cases an adequate precedent for future cases and where different perceptions of the problems and their solutions will need to be tolerated and respected.
>
> (Quicke, 1996, p. 370)

Introduction

Central to the project of liberal education in its Western sense are the concepts of individual freedom, independence, and autonomy through the enculturation of the mind. This process gives rise to the widening of opportunities for self-development, self-enrichment, and self-fulfillment in society. Content knowledge and specific pedagogical approaches—very often associated with learner-centeredness and critical thinking, particularly in the area of arts, the humanities, and the social sciences—have been privileged as instrumental for the achievement of such an ideal. However, while celebrated in the Western world, this concept's success in the developing countries requires conceptualizing curricula and pedagogy grounded in "an appreciation of the contemporary experience of the self in its social world and embedded in its deep historical roots" (Quicke, 1996, p. 1).

It is essential, in understanding the nature of liberal education in these countries, to think outside the box of the traditional universalizing approaches to grasp the variety, complexity, and significance it assumes in these settings. This requirement is particularly true in South Africa where liberal educational ideals have been either absent from the curriculum (Afrikaans-medium and historically black universities) or highly contested across the political spectrum where they have been attempted (English-medium also known as "liberal" universities). In recent times, these ideals have been underlined in the context of attempts to identify the defining characteristics of the knowledge, curriculum, and educational experiences that translate into an improved awareness of the principles and values of social justice, equity, and human rights without making direct reference to "liberal education." Attempts are being made to explore the ways in which higher education content could be reformed to take into account appreciation of the discourses of democratic citizenship, human rights, and social justice (Enslin, 2003).

Against this background, we argue that our understanding of current academic practices that could well lay claim to the notion of "liberal education" has deep historical roots that allow us to speak of the pursuit of the same or similar ideals through alternative pathways. While such pathways embrace individual liberties, they do so with reference to the discourse of "group rights" and "cultural diversity" that is deeply embedded in the South African politics, including its constitution. In this discourse, the individual appears somewhat decentered or thought about, not as an egocentric subject unable to engage with the surrounding social world in other words and other worlds, but rather as a reflection or individuation of this social world.

Put differently, such pathways imply socialization into liberal ideals insofar as these are for the public good or rooted in the African communitarian ideal of education. This ideal is frequently termed *ubuntu*, which is captured in the maxim "a person is a person through other persons" (*umuntu ngumuntu ngabantu*). Little emphasis is put on the self, the individual, and individuation in contrast to the liberal education tradition in which "the individual's experience of himself becomes more real to him than his experience of the objective social world" (Berger, Berger, & Kellner, 1973, p. 74). The South African communitarian focus makes the individual more aware, reflective, and accountable to the wider society both discursively and in terms of practical consciousness in response to the legacies of apartheid and to avoid falling into asocial and reductionist individualism. In this perspective, "self-identity cannot be taken as given, but has to be accomplished and sustained through reflexive activity" (Quicke, 1996, p. 366), which requires social responsibility and an understanding of wider social narratives beyond the narratives of the self. The implication is not that of the "homeless mind," as suggested by Berger et al. (1973), but rather of the critical mind that finds its home in the social world and which is not blind to the embeddedness and social character of its self-conceptions.

Higher Education Institutions

A close look at the legacies in South Africa's higher education landscape shows that generally students had more exposure to liberal arts education in universities than in other sectors of higher education, which focused mainly on vocational training. In 1994, the South African higher education system comprised 36 public institutions structured along "racial" and ethnic lines. These institutions, characterized by a binary divide between the 21 universities and 15 technikons (similar to polytechnics), functioned under the administration of different education departments. There were four different departments in the so-called white South Africa and four in each of the Bantustans.[1] The 36 included: (a) four English-medium universities originally reserved for white students; (b) six Afrikaans-medium universities originally reserved for white students; (c) seven technikons reserved for white students; (d) four universities and three technikons located in the Bantustans and self-governing territories and reserved for African students; (e) four urban universities and two technikons reserved for black students; (f) one university and one technikon for Coloureds (people of mixed race) and one university and one technikon for Indians; and (g) one distance university and one distance technikon.

The binary distribution of higher education institutions was not just an institutional or technical divide. It reflected a difference in admission requirements, a difference of knowledge types and institutional organization, and a difference of pedagogical approaches and epistemologies. These institutions had differences in access (lower entry requirements in technikons than in universities), in qualifications (vocational certificates, diplomas, and degrees in technikons while universities awarded academic diplomas and degrees), in orientation (outward to application and practice for technikons but inward to the discipline for universities), in research (applied and responsive to industry, business, and government for technikons while universities focused on basic research that was responsive to the academic discipline), and in knowledge structure (with the universities providing more room to acquire general knowledge, the arts, and the humanities than technikons, which focused on training and marketable skills). Consequently, the students who opted for technikon education had very limited exposure to the humanities and social sciences compared to their counterparts in the university system.

From 2004 onwards, the higher education system was restructured through a series of mergers to rationalize the 36 universities and technikons into 22 institutions in three categories: 11 "traditional universities," five "universities of technology," and six "comprehensive universities" (Badat, 2007; Jansen, 2003). Accompanying these changes in public higher education was a considerable expansion of private education. Jansen (2004) notes that the number of private schools increased from 518 in 1994 to around 1,500 in 2001, while more than 100,000 students were registered in 145 private higher education institutions by 2004 (p. 6; see also Mabizela, Subotsky, & Thaver, 2000). Private providers concentrate primarily on further education and training in commercial and business subjects; they do not constitute significant competition to the public sector.

Government's Role in Higher Education

In 1994, the national constitution granted institutional autonomy to all higher education institutions, which left the government with steering as the sole mechanism for influencing change. Nonetheless, the state's role in driving higher education change through policy has been more significant than initially anticipated (Adam, 2009, p. 73). The notion of relative autonomy, which the new government bestowed upon institutions, soon came under scrutiny and prompted a slight shift in the government's position on autonomy. It argued that, after 10 years of transition to democracy, many institutions still continued to reflect apartheid historical divisions and needed to be made accountable to democratic goals. In 2004, the Minister of Education, Naledi Pandor, put it this way: "We cannot stand by and watch institutions collapse." From the late 1990s into the mid-2000s, the government shifted away from benign steering toward higher levels of control and even interference (Johnson, 2006), drawing on new forms of planning, funding, and quality assurance—particularly program review and accreditation. This new emphasis has been referred to as the "highly active state supervision model" (Johnson, 2006; Kraak, 2001), concerned primarily with transformation through standardization. Not surprisingly, a wide range of stakeholders believed that institutional autonomy was being eroded and strongly contested these developments (Jansen, 2004, p. 296).

The drive toward standardization as a measure of quality in higher education is linked to the regulatory frameworks emanating from statutory bodies that are very often perceived as operating outside government. These bodies include the Council on Higher Education (CHE), the National Research Foundation, the National Science Foundation and other science councils, and the South African Qualifications Authority. For example, through registration of qualifications, the South African Qualifications Authority ensures compliance with the provision of the National Qualifications Framework (NQF) and its outcomes-based philosophy in curriculum structuring. Similarly, the Council on Higher Education sets criteria and standards for program accreditation which include, among other provisions, compliance with national policies and regulations regarding higher education qualifications; program strategy and coordination; student recruitment, admission, and selection; staffing; teaching and learning; supervision and research targets; student assessment; infrastructure and library resources; student retention and throughput rates;

and program reviews (CHE, 2005). These bodies exert external pressures toward institutional compliance with government policy. Institutions and academic staff are now required to review their programs and curriculum and align them with the national policy framework.

Those who resist these external pressures make the legitimate argument that the establishment of new national accreditation schemes, renewal strategies, and the encouragement of innovation contrasts with the political ambitions of institutional autonomy and academic freedom. The two logics seem to collide. While program accreditation and concerns with standards or standardization may be interpreted as an invitation for more integration and coherence across the system, they also reflect the complex ways in which the relationship between the state and academia has been redefined and reorganized to the disadvantage of the latter, particularly at the level of curriculum choice.

Funding in Higher Education

Central to our argument in this section is the fact that government funding policy is designed to privilege science, maths, and technology at the expense of the humanities and social sciences. Higher education in South Africa is funded in three ways: by the state, by student fees, and by "third-stream" income including entrepreneurial activities, donor contributions, and research activities (Steyn & de Villiers, 2006, pp. 89–91). Overall the proportion of income derived from state funding has declined and the proportion derived from student fees has increased from the late 1980s to the early 2000s. In the early 1990s, the private sector and market-orientation protagonists severely criticized the government about the character of the country's universities and the imbalanced trends in the numbers of degrees awarded in the sciences versus those awarded in the arts and humanities (Pouris, 1991). They argued that South African universities were training an increasing percentage of arts and humanities graduates while the numbers of science graduates remained constant, a trend that could compromise the economic development goals of the country. In response, the government introduced a new funding mechanism in 2003 that favors maths, science, and technology. Since then, this pattern has become widespread, in both public and private student support, including research funding.

Underpinning the new funding formula was the division of the courses into four broad categories with the arts and humanities largely located in the lowest level of funding and the sciences largely located in the highest funding levels, to encourage the enrollment of larger numbers of students in the sciences and business qualifications. As discussed below, this strategy has not, apparently, significantly reduced enrollments in the arts and humanities (Cloete & Bunting, 2000, p. 24).

The Arts, Humanities, and the Liberal Education Curriculum: Institutional Legacies

Historically, liberal education in South Africa has been under fierce attack from both the conservative and radical sides of academia (Cross, 1986; Cross, Carpentier, & Ait-Mehdi, 2009). On the one hand, the Afrikaner regime and its academic circles perceived liberal education as a threat to Afrikaner nationalist ideals and the project of apartheid. Afrikaans-medium and historically black universities, which were the main centers of conservative Afrikaner Christian Nationalist ideology, met liberal education with militant hostility. Instead of liberal education, the humanities and social sciences became academic disciplines designed to indoctrinate students in apartheid ideologies. These social elements strongly contested progressive pedagogy, with its emphasis on "student-centeredness," "critical thinking," and the development of "independent and autonomous citizens." Similarly, radical scholarship in its neo-Marxist and Africanist strands (e.g., the Black Consciousness movement), challenged liberal education either as redundant in the context of the struggle against apartheid and/or as failing to account for the specificity of African cultures, given their emphasis on the collective and not the individual.

At the center of the radical–liberal debate of the 1980s was a fierce contestation of the alleged hyper- or atomistic individualism in the liberal conception of autonomy, claims to neutrality as politically inimical to social justice, and perceived epistemological weakness as unable to uncover the complexities of the apartheid project. Nonetheless, small pockets could be identified in English-medium universities—University of the Witwatersrand, University of Cape Town, Rhodes University, and the University of Kwa-Zulu Natal—in which forms of liberal education developed that were associated with the concept of social inquiry as a disinterested/disengaged enterprise or with the liberal cult of personal autonomy or independence. English-medium universities came to be labeled "liberal" (with pejorative connotations) due to their defense of Western-style liberal education, particularly their commitment to a disinterested pursuit of knowledge in the arts and humanities.

Liberal Education in Secondary Education

On March 24, 1997, Sibusiso Bengu, the Minister of Education, launched Curriculum 2005 (C2005), a movement that would represent the national curriculum framework for basic education in post-apartheid South Africa. It was a dramatic departure from the apartheid curriculum and a significant paradigm shift from content-based teaching and learning to outcomes-based education. It also marked a departure from "fundamental pedagogics" (a racially based set of prescribed learning objectives) to progressive pedagogy and learner-centered teaching and learning strategies. Debates within the labor movement resulted in borrowing the outcomes-based approach to curriculum from Australia and New Zealand as a solution to concerns about skills and jobs among workers.

In broad terms, Curriculum 2005 had the following aims: (a) to align school work with workplace, social, and political goals; (b) to emphasize experiential and cooperative learning; (c) to pursue diversity in race, gender, and culture; and (d) to develop citizens who are imaginative and critical problem-solvers. The Natural Science Learning Area encapsulates the theory of knowledge underpinning Curriculum 2005: that theoretical knowledge is necessary but not sufficient and that the intended outcome is the ability to apply theoretical knowledge, concepts, and principles to practical daily life situations and issues (Department of Education (DOE), 2002, pp. 3–9).

The objectives of secondary education stated by government and private providers make the point that the new order inherited "a situation in which an entire population needed to adjust to democracy" (Enslin, 2003, p. 79). The educational system came to be seen as both a prerequisite for the full exercise of citizenship and as a site for citizenship education to counter the legacy of disfranchisement. These perceptions are reflected in the main policy instruments regulating the curriculum in basic education. Both the 1997 *Education White Paper 3: A Programme for the Transformation of Higher Education* (DOE, 1997, p. 5) and the later Curriculum 2005 embraced the principles of common citizenship and educational rights enshrined in the Interim Constitution of 1995. The South African Schools Act (SASA) of 1996 also supported the same policy provision, emphasizing the participatory model of governance and encouraging teachers, learners, and parents to be represented in school-governing bodies.

Concerns about violence and social disintegration in schools led the Minister of Education to release a *Manifesto on Values, Education, and Democracy* in 2001 to show how the constitution can be taught as part of the curriculum and applied in programs and policy-making by educators, administrators, governing bodies, and other officials (DOE, 2001, p. 1). The manifesto outlines 10 values: democracy, social justice and equity, equality, non-racism and non-sexism, *ubuntu* (human dignity), sustaining an open society, accountability (responsibility), the rule of law, respect, and reconciliation.

Secondary Education: Courses in the Arts, Humanities, and Social Sciences

Secondary education includes the senior phase of General Education and Training (grades 5–9) and Further Education and Training (grades 10–12). The National Senior Certificate is the new school-leaving qualification, which replaces the matriculation examination. This certificate is based on a new curriculum for grades 10–12. To qualify for the certificate, a learner needs to take seven subjects, four compulsory and three elective. In the compulsory section, every learner takes two languages; one is his or her home language and the other is a first additional language. The other three required courses are life orientation and either mathematics or maths literacy. For the three electives, the learner has a choice among 27 subjects, some of which have been classified as "designated subjects," meaning that they are more suitable for tertiary study. The electives include agricultural sciences, dramatic art, music, the visual arts, accounting, business studies, economics, engineering graphics and design, geography, history, religious studies, information technology, life sciences, physical sciences, consumer studies, all official languages, and a number of non-official languages. The learner has to achieve a rating of at least 4 (50–59%) in four designated subjects to be eligible for university entrance. This rating is over and above the minimum requirements. Institutions can also set institutional requirements (DOE, 2005).

Within this structure, the social sciences, history, arts and culture, languages, and life orientation subjects are the home of "liberal" learning. They are designed to produce "responsible citizens in a culturally diverse, democratic society" (DOE, 1997, p. 49). However, students may choose combinations for the purposes of specialization that exclude such liberal arts subjects as the humanities, social sciences, and the arts. The Further Education and Training (FET) program for grades 10–12 provides different pathways resulting in a Further Education and Training Certificate: general vocational and trade, and occupational and professional. Offered mainly in FET colleges, the general vocational and trade area contains programs that cover broad vocational skills and prepare learners for work and self-employment. Trade, occupational, and professional subjects are designed to meet needs of local communities and the workplace, are offered by colleges and industry-based providers, and include learnerships.

In elite independent or private schools, learners choose 14 subjects taught in grade 9, and 20 at the FET level. These subjects are English, Afrikaans, Zulu, French, Portuguese, maths, advanced maths, physical science, life science, guidance and counseling, visual arts, business studies, music, geography, history, information technology, speech and drama, accounting, and physical education. Elite schools offer a wider range of subjects and more depth in maths, science, and English—subjects that allow for access to the most competitive programs in universities. Most of these schools are denominational (usually Catholic or Anglican). Christian or denominational concerns prevail over liberal learning concerns, although they embrace a more liberal stance than public schools.

Course Work in the Humanities: National History, Literature, Arts, and Cultural Diversity

It was in line with apartheid policies that students in the secondary school system were systematically exposed to subjects in the arts, the humanities, and social sciences. History, geography, and civic education in particular represented the main sources of apartheid indoctrination. For similar reasons, the school curriculum was also heavily academic and left little room for science, mathematics, and technology. Today the key subjects in the humanities and social sciences are history and geography. The history syllabus aims at rigorous inquiry into the past and its relevance to the present (e.g., to support democracy or as a vehicle for promoting a culture of human rights). It supports the view that historical truth consists of a multiplicity of voices expressing varying and often contradictory versions of the same history. It deliberately introduces the concept of indigenous knowledge systems to acknowledge the richness of South Africa's history and heritage and the contribution of those knowledge systems as a source of inspiration for change to help transform learners' values.

The history syllabus has three main areas of focus. The first deals with national history (e.g., How unique was apartheid South Africa? How did South Africa emerge as a democracy?). The second looks at regional issues and the rest of the continent (e.g., competing nationalisms and identities in Africa). The third reviews aspects of global history (e.g., the cause and impact of the collapse of the USSR).

Geography starts in grade 10 with information on world geography, weather and climate, and changing landforms, populations, and organizations. It focuses on general concepts and theories that are universally applicable. Grade 11 instruction concentrates on the African continent with emphasis on the significance of water masses, ecosystems, development and sustainability, and the people and their needs. Grade 12 is dedicated to South Africa itself: geographical skills and techniques, climate and weather, fluvial processes and landforms, people and places, rural and urban settlement, and the country's people and their needs. The three components give particular attention to geographical skills and techniques.

"Liberal" Learning in Secondary School Curricula

It must be stressed from the outset that liberal education is foreign to most South African learners and does not represent a concern in their selection of subjects. Seen as a sort of heresy within dominant educational spheres throughout South African history, it still remains marginal in current discourses. As in the apartheid school curriculum, the current secondary curricula do not refer specifically to liberal education. However, repeated references to "critical thinking," "responsible citizenship," etc., and the principles and values outlined in the 2001 manifesto could be read as endorsing key attributes of liberal learning, although neither refers to individual liberties or education for autonomy.

Overall, critics point to several tensions in the secondary school curriculum that have implications for liberal learning. Some point to the need to separate the curriculum from human resource development strategies that are grounded in an ideology of skills shortage. They thus advocate the politics of liberal learning to the degree that such learning is located in a discourse of human rights and social justice. Some challenge the theory of knowledge that under-pins the curriculum (constructivism manifested in learner centeredness) and call for providing content knowledge and content pedagogical knowledge.[2] They argue for reinstating textbooks that had earlier been banned because of their association with apartheid curriculum. For them, it is not clear what clus-ters of knowledge or content should be brought together to facilitate learning, in what sequence, and at what level of competence (Muller, 2000, p. 15). Cur-riculum 2005, by deemphasizing subject matter, reduced knowledge in the classroom to the constructs brought in by individual teachers and learners (personal knowledge embedded in personal experience) or to the knowledge produced by interactions in the classroom through such forms of progressive pedagogy as group work or integrated studies. Muller (2000) appraises the success of this approach:

> A success can be made of such an under-stipulated curriculum, but only if the teacher has a well-articulated mental script of what should be covered, and if the pupils come from homes where they have been well prepared to respond to such putative freedom, in other words, only in schools by and for the middle class.
>
> (p. 14)

Enslin (2003) also calls for caution lest the danger of indoctrination reemerges in promoting values in schools. For example, one such value would be "nurtur-ing the new patriotism," which is one of the 16 strategies formulated in the 2001 manifesto, by promoting reverence for anthems, flags, mottoes, sports insignia, and national symbols (Enslin, 2003, p. 82). Now that the government has officially recognized the failure of Curriculum 2005 and shifted away from outcomes-based education, textbooks will be reintroduced beginning in 2011. More radical criticism came from Jansen (1999) who argued from the outset that Curriculum 2005 was doomed to failure for giving primacy to political imperatives—policy symbolism and political expediency—over policy and pedagogical imperatives.

Curricula and the Liberal Arts in Higher Education

Two critical policy milestones were instrumental in shaping South Africa's higher education vision. The first included the National Qualifications Frame-work (NQF), a provision for articulating qualifications introduced in 1995 through the South African Qualifications Authority Act. The NQF was designed to allow learners to have greater vertical and horizontal mobility within each education track and between academic and vocational programs while preparing them more effectively for the workplace. Advocates also expected the framework to promote "responsible citizenship." Ensor (2004) argues that "the NQF encapsulates the desire of education policy-makers to erode three sets of boundaries: between education and training, between academic and everyday knowledge, and between different knowledges, disciplines or subjects within the academic domain." Furthermore, he continues, "the weakening of these three sets of boundaries was intended to erode a fourth set—the boundaries between social groups on the basis of race and social class—thereby incorporating a powerful agenda for social justice" (p. 340).

The second policy milestone consisted of four policy documents that expanded and consolidated the ideas articulated in the NQF: the National Commission on Higher Education Report of 1995, the Green Paper on Higher Education of 1996, the White Paper of 1997, and the National Plan for Higher Education of 2001. Emerging from these documents are such principles and values as equity and redress, democratization, economic and socio-cultural development, quality, effectiveness and efficiency, academic freedom, accountability, and autonomy (DOE, 1997). The vision entails the following goals: (a) creating an integrated and coordinated higher education system from the fragmented apartheid legacy, (b) thinning the rigid boundaries between the institutional types of universities and technikons, (c) addressing the legacies of racially and ethnically engineered institutional histories, (d) establishing a more diverse and differentiated higher education landscape, (e) making changes in curricular programs and qualification offerings, and (f) increasing higher education enrollments (Cloete, 1998).

Although heavily criticized for not paying enough attention to curriculum, the higher education vision has profound implications for curriculum reform. First, it identified three key organizing concepts for structuring curricula: modularization, credit accumulation, and the shift from departments to programs (National Commission on Higher Education, 1996). The discourse to which Ensor (2002, p. 279) refers as credit accumulation and transfer or credit exchange discourse came to be privileged as providing greater flexibility to work with both traditional forms of knowledge organization based on disciplinary discourses and innovative interdisciplinary and professional approaches to curriculum. The White Paper of 1997 also signals a need to shift the focus from the arts and humanities toward the sciences and technology and to shape a curriculum that is more directly linked to the nation's economic needs (DOE, 1997, p. 3).

Government and Private Providers: Policy Pathways for Curriculum Reconstruction

The argument in this section about the interface of higher education policy and the liberal arts education curriculum in South Africa has three dimensions. First, the South African policy environment reflects a dynamic tension between global priorities (global competitiveness, high skills, and the demands of a knowledge economy) and national priorities (social and economic development within a framework of redress, equity, access, and efficiency) (Kraak, 2000, p. 16; Maassen & Cloete, 2002, p. 30). South Africa's neo-liberal macroeconomic policy framework was articulated through its Growth, Employment, and Redistribution (GEAR) policy introduced in June 1996. Many analysts take the position that this policy is more strongly influenced by global pressures than by national concerns (Jansen, 2000, p. 156; Kishun, 1998, p. 61). This bias, they argue, compromises national agendas (Alexander, 2001, p. 139).

Second, South Africa lacks a clear national policy concerning curriculum reform in higher education. Institutions must rely on a series of incoherent and fragmented statements scattered through a variety of policy documents. Where policy guidelines exist (e.g., those from the National Qualifications Framework and the Council on Higher Education), they are diluted in the context of political, economic, and institutional mediation (Ensor, 2004; Kraak, 2004). Clearly, the government's policy on curriculum is broad and vague in its attempt to be inclusive, making it open to a wide variety of interpretations at the implementation level (Ensor, 2002, p. 279). This broad policy framework has resulted in the emergence of competing curriculum discourses, discussed below.

Third, curriculum choices in the arts, humanities, and social sciences reflect largely local contextual complexities and differing institutional legacies. It appears that the major inhibitors of change and accommodation of liberal education remain the different political values embedded in these legacies, the values and visions advocated by political leaders and institutional stakeholders, the value differences held within and across individual institutions, and their consequent value conflicts, which are often not explicit, recognized, or understood. For example, emphasizing the arts and humanities as the preserve of cultural and linguistic diversity or group rights remains an attribute of historically Afrikaans-medium universities where the mergers have taken place (e.g., Stellenbosch, University of Pretoria) while historically English-medium universities claim new forms of liberal learning.

Student Development as Part of Curricular Development

Generally changes in the demographic profile of the campuses had multiple effects on curriculum reform, though no fundamental changes were undertaken in this regard. Enrollment in South African universities numbered 159,756 in 1980, increased to 304,625 in 1990, and stood at close to 490,000 by 2003. Because institutions were restructured, it is difficult to determine the number of students in universities and in technikons after 2007, the last year for which complete data are available. However, the total population of students in higher education in the country can reliably be estimated at around one million in 2010.

By contrast, technikon enrollments increased by 119% between 1990 and 2000 (Steyn & de Villiers, 2006, p. 25). The most significant increase began in 2000 and had reached 761,087 in 2007. The increase in technikons has been interpreted as reflecting students' perceptions that the technikons offered a curriculum that was more practical and more closely tied to the labor market.

However, the main aspect of student participation does not lie in the upward trend of enrollments but in the racial recomposition of the student body, with a significant increase of black students and a decline of white students, who numbered 220,000 in 1993 but 164,000 by 1999. The proportion of African students enrolling in universities increased from 40% in 1993 to 65% in 2002 (Bundy, 2006, p. 12). In addition, the number of international students increased from 30,943 in 2000 to 52,453 in 2004 (Department of Education, 2000, 2004), according to HEMIS (Higher Education Management Information System) data. In 2000, 47.2% were from the Southern African Development Community (SADC) region, a percentage that had increased to 68% by 2004. Currently South African universities attract almost 70,000 students from countries on all continents, but particularly Africa (Nzimande, 2010).

The changing student demographic profile had several implications for curriculum reform. The increase of black students had the unintended effect of reproducing the existing patterns of enrollment in the arts and humanities where a large number of these students were admitted. Most of these students were considered unsuitable for courses in science and engineering. We saw the increasing commodification of the curriculum as universities tried to respond to perceived student needs and market demands, with Afrikaans-medium institutions championing this trend. English-medium universities adopted a more conservative attitude. The consequence has been the restructuring of the arts and humanities, the elimination of classical languages, the decline of history courses, and the increasing professionalization or vocationalization of the humanities curriculum. Among developments in the latter trend has been, for example, the introduction of four-year B.A. professional programs in law and market-oriented courses such as information and communication technology (ICT) in the humanities, history and tourism, heritage studies, and so forth (Jansen, 2004, p. 308). In the following section, we will explore the main discourses underpinning these changes.

Competing Faculty Discourses in Curriculum Development

Many curriculum developments can be attributed to the complex interplay of curriculum policies and strategies, and the diversity of institutional histories, cultures, and capacity as discussed earlier (Jansen, 2000; Moore, 2003). However, while these legacies are useful in providing a framework for locating institutional responses, they do not fully explain the changes taking place across departments, where different approaches can be identified (Ensor, 2002, p. 285; Jansen, 2000, p. 164). South African universities are loosely coupled organizations with no single authority on curriculum. Their academic staffs enjoy relative autonomy from state control. Therefore, it is not easy to control and predict curriculum responses in different departments (Maassen & Cloete, 2002, p. 27) without delving into the domain of competing discourses that underpin academic practice and curriculum choices at universities, which exists in dialogue with the standardization discourse driven by the government and its agencies.

Two other discourses that separate academics are the global competitiveness and knowledge innovation discourse (also known as high-skills discourse) and the popular democratic discourse with its different nuances.

Internationally, the discourse of global competitiveness and knowledge innovation responds to the global knowledge economy. Nationally, it responds to the government's neo-liberal macro-economic framework of GEAR, which emphasizes fiscal controls, efficiency, cost-effectiveness, and the standardization and rationalization of higher education. Institutionally, there is plenty of evidence to suggest that the rise of managerialism in South African universities has eroded the autonomy of academic work and reconfigured the identities of academic staff (Henkel, 2005, p. 155). The implementation of efficiency, planning, and quality assurance mechanisms within the narrow framework of managerialism has also affected the traditional role of academics (Henkel, 2004; Kletz & Pallez, 2002, p. 9) by undermining the academic and intellectual project and relocating power from academics to administrators. New layers of university management have strengthened national and institutional compliance with curriculum goals; academics are now focusing much more on administrative tasks (Johnson & Cross, 2005).

Freedom to teach in their preferred areas of research is being eroded as academics are expected to align courses with national and institutional goals dictated by cost and the markets. Therefore, if a more skills-based curriculum attracts more students and more money, then that curriculum is adjudged "better." If the curriculum seems removed, abstract, and not useful, then students will not register for those courses and it must be changed. Johnson (2006) notes that, where these skills-based curricula have become entrenched, academic staff feel increasingly overworked, less supported by their institutions, marginalized in decision-making, and at odds with the "managers," "newly appointed executive deans," and "executive heads of schools," some of whom have little academic experience. These changes have led to a loss of a sense of community and feelings of powerlessness, which in turn influence the relationship between academics and students (pp. 61–67).

Another significant trend is the shift toward interdisciplinarity in research and in the organization of the curriculum, even though disciplinary-based curriculum remains the dominant model. Interdisciplinarity is conceived of either as a collection of curriculum components, which maintains some level of disciplinary boundaries, or as a more integrated approach to curriculum selection and design (Ensor, 1998). In some cases, entire programs have been restructured along interdisciplinary lines. For example, the sociology of education, the psychology of education, philosophy of education, history of education, and comparative education have been replaced by curriculum studies, leadership and management studies, adult education, maths and science education, and democratic citizenship and education. At the national policy level, such restructuring was facilitated by adopting the "program" as the organizing concept of qualifications and "modularization" as the basis for course packaging (National Commission on Higher Education, 1996). These two concepts provided a basis for the horizontal organization of knowledge alongside traditional vertical and hierarchical knowledge structures (Ensor, 2004).

Challenging global competitiveness and knowledge innovation discourses is the second mode—those discourses clustered around popular democratic values and principles generated by the mass struggle in the 1970s and 1980s against apartheid. Now enshrined in the national constitution, these values are nonracism, nonsexism, human dignity, equality, and advancement of human rights and freedoms. In contrast to traditional liberal education which promotes the ideal of personal autonomy and individual development, the democratic discourses tend to decenter the self and to experience it as a reflection of the social. They have given rise to strategies geared at promoting democratic citizenship, a culture of human rights and social justice, critical thinking, learner centeredness, interdisciplinarity, engaged scholarship, community involvement, and strong links between formal education and work. Adam (2009) argues that their impact is more felt at the pedagogical level than at the level of content—hence, the sparse references to the arts or humanities, let alone to liberal arts education. Important ramifications of popular democratic discourses are curriculum responsiveness to economic, cultural, disciplinary, and learner-related concerns (Moll, 2004).

Overall, the various discourses on curriculum reform in South Africa suggest that curriculum strategies are not implemented in a linear way but are mediated within a complex institutional medium (Ensor, 2004; Kraak, 2004). This phenomenon gives rise to diverse conceptions of curriculum, which operate within a continuum ranging from a strong market-oriented approach to a strong traditional approach (Cloete & Fehnel, 2002, pp. 282–283).

The Arts, Humanities, and Social Sciences

While some programs in both science and the humanities make provision for general education, including liberal arts, when the choice of subjects is compulsory or not part of degree "majors" (dictated by the rules of combination), the choice is left to individual students. The choices students make cannot be separated from their learning and knowledge identities. Some students define the value of what they study as a better understanding of themselves or others (Cross, Shalem, Backhouse, Adam, & Baloyi, 2010). This learner identity is grounded in the classic liberal view of education, which values knowledge for the sake of knowledge. Some attach their choices to altruistic concerns and seek to improve society through their study. This learner identity values social justice or social responsiveness. In our view, these differing identities reflect alternative pathways to "liberal" learning in the South African context. However, most students are increasingly making choices informed by the discourse of market responsiveness at the expense of general knowledge or citizenship education. This market-related identity is grounded in the globalization discourse, which determines the selection of knowledge on utilitarian grounds or with reference to the economic advantage that a degree can purchase. Increasing numbers of students share this identity, which militates against the future of liberal education.

The discourse of credit accumulation and transfer allows students greater flexibility in choosing and packaging curriculum content through modularization. Thanks to the revised rules of combination, they can accumulate credits toward academic qualifications—whether certificates, diplomas, or degrees (Ensor, 2004, p. 344). In this context, the National Qualifications Framework allows students to match and exchange modules and credits across various learning sites, thus providing greater educational portability. Cross-field course work opportunities and practices are thereby limited only by the rules of combination in certain fields. This practice goes against the grain of the liberal curriculum which focused on disciplinary enculturation through years of engagement with the discipline and is further complicated by the fact that the government is privileging enrollments in business, science, engineering, and technology over the humanities (Jansen, 2004, p. 309). In addition to institutions' greater emphasis on science and technology in recruiting students, there is certainly a growing perception that the ultimate career benefits of a qualification in the humanities or social sciences do not justify the costs of education in these fields that students and their families must pay (Cloete & Bunting, 2000, p. 24).

Analysts are divided on their assessment of current trends. Muller (2005) suggests that the humanities are in a tight corner—"damned if they do" succumb to markets and "damned if they don't" (pp. 14–15). Jansen (2004) notes that "not a single university in South Africa has escaped the sharp downward spiral in humanities enrollments in the past decade" and that "humanities and social science faculties bore the brunt of the unexpected decline in matriculants from the school system" (p. 308). He identifies five reasons for this decline: (a) the perceived demand by students and the general public for vocationally oriented courses; (b) the opening of new opportunities for, especially, black students in non-humanities that, under apartheid, were fields previously limited to white graduates; (c) the growing status of the commercial sciences and allied subjects (e.g., actuarial science) as high-income, rewarding fields for new graduates; (d) the declining status of the teaching profession (teacher education was the single largest field of enrollment in post-school education prior to the 1990s); and (e) the declining numbers of graduates from the school system, most of whom are absorbed in non-humanities faculties. In many universities, faculties of humanities were restructured, the humanities academics were retrenched, and foreign language, music, art, and drama departments were closed (Adam, 2009; Ensor, 2002, p. 287). For Jansen (2004), the consequences are dramatic: "Senior academics have been lost, powerful intellectual traditions have been terminated, and a culture of critical and creative thought in the social sciences and humanities has been eroded" (p. 309).

However, while Muller and Jansen lament the downsizing of some fields of the arts and humanities, which they associate with decline, student enrollments have remained relatively stable in the arts and humanities. The overall trend in South African universities since the 1990s has been to train even more arts and humanities graduates compared to those completing science and technology courses (Inglesi & Pouris, 2008, p. 347). The total head count of students majoring in the humanities followed the apartheid pattern of growth and peaked at 329,000 in 1995, then fell by 52,000 between 1996 and 1999. The number of students majoring in science and technology increased between 1993 and 1999, but at a slower pace than majors in business and commerce (Cloete & Bunting, 2000, p. 24). In 2007, out of a total of 760,009 students enrolled in public higher education institutions, 41.7% (316,933) were enrolled in teacher education, the humanities, or the social sciences; 30.1% of students (228,735) were enrolled in business and management; and 28.2% (214,341) were enrolled in science, engineering, and technology (DOE, 2009).

The enrollments in 2008 also show the dominance of the humanities and social sciences as well as business, commerce, and management science. Among the reasons for the continuing prevalence of the humanities is the fact that the secondary school system has not been able to produce adequate numbers of matriculants qualified for science and engineering professions. What the funding formula has done is not necessarily to redirect students to science and engineering fields but to allow them to make choices guided by their perceptions of the needs of the labor market. Indeed, it seems that the main change so far is less a "decline" than a restructuring of the field in response to the different levels of responsiveness.

The Revival of the Liberal Arts in South Africa

The neglect of the social sciences and humanities is leading to a change of attitude that may result in future policy changes. Dr. Blade Nzimande (2010), Minister of Higher Education and Training, has launched an initiative to revive and strengthen the social sciences and humanities: "Now is the time for the teaching of and research in the social sciences and the humanities to take their place again at the leading edge of our struggle for [the] transformation and development of South African society." He sees the social sciences and humanities as playing a leading role in helping people deal with the scourges of poverty, unemployment, racism, discrimination of all kinds, and HIV/AIDS. He also sees these educational emphases as important in rebuilding a sense of nationhood and independence and enhancing the ability of South Africa to take its place in the community of nations.

For this purpose, the minister established a Task Team to prepare a charter of recommendations to be published in mid-2011, which should highlight the neglected areas of study and emphasize the critical role of the liberal arts in creating responsible, ethical, and broad-minded citizens. According to Ari Sitas (2010), Chair of the Task Team, the deemphasis of the social sciences and humanities has

> not only … affected the ability of graduates to think critically about key issues, but it has also led to a decline in the quality of leadership in the country, especially in the context of a post-conflict society where subjects such as history, anthropology, literature and the fine arts can go a long way toward bridging differences and creating unity among former enemies.

The Task Team draws on an advisory group of stakeholders, including the Academy of Science of South Africa, Higher Education South Africa, the Harold Wolpe Memorial Trust, and research directors, deans, and vice-chancellors from South African universities. In addition, at an international forum, leaders from overseas universities will share their experiences and expertise. Two key UNESCO bodies (the International Social Science Council and the International Council of Philosophy and the Humanities) will be part of the process, as will Latin American, African, Indian, and Chinese centers of social scientific and humanities research. An e-portal will support the interaction among the various local and international participants. It has been made clear that, although the team is looking abroad for advice, the charter will be a homegrown initiative. Nonetheless, some academics are skeptical about whether the government is truly interested in free thought and the diversification of the liberal arts curriculum.

Preparing Students for Effective Citizenship

One of the challenges facing higher education in South Africa is how to interrupt the "bitter knowledge" resulting from apartheid indoctrination that students bring to university campuses (Jansen, 2009). Recent racist incidents have occurred on some campuses, a testimony of the consequences of this phenomenon. At the University of Free State, for instance, a group of white students made a movie in which they are shown serving food in which they had urinated to black cleaners. It could be that liberal arts curricula could play a critical role in this regard. The B.A. degree in South Africa is generally referred to as part of the liberal arts tradition. This degree provides students with extensive choices of disciplines and subjects, in general focusing more heavily on social sciences and the humanities, but also including maths and sciences. It offers four types of curriculum organization for the first degree, one of which has enough flexibility to integrate liberal arts before specialization.

Beyond the B.A. degree, universities are increasingly moving toward adopting a core curriculum to provide all students with general knowledge and aspects of liberal learning. For example, the University of North-West has introduced a compulsory two-module curriculum for all students. The first module, "Understanding the World," has two objectives: (a) to portray knowledge about and a comprehensive understanding of the nature and function of worldviews, the nature of ideologies, and their relationship to phenomena and problems of our times (e.g., poverty, change, human rights, AIDS, power abuse, corruption, science); and (b) to obtain and apply knowledge through applicable forms of analysis and synthesis and to formulate a coherent personal view on the core issues and problems of contemporary times. The second module aims at providing general knowledge about the student's chosen field of study. Beginning in 2011, all programs at the University of Johannesburg will include some level of citizenship education to provide students with a strong sense of ways in which they can actively contribute to the development of South African society through the proper exercise of their rights and responsibilities as citizens.

Pedagogy and Classroom Interaction

Depending on specific institutional histories and legacies, South African universities display three competing categories of pedagogic practices: performance-driven, competence-driven, and hybrid. Performance-driven pedagogic practices characterized the learning environments of the "liberal" universities (University of the Witwatersrand, University of Cape Town, University of Natal, and Rhodes University just before the mergers) and still dominate many departments after the mergers, as discussed earlier (Bernstein, 2000). Performance-driven pedagogies are linked to a low-participation environment. Their defining aspects include a particular conception of the specialization of knowledge within strong disciplinary boundaries. They require a great deal of general knowledge as a requirement and use modes of transmission and evaluation based on a particular relationship between students and lecturers that emphasize individual responsibility for performance. The environment is competitive, with limited peer collaboration or faculty support. These pedagogies define, as the key resource for success, the student's accumulated social and cultural capital, his or her ability to work independently, and individual autonomy. These approaches are in line with an institutional culture that emphasizes individual self-regulation. Students are tasked with the responsibility of working hard as individuals, displaying initiative, and getting desired results. Chief among these results is an expansion of the self as the center of power, action, change, and responsibility.

While performance-driven approaches are dominant in elite universities, meaningful pockets of innovative, competence-driven pedagogy are rooted in the discourse of social justice and are perceived as more effective for addressing the needs of nontraditional students. The benchmarks here are "inclusion" and "integration." Success is not only predicated on personal effort and hard work but also on help from caring others. Economically, such pedagogies are expensive, since they require small, interactive classes, academic support, mentoring, and academic enrichment initiatives. In curricular terms, this approach allows for loose boundaries between academic knowledge and everyday life. While pockets of these practices exist in all elite institutions, this model is being developed more systematically in the academic support programs of the University of Kwa-Zulu Natal and the University of the Western Cape.

From a liberal learning perspective, these pedagogical practices have

> the tendency ... to emphasize the social and in particular the socially constructed nature of the self—"the social individual"—but in so doing [fail] to give special emphasis to the self as a reflexive constructor of a "narrative" of the self.
>
> (Quicke, 1996, p. 369)

Both sets of pedagogies—performance-driven and competence-driven—assume more specific modes, and their construction in specific historical circumstances "may give rise to what could be called a pedagogic palette where mixes can take place" (Bernstein, 2000, p. 56).

Conclusion

The lack of systematic national policy on higher education curriculum reform leaves considerable space for the emergence of competing curriculum discourses, which either constrain or widen the possibilities of liberal learning.

These discourses create tensions within the system that are sometimes productive and are very often unproductive. The first is the tension between the discourse of standardization as a measure of quality on the one hand and on academic freedom and institutional autonomy on the other. The second is between performativity and efficiency discourse and concerns with equity, redress, human rights, and social justice. A general perception is that South African higher education policies tend to privilege neo-liberal ideology and its celebration of the markets, which compromises the national agenda of equity and social justice. The third is between the vision that privileges disciplinary approaches vis-à-vis interdisciplinary knowledge, particularly in the humanities and social sciences, and the emphasis on formative and academic concerns vis-à-vis the professionalization of the curriculum (e.g., law, business, economics, education). Specific curriculum responses in this regard depend on institutional cultures and academic identities.

In the past, content knowledge in the arts, humanities, and social sciences was a source of apartheid indoctrination in Afrikaans-medium and historically black universities. Only in English-medium universities were the arts, humanities, and social sciences associated with the Western idea of liberal education, though highly contested within radical scholarship. Today there seems to be a clear distinction between critical pedagogy and the arts, humanities, and social sciences. These fields are still contested, either because of the conservatism that still dominates their teaching or because of their Eurocentric orientation. Critical pedagogy—an attribute of progressive scholars—draws on specific pedagogical content knowledge, within and beyond the liberal arts domain. Thus, in contrast to the apartheid era, we have argued that liberal learning is now primarily linked to the practices driven by popular-democratic discourses that emphasize access, equity, and social justice. The emphasis is placed on the pedagogical domain (pedagogical content and practice) rather than the intrinsic value of the arts, humanities, or social sciences. In other words, general education and liberal arts were not always connected to such key attributes of liberal education as student-centered pedagogy, training in critical thinking, individual autonomy, and independence in reasoning.

South African government authorities have committed themselves to reducing enrollments in the arts, humanities, and social sciences in favor of maths, science, and technology—fields to which black students were denied access under apartheid. Where possible, students have responded positively and have come to regard maths, science, and technology as gateway subjects—that is, as skills that provide access to many career and job opportunities. At the curriculum level, the changing student choices are accompanied by increasing professionalization or vocationalization of the liberal arts programs and the consequent thinning of general education. In fact many disciplines such as history, anthropology, and philosophy that, in the past, had no need to forge links between their curriculum and the world of work are experiencing increasing pressure to do so now. They must justify their existence through new conceptions of what constitutes valuable knowledge within a utilitarian framework, most frequently measured by, for example, the kinds of jobs that history graduates can do. Nonetheless, the arts, humanities, and social sciences still outstrip maths, science, and technology in terms of enrollments and graduation rates. As a result, we challenge claims about the decline of the arts, humanities, and social sciences. Instead, we argue that these fields have essentially undergone a profound restructuring characterized by the increasing professionalization and commodification of the curriculum.

Against this background, the future of liberal education will certainly depend on its ability to integrate a theory of the cultural recognition of individual liberties, personal autonomy, and independence with the theory of social justice. In other words, liberal education in South Africa depends on its ability to reconcile the cultural politics of individual liberties with the social politics of equity. It rests with South African scholars to develop a critical theory of liberal learning, distinguishing those claims for the recognition of individual autonomy that advance the cause of social equality from those that retard it or undermine it. To borrow from Mackenzie and Stoljar (2000), this is a theory that recognizes that "persons are socially embedded and that agents' identities are formed within the context of social relationships and shaped by a complex of intersecting social determinants, such as race, class, gender, and ethnicity" (p. 4). We suggest that, in contexts where social life is permeated by legacies of conflict and social discrimination warranting commitment to social justice and human rights, liberal education in South Africa is embracing new goals and pointing toward new developments deeply rooted in the specific history of these contexts. Overlooking this aspect runs the risk of ignoring the variability, contingency, and peculiar forms of social existence that warrant rejection of old-style hyper-individualism in liberal education. In this regard, South Africans should see themselves as presented with a new intellectual and practical opportunity: that of developing a context-sensitive critical theory of promoting liberties—a theory that identifies and defends only those versions of liberal education that can be coherently combined with the social politics of equality.

Notes

1 Bantustans were ethnically defined separate geographical areas set aside by the apartheid government for African communities. The purpose was to exclude African communities from the political system in South Africa and strip them of political power.
2 Shulman (1987) introduced the concept of pedagogical content knowledge to argue for the inextricable link between what is taught and how it is taught. This was in response to the fact that teacher training often viewed the two as mutually exclusive, focusing on either the subject matter or on teaching methodologies.

References

Adam, F. (2009). *Curriculum reform in higher education: A humanities case study*. Ph.D. thesis, University of the Witwatersrand, Johannesburg, South Africa.

Alexander, N. (2001). The politics of identity in post apartheid South Africa. In J. Muller, N. Cloete, & S. Badat (Eds.), *Challenges of globalisation: South African debates with Manuel Castells*. Pinelands, Cape Town: Maskew Miller Longman.

Badat, S. (2007). *Higher education change in post-1994 South Africa: The dynamics of change and questions and issues in search of sociological inquiry*. Princeton, NJ: Princeton University, African Studies Program.

Berger, P., Berger, B., & Kellner, H. (1973). *The homeless mind: Modernization and consciousness*. Harmondsworth, UK: Penguin.

Bernstein, B. (2000). *Pedagogy, symbolic control, and identity: Theory, research, critique* (rev. ed.). Lanham, MD: Rowman and Littlefield.

Bundy, C. (2006, Winter). Global patterns, local options? Changes in higher education internationally and some implications for South Africa. *Kagisano*, No. 4, 1–20.

CHE. Council on Higher Education. (2005). *National review of master of education programs by dissertation criteria and minimum standards*. Pretoria, South Africa: Council on Higher Education.

Cloete, N. (1998, August). Paper presented at the first national conference for student services practitioners. Photocopy in our possession, courtesy of Cloete.

Cloete, N., & Bunting, I. (2000). *Higher education transformation: Assessing performance in South Africa*. Pretoria, South Africa: Center for Higher Education Transformation.

Cloete, N., & Fehnel, R. (2002). The emergent landscape. In N. Cloete, R. Fehnel, P. Maassen, T. Moja, H. Perold, & T. Gibbon (Eds.), *Transformation in higher education: Global pressures and local realities in South Africa*. Center for Higher Education Transformation. Lansdowne, Cape Town, South Africa: Juta and Co.

Cloete, N., Fehnel, R., Maassen, P., Moja, T., Perold, H., & Gibbon, T. (Eds.). (2002). *Transformation in higher education: Global pressures and local realities in South Africa*. Center for Higher Education Transformation. Lansdowne, Cape Town, South Africa: Juta and Co.

Cross, M. (1986). A historical review of education in South Africa: Toward an assessment. *Comparative Education, 22*(3), 185–200.

Cross, M., Carpentier, C., & Ait-Mehdi, H. (2009). Unfulfilled promise: Radical discourses in South African educational historiography, 1970–2007. *History of Education, 38*(4), 475–503.

Cross, M., Shalem, Y., Backhouse, J., Adam, F., & Baloyi, H. (2010). "Wits gives you the edge": How students negotiate the pressure of undergraduate study. *Access and throughput in South African higher education studies: Three case studies*. Pretoria, South Africa: Council of Higher Education. *Higher Education Monitor*, Issue 9, 54–94.

DOE. Department of Education. (1997). *Education White Paper 3: A programme for the transformation of higher education*. Pretoria, South Africa: DOE.

DOE. Department of Education. (2000). *Statement on higher education funding 2000/01 to 2001/03*. Pretoria, South Africa: DOE.

DOE. Department of Education. (2001). *Manifesto on values, education, and democracy*. Pretoria, South Africa: DOE.

DOE. Department of Education. (2002). *Revised national curriculum statement*. Pretoria, South Africa: DOE.

DOE. Department of Education. (2004). *Statement on higher education funding 2004/05 to 2006/07.* Pretoria, South Africa: DOE.

DOE. Department of Education. (2005, August). *Minimum admission requirements for higher certificate, diploma and bachelor's degree programmes requiring a national senior certificate.* Pretoria, South Africa: DOE.

DOE. Department of Education. (2009). *Education statistics in South Africa.* Pretoria, South Africa: DOE.

Enslin, P. (2003). Citizenship education in post-apartheid South Africa. *Cambridge Journal of Education, 33*(1), 73–83.

Ensor, P. (1998). Access, coherence and relevance: Debating curriculum in higher education. *Social Dynamics, 24*(2), 93–105.

Ensor, P. (2002). The South African experience: Curriculum. In N. Cloete, R. Fehnel, P. Maassen, T. Moja, H. Perold, & T. Gibbon (Eds.), *Transformation in higher education: Global pressures and local realities in South Africa* (pp. 179–193). Center for Higher Education Transformation. Lansdowne, Cape Town, South Africa: Juta and Co.

Ensor, P. (2004). Contesting discourses in higher education curriculum restructuring in South Africa. *Higher Education, 48*(3), 339–359.

Henkel, M. (2004). The impacts of evaluation on academic identities and links with managerialism. In *Managerialism and evaluation in higher education* (pp. 86–101). UNESCO Forum Occasional Papers Series, ED-2006/WS/47. *Collected papers of the First Regional Research Seminar for Europe and North America.* Paris: UNESCO.

Henkel, M. (2005). Academic identity and autonomy in a changing policy environment. *Higher Education, 49*(1–2), 155–176.

Inglesi, R., & Pouris, A. (2008). Where are our universities going? A review, twenty years later. *South African Journal of Science, 104*(9–10), 345–348.

Jansen, J. D. (1999). Why outcomes based education will fail: An elaboration. In J. D. Jansen & P. Christie (Eds.), *Changing curriculum: Studies on outcomes-based education in South Africa* (pp. 145–156). Cape Town, South Africa: Juta and Co.

Jansen, J. D. (2000). Mode 2 knowledge and institutional life: Taking Gibbons on a walk through a South African university. In A. Kraak (Ed.), *Changing modes: New knowledge production and its implications for higher education.* Pretoria, South Africa: Human Science Research Council.

Jansen, J. D. (2003). Mergers in South African higher education: Theorising change in transitional contexts. *Politikon: South African Journal of Political Studies, 30*(1), 27–51. Retrieved on January 11, 2011, from www.tandf.co.uk/journals/carfax/02589346.html.

Jansen, J. D. (2004). *Changes and continuities in South Africa's higher education system, 1994 to 2004: Changing class.* Pretoria, South Africa: Human Sciences Research Council Press.

Jansen, J. D. (2009). *Knowledge in the blood.* Palo Alto, CA: Stanford University Press.

Johnson, B. (2006). *Towards post-managerialism in higher education: The case of management change at the University of the Witwatersrand, 1999–2004.* Ph.D. thesis. Wits University, Johannesburg, South Africa.

Johnson, B., & Cross, M. (2005). Academic leadership under siege: Possibilities and limits of executive leadership. *South African Journal of Higher Education, 18*(2), 34–58.

Kishun, R. (1998). Internationalization in South Africa. In P. Scott (Ed.), *The globalization of higher education* (pp. 58–69). Buckingham, UK: Society for Research into Higher Education and Open University Press.

Kletz, F., & Pallez, F. (2002). Taking decisions on new curricula in French universities: Do disciplinary criteria still prevail? *European Journal of Education*, 37(1), 57–70.

Kraak, A. (2000). Changing modes: A brief overview of the mode 2 knowledge debate and its impact on South African policy formulation. In A. Kraak (Ed.), *Changing modes: New knowledge production and its implications for higher education* (pp. 1–37). Pretoria, South Africa: Human Science Research Council.

Kraak, A. (2001). *Policy ambiguity and slippage: Higher education under the new state, 1994–2001.* Pretoria, South Africa: Human Sciences Research Council.

Kraak, A. (2004). Discursive tensions in South African higher education, 1990–2002. *Journal of Studies in International Education*, 8(3), 244–281.

Maassen, P., & Cloete, N. (2002). Global reform trends in higher education. In N. Cloete, R. Fehnel, P. Maassen, T. Moja, H. Perold, & T. Gibbon (Eds.), *Transformation in higher education: Global pressures and local realities in South Africa* (pp. 7–33). Center for Higher Education Transformation. Lansdowne, Cape Town, South Africa: Juta and Co.

Mabizela, M., Subotsky, G., & Thaver, B. (2000). *The emergence of private higher education in South Africa: Issues and challenges.* Discussion document presented at the Council on Higher Education (CHE) Annual Consultative Conference. Pretoria, South Africa: CHE.

Mackenzie, C., & Stoljar, N. (Eds.). (2000). *Relational autonomy: Feminist perspectives on autonomy, agency, and the social self.* New York: Oxford University Press.

Moll, I. (2004). Curriculum responsiveness: The anatomy of a concept. In H. Griesel (Ed.), *Curriculum responsiveness: Case studies in higher education* (pp. 1–20). Pretoria, South Africa: South African Universities Vice Chancellors Association (SAUVCA).

Moore, R. (2003). Curriculum restructuring in South African higher education: Academic identities and policy implementation. *Studies in Higher Education*, 8(3), 303–319.

Muller, J. (2000). *Reclaiming knowledge: Social theory, curriculum, and education policy.* London: RoutledgeFalmer.

Muller, J. (2005). *The world is not enough: Responsiveness, innovation, and the limits of policy in higher education.* Paper presented at a seminar at Wits University. Johannesburg, South Africa: University of the Witwatersrand. Retrieved on January 21, 2011, from wiredspace.wits.ac.za/bitstream/handle/10539/1806/05Chapter5.pdf. Also published in (2005), *South African Journal of Higher Education*, 19(3), 497–511.

National Commission on Higher Education. (1996). *An overview of a new policy framework for higher education transformation.* Pretoria, South Africa: Council of Higher Education.

Nzimande, B. (2010, April 22). Keynote address by Minister of Higher Education and Training Dr Blade Nzimande to the Stakeholder Summit on Higher Education Transformation, Cape Peninsula University of Technology. Retrieved on January 21, 2011, from www.education.gov.za/dynamic/dynamic.aspx?pageid=306&id=9880.

Pandor, N. (2004, October 24). We cannot stand by and watch institutions collapse: Universities and technikons should not use the principle of institutional autonomy as a pretext for resisting democratic changes. *Sunday Independent.*

Pouris, A. (1991). Where are our universities going? *South African Journal of Science*, 87, 218.

Quicke, J. (1996). Self, modernity, and a direction for curriculum reform. *British Journal of Educational Studies*, 44(4), 364–376.

Shulman, L. (1987). Knowledge and teaching: Foundations of the new reform. *Harvard Educational Review, 57,* 1–22.

Sitas, A. (2010). Quoted by Alison Moodie. Initiative to strengthen the liberal arts. *University World News: South Africa.* Retrieved on February 13, 2011, from www. universityworldnews.com/article.php?story=2010102922422770.

Steyn, G., & de Villiers, P. (2006). *The impact of changing funding sources on higher education institutions in South Africa.* Pretoria, South Africa: Council on Higher Education.

9

TURKEY

Obstacles to and Examples of Curriculum Reform

Kemal Gürüz

The History of Education in Turkey

Until the late 18th century, Ottoman educational institutions consisted only of the district school and the *madrasa*. The former was a sort of primary school where instruction included reading, writing, and arithmetic, with emphasis on memorizing the Qur'an. The *madrasa* was essentially a college of Islamic law, the *sharia*.

In its rituals and outlook, the *madrasa* was similar to the medieval university of Western Europe. The critical difference, however, was in the curricular content. The academic backbone of the medieval university was the Faculty of Arts, which, in today's parlance, was the undergraduate school that prepared students for the professional schools of theology, law, and medicine at the graduate level. The undergraduate curriculum consisted of the *artes liberales*. The term *arte*, as used in this context, connotes all of the natural, social, and human sciences as we know them today. In addition, it also connotes both the fine arts and the performing arts, but also refers to practical applications of the seven courses, as in the art of doing or being skilled at something.

The connotation of *liberales* is even more important and relevant. It refers to the so-called free part of the human mind in contrast to the part related to manual or mechanical skills, collectively expressed by the term *artes mecanicae*. None of these curricular features existed in the *madrasa*.

It was only after Turkey's navy was annihilated by the Russian navy in the Aegean Sea in 1771 that the Ottomans realized the need for new types of educational institutions with curricula that included natural sciences. The result was the founding in 1773 of the Imperial Naval College, the precursor to today's İstanbul Technical University. Also, as part of the reforms in the 19th century, a university-type institution was first conceived and planned in 1846, although it was not instituted until 1901. This new tertiary-level institution was named *Darülfünun* (the House of Sciences), rather than "university" to deflect further resistance by the conservative religious reactionary scholars in the *madrasas*. Under French influence, the imperial government opened a number of tertiary-level vocational schools in the 1800s that were similar to the *grandes écoles* in a wide range of fields, including engineering, fine arts, commerce, and public administration. Medicine remained part of military education until the 1930s.

It is interesting and pertinent to the topic of this study that the *Darülfünun* in 1901 consisted of three Faculties: the Faculty of Letters and Philosophy, the Faculty of Mathematics and Natural Sciences, and the Faculty of Divinity. (I capitalize Faculty to refer to the administrative unit and lower-case it to refer to the teaching staff.) The *Darülfünun* was clearly conceived as an institution of liberal arts similar to the Faculty of Arts of the medieval university, while vocational and professional education at the tertiary level was confined to the individual schools affiliated with the various ministries in their respective fields.

On October 29, 1923, the Republic of Turkey rose from the ashes of the Ottoman Empire. Since then, the Turkish national education system has undergone a number of major structural changes at all of its levels (Barblan, Ergüder, & Gürüz, 2008; Gürüz, 2008a).

The Turkish National Education System: Primary and Secondary Levels

Compulsory basic education starts at age six and comprises the primary education stage that lasts eight years. Students who complete this primary stage have three options: apprenticeship, the general (academic) secondary track, or the vocational secondary track. Until 2008, both the academic and the vocational tracks lasted three years; but in 2008, the duration of both was increased to four years. Currently, 61% of the students at the secondary level are in the general education track (National Ministry of Education, 2009).

Secondary schools include the regular general secondary schools and schools specializing in science, social science, sports, fine arts, and teacher training. First-year students in all of these schools follow a common curriculum that includes oral and written communication, Turkish literature, religion and ethics, history, geography, mathematics, physics, chemistry, biology, hygiene, foreign languages, physical education, and guidance and counseling. The curricula in subsequent years depend on the type of school and reflect the school's specialty.

The vast majority of the students in the secondary general education track are in the regular schools. Students who complete the first common year in a regular secondary school have several options for concentrated study: natural sciences, social sciences, Turkish language and mathematics, and foreign languages. (Turkish language and mathematics as a concentration area is peculiar to the Turkish system; its putative purpose is to prepare students for tertiary-level programs like law and business administration.) Studies in subsequent years continue the area of concentration. Mathematics, physics, chemistry, and biology constitute most of the natural sciences concentration area. Similarly, oral and written communication, Turkish literature, history, and geography are the major subjects in the social sciences concentration area; oral and written communication and mathematics constitute the Turkish language–mathematics option; and oral and written communication and foreign languages form the major part of the curriculum in the foreign languages concentration area. Students also have to take elective courses, which correspond to about a quarter of the total credit requirement in each year. Information technologies, democracy and human rights, physical education, independent study, a second foreign language, and community engagement are electives common to all four options. The remaining electives must be from outside the concentration area.

Secondary vocational schools are grouped into four broad areas. The curriculum in the first year in all vocational schools is the same as that in the regular general schools, while the vocational specialization governs course-taking in subsequent years.

In summary, secondary-level curricula in Turkey include a significant amount of material that can be regarded as liberal arts. However, Turkey's traditional approach to curriculum design at the secondary level relies on the Continental European model, rather than the Anglo-Saxon model. Unfortunately, the system of admission to higher education in Turkey precludes the establishment of meaningful links between secondary- and tertiary-level curricula. More importantly, the current admission system uses multiple-choice standardized tests to evaluate subject matter knowledge rather than evaluating reasoning capabilities. This factor, combined with tracking, forces students into early specialization that, over time, has eroded the general education base even at the secondary level. Although some argue that there is no need for liberal arts education at the tertiary level because those topics are extensively covered in the secondary-level curricula, that argument is certainly no longer valid.

Higher Education in Turkey Today

In 1933, the *Darülfünun* was transformed into İstanbul University with a Continental European character in terms of governance, academic structure, and curricula. The Imperial Naval College, having undergone a number of reorganizations in its history, was restructured as İstanbul Technical University in

1944, and Ankara University was founded in 1946. These institutions, too, developed along Continental European lines (Barblan et al., 2008; Gürüz, 2008a, 2008b).

Robert College, founded in 1863, the precursor to today's Boðaziçi University, was a typical New England liberal arts college in its curriculum, but it also had a strong industrial arts program that developed into a separate School of Engineering in 1912 (Freely, 2000a, 2000b). Following a change in government in 1950, the new Democrat Party founded four new universities in 1953–1958. Two of them—Middle East Technical University (METU) and Atatürk University—were patterned after U.S. land-grant state universities, while Karadeniz Technical University was modeled after German technical universities, and Ege University drew on the Continental European model.

The Turkish higher education system expanded during the 1960s and the 1970s. Many new universities were established across the country; and when they failed to keep up with the increasing demand for access, new types of non-university institutions were founded. In 1981, a major restructuring of the system took place under the comprehensive Higher Education Law, Law No. 2547, enacted on November 6, 1981. Two key provisions are pertinent to liberal education. First, this law established the Council of Higher Education as a constitutional body charged with the planning, coordination, and governance of all higher education institutions, including private providers. Second, admission to associate- and bachelor-level programs is by a central competitive multiple-choice test prepared, administered, and proctored by the Student Selection and Placement Center (SSPC; Turkish acronym ÖSYM), which is affiliated with the Council of Higher Education.

The Council of Higher Education functions much like a national board of governors, more akin to the statewide boards in New York and California. The key difference that directly bears on matters related to curricula and degree programs stems from the system of student admissions, discussed below.

According to the statistics annually reported by the Student Selection and Placement Center, in the period 1981–2009, student enrollment in the Turkish higher education system grew by a factor of more than 10. As of October 2009, student enrollment at all levels in the system stood just below three million, with a gross enrollment ratio just over 50%. Approximately a third of the students were enrolled in distance education programs. Since 1981, these programs have been administered by the Faculty of Open Education of Anadolu University, a state university, under Council of Higher Education regulation like all other institutions and programs. The system, one of the largest in the world, comprised 102 state universities, 52 private universities, and four private two-year vocational schools not affiliated with any university. Total academic staff of all ranks numbered nearly 100,000. Despite their relatively large number, private institutions accounted for only 5% of the national enrollment (ÖSYM, 2009).

Since 1981, the basic academic unit is the department, a number of which make up each Faculty. Faculties are responsible for bachelor-level programs, while master- and doctoral-level programs are coordinated by graduate schools. In 1981, the two-year vocational schools became part of the universities. There are now more than 500 such schools, carrying out the associate-level programs in distinct vocational areas. The university senate, presided over by the rector of the university and consisting of vice rectors, deans, school directors, and elected faculty representatives, has the power to issue rules and regulations that pertain to the university as a whole, while curricula and individual course contents are normally determined at the department and the Faculty levels.

Thus, the academic structure of a typical Turkish university is more like that of a U.S. state university than that of a Continental European institution. However, in practice, the older universities—İstanbul University, İstanbul Technical University, Ankara University, and Ege University—have retained much of their previous structures.

Admissions to the Tertiary Level

As the number of applicants to Turkey's higher education system started to grow exponentially during the late 1960s and the early 1970s, the supply of places failed to keep up with demand. In 1974, the Student Selection and Placement Center (ÖSYM) was established to standardize and unify admissions. Since 1981, the Council of Higher Education has had full powers over the scope and content of the multiple-choice admission test to determine the relative contributions of secondary school performance and set the test score necessary for admission. Furthermore, the council determines the number of students to be admitted to each degree program at the bachelor and the associate levels, including those in private universities. Admission to master- and doctoral-level programs depends partly on scores obtained in a GRE-type multiple-choice test administered by the Student Selection and Placement Center, but universities have freedom in the relative weight they assign to test scores in making admission decisions.

The names of undergraduate-level programs and the number of students to be admitted to each program are controlled centrally by the Council of Higher Education. Each year, the council announces each degree program of every university at the undergraduate level and the number of students to be admitted in the coming year; it mails this information to all candidates who have registered to take the entrance exam. Close to 5,000 programs are announced every year, with more than 1.5 million applicants vying for about 40% of that number of places. There are no restrictions on the numbers of students admitted to distance education programs.

What has happened in Turkey over the past 35 years is a classical case of the collateral damage that the injudicious use of standardized tests inflicts on the lower stages of the country's education system. A private coaching and tutoring industry has developed, the revenues of which are currently estimated at billions of dollars. Students start to cut classes, especially in their senior year, to prepare for the tests in cram schools where tutoring amounts to little more than coaching in test techniques. The result has been generations of students with poor communication, reasoning, and analytical skills.

As a result of a comprehensive study in 1998, in 1999 subject matter tests were eliminated, and admission was based on the score obtained in a comprehension/reasoning test. This test examined proficiency in Turkish language, mathematics, natural sciences, social sciences, and the humanities plus secondary school performance, the contribution of which was increased in a manner that established a relationship between curricula at the two educational levels. The underlying philosophy was that students who took a broad-based test rather than narrow subject-area exams would be better prepared for the higher education curricula of the knowledge economy which is rooted in a much broader epistemic base.

The coaching and tutoring industry campaigned very effectively against these changes, and the council's subsequent administration succumbed to claims that students lacked adequate preparation in subjects. From 2006 on, subject matter tests were reintroduced, but in an abbreviated form.

This section has described how the injudicious use of standardized admission tests has adversely affected secondary education. The next section also indirectly deals with the potential negative effects on tertiary-level curriculum of the procedures governing the transition from the secondary to the tertiary levels. In brief, however, Turkey's current admissions system has had the unintended consequence of creating a culture of degree programs at the higher education level that are uniform and vocationally oriented in narrowly defined areas.

Core Curricula and Liberal Arts Education in Turkey

Historical Background

Although the Faculty of Arts was the academic backbone of the medieval university, higher education developed along different paths in the Anglo-Saxon world, particularly in the United States and in Continental Europe, both in degree structures and in curricular content and governance patterns.

Two pertinent points need to be underscored. (a) Liberal arts is at the center of modern American higher education; its importance to both professional and vocational paths was emphasized as early as the Morrill Land Grant Act of 1862. Viewed from this perspective, the modern American research university is, in fact, quite similar to the medieval university in academic organization. (b) Certainly, liberal education and core programs are offered in all institutions of higher education worldwide. However, no country outside the United States has a cohesive liberal arts education as an integral, compulsory component of curricula, even in programs that lead to highly specialized professional degrees in the regulated professional areas. It is, therefore, not unrealistic to state that liberal arts education is a uniquely American concept whose roots can be traced back to the medieval university in Europe. This view should not be interpreted as taking the position that liberal arts are culture-specific to the United States. Rather, I argue that a strong liberal arts component in undergraduate curricula is essential in meeting the job market requirements of the global knowledge economy.

Liberal Arts in Turkish Universities

According to Law No. 2547 (1981)'s Article 4, the purpose of higher education is to educate and train individuals who are responsible citizens aware of their civic duties and committed to Atatürk's republican ideals, can think independently with a broad worldview and respect for human rights, and have acquired the skills and knowledge of a profession that will enable them to sustain a happy and prosperous life. Thus, no clause in this article precludes a liberal arts education. On the contrary, phrases such as "independent thinking with a broad worldview" and "respect for human rights" (my translation) do indeed imply an education predicated upon liberal arts. However, as things have turned out, vocational and professional aspects have come to dominate the curriculum in Turkish higher education. In my opinion, this situation results from the fact that the idea of a general educational base, though almost totally eroded over time, has always existed at the secondary level, but such a philosophy of curriculum has never existed at the tertiary level. These key phrases in Article 4 therefore stem from a traditional view of higher education's nation-building role rather than a philosophy of curriculum.

From the outset, there were separate Faculties for the natural sciences and mathematics, and for the social sciences and humanities at both İstanbul University and Ankara University. These arrangements did not change even after the restructuring of 1981 and continue to the present. At İstanbul University, letters, the humanities, and social sciences are in the Faculty of Letters, while its Faculty of Sciences comprises natural sciences and mathematics. Its Faculty of Economics also includes business, and it has since added a Faculty of Business Administration and a Faculty of Political Sciences.

Ankara University has three Faculties in disciplines related to liberal arts: a Faculty of Languages, History, and Geography, a Faculty of Science, and a Faculty of Political Sciences that includes economics, management, international relations, and public administration. İstanbul Technical University (İTU) was modeled after German technical universities. Before 1981, it had a Faculty of Basic Sciences, which did not include social sciences and humanities.

In 1981, that Faculty was reorganized and renamed as Faculty of Sciences and Letters, but 15 years elapsed before departments of social sciences and humanities were established in that Faculty. In addition to separate Faculties for various engineering disciplines, İstanbul Technical University today also has a Faculty of Business Administration.

In all three of these oldest universities, first degrees in the closely regulated professional areas of law, medicine, pharmacy, dental medicine, veterinary medicine, engineering, architecture, and agriculture were at the bachelor level in the European tradition—still the case in all universities throughout the country today.

Thus, courses that form part of a liberal arts education were offered in all of the three universities, but they did not constitute a coherent liberal arts core program. In contrast, all three had a sort of coherent core program in the natural sciences and mathematics. The first year was devoted to physics, chemistry, biology, and mathematics for students in technical fields and health sciences; this program did not include a social sciences and humanities component. The programs offering degrees in economics, law, and business likewise did not offer a core program in the social sciences and humanities areas. This continues to be the case throughout the country today, except for the cases I describe below.

The case of Robert College is an interesting experiment in liberal arts education in Turkey. Its 1878–1879 catalogue stated its mission as "to give its students, without distinction of race and religion, a thorough education equal in all respects to that obtained at a first class American college and based upon the same principles." In 1864, Robert College was granted a charter by the Board of Regents in the State of New York to confer the bachelor of arts degree and was included in the state's list of educational institutions. The curriculum was similar to that of other American colleges. The medium of instruction was English. Other languages—including French, Turkish, Latin, Armenian, Greek, and Bulgarian—were also taught. The curriculum eventually included philosophy, theology, mathematics, science, history, engineering, commerce, and law, as well as ancient and modern languages; and from the sophomore year on, it was divided into an arts and a science option leading to a bachelor of arts and a bachelor of science degree. The college included a preparatory division, whose purpose was to bring the incoming students up to the level of an American college freshman. In retrospect, Robert College may fairly be described in those years as an institution that was at an intermediate educational level between a prep school and a liberal arts college. However, many prestigious U.S. institutions accepted the Robert College degree as equivalent to an American B.A. degree.

The college became more of a tertiary-level institution with the addition of an engineering program in 1912. The engineering school was initially intended to be at the graduate level, accepting students after their sophomore year.

Interestingly, older members of the Faculty resisted the engineering school because the manual labor required of engineering students did not conform to the genteel tradition associated with scholarship. This attitude was reminiscent of the inferior status ascribed to mechanical arts, in contrast to liberal arts, in medieval Europe (Freely, 2000a, p. 182). Thus, after 1912, Robert College comprised the College of Arts and Sciences and the Engineering School. To my knowledge, this was the first time the term "arts and sciences" was used in Turkey as the name of an academic unit.

The status of Robert College—whether it was a prep school, an institution of higher education, or both—was resolved in 1957, when Turkish authorities granted permission to establish a "higher section" of the college in addition to its secondary level schools. This "higher section" consisted of the School of Engineering, the School of Business Administration and Economics, and the School of Languages and Sciences. Although social sciences, the humanities, and natural sciences were in different schools, Robert College was able to offer a coherent, two-year liberal arts core program. This bilingual, bicultural humanities program was compulsory for all students, including engineering students. Designed by a group of distinguished scholars in both Western and Islamic humanities, it provided a survey of both Western and Islamic (primarily Turkish) culture, with half of the lectures and seminars in Turkish and half in English (Freely, 2000b, p. 117). Humanities 101, offered in the freshman year, and the various history courses formed the backbone of the program.

Students were admitted to the three schools, not to the individual programs offered by the separate schools. At the end of the two-year core program, however, they were allowed to change programs and schools, largely because, in those years the college was small and compact. As the institution grew in size after it was transformed into Boðaziçi University in 1971, a state institution, that core program started to wane (Ergüder, 2009; Freely, 2000b, pp. 124–125).

Obviously, Robert College, by and large, did not serve as a model for Turkish higher education, but its liberal arts tradition has recently been carried over to two new private universities, Koç University and Sabancí University, whose founders and initial faculty members had close affiliations with Robert College and Boðaziçi University.

Middle East Technical University (METU), founded in 1956, was the first campus university with an integrated academic structure modeled after U.S. state universities. English was the language of instruction, and it was governed by a lay board of trustees, with nearly complete autonomy in administrative, financial, and academic matters. The university comprised an English Language Preparatory School, a Faculty of Engineering, a Faculty of Architecture, a Faculty of Administrative Sciences, and, last but not least, a Faculty of Arts and Sciences. (Interestingly, this Faculty was listed as the "Faculty of Arts and Sciences" in university catalogues published in English but as the "Faculty of

Sciences and Letters" in Turkish. I see the latter term as something of a misnomer for the Faculty designated as the academic backbone of the university. "Letters" was meant to include the humanities and social sciences, while "Sciences" meant natural sciences and mathematics.) Still, this was the first time in Turkey that natural sciences, the social sciences, and the humanities were all in one Faculty. Oddly enough, the departments of economics, political science, and statistics were in the Faculty of Administrative Sciences, not in the Faculty of Arts and Sciences.

Another curricular novelty introduced by Middle East Technical University was the requirement that students in technical fields take four non-technical electives and that students in the social sciences and humanities take four technical electives—approximately 10–15% of the credits required for graduation. However, other than the common core program of basic natural sciences and mathematics courses in the first year of engineering curricula, there was no liberal arts core program even at Middle East Technical University.

The Faculty, comprising various chairs, was the basic unit of academic organization in the older Turkish universities. The basic academic unit at Middle East Technical University was the department, and it was this academic structure that served as a template during the 1981 reorganization. The Faculty structure of the older universities was left intact, while a Faculty of Sciences and Letters was established in the younger institutions. The 1981 regulations required that private institutions seeking the title of "university" have programs in the arts and sciences.

Although the reorganization of 1981 clearly intended to transform the Turkish higher education system to more closely resemble its American counterpart, the Faculty rather than the department continued to be the main academic administrative unit of Turkish universities. Currently, Faculties offer bachelor-level programs through their various departments, covering the whole spectrum from medicine, law, and theology, to pharmacy, dentistry, engineering, architecture, economics, business, public administration, political science, the fine arts, industrial arts, communication and journalism, education and teacher training, agriculture, veterinary medicine, and fisheries. Some Faculties also offer bachelor-level programs in basic natural and social sciences and the humanities in addition to offering courses to students enrolled in other Faculties. Faculties also offer degree programs in economics, business, political science, public administration, and international relations; such educational units are generally named the "Faculty of Economic and Administrative Sciences." These are the basic academic units in the Turkish higher education system, the subject matter of which is closely related to the liberal arts.

Table 9.1 displays the numbers of students enrolled in bachelor-level programs carried out in these Faculties in the 2007–2008 academic year, according to the International Standard Classification of Education.

TABLE 9.1 Student enrollment in 2007–2008 by bachelor degree programs

Program	Enrollment (%)
Education	14.9
Humanities	4.6
The arts (fine arts, performing arts, etc.)	1.5
Social and behavioral sciences	23.8
Mass communication and mass media	1.4
Business and management	27.0
Law	1.4
Life sciences	1.3
Physical sciences	3.5
Mathematics and statistics	2.1
Computer sciences	1.1
Engineering	3.9
Production and production processing	2.3
Architecture and construction	2.2
Agriculture, forestry, and fisheries	1.8
Veterinary medicine	0.5
Health (medicine, dentistry, pharmacy, nursing)	4.8
Social services	0.3
Services	1.6

Source: Student Selection and Placement Center (ÖSYM, 2008).

As these figures show, close to 40% of the students in bachelor-level programs are in liberal arts fields: e.g., the humanities, arts, social and behavioral sciences, physical sciences, life sciences, and mathematics. If education and management fields are also even partly included in this list, the liberal arts fraction moves up to well over half of all bachelor-level enrollments. Yet except for the few programs that I discuss in the next sub-section, there are no liberal arts programs in Turkey, nor are there coherent core programs outside the medical and the engineering fields, which as already noted, cover only the natural sciences and mathematics.

According to my analysis, three factors have led to Turkey's current undergraduate curricula. First, all first degrees in professional fields such as law, medicine, engineering, and architecture are offered at the bachelor's level. Thus, there are no prospects for entering a vocational field after taking a liberal arts degree or core program—with two exceptions. MBA programs are normally open to anyone with a bachelor's degree. Also, master's programs that lead to teaching certificates in secondary school subjects are likewise open to those with a bachelor's degree. (These programs began in 1998. Unfortunately, they are now being replaced by teaching certificate programs that comprise a few courses in pedagogy, which candidates can take while they are pursuing undergraduate degrees in other fields.)

Second, the concept of specializing in a major and a minor after a liberal arts core program is not part of Turkish higher education. Third, students are admitted to narrowly defined individual programs at the undergraduate level, each conducted by its own department. The result has been a very high degree of compartmentalization, accompanied by very weak curricular relations between departments, even within a given Faculty—and naturally such relationships are even weaker between departments in different Faculties.

For example, programs in medicine, dentistry, pharmacy, and law are carried out in their respective Faculties independent of departments, and students are admitted to these Faculties as a whole rather than to individual departments. Even in those cases, the basic science courses in the earlier years of these programs are generally taught by members of those particular Faculties rather than being offered by the respective departments in Faculties of Letters and Sciences. Thus, organic curricular relations among the various Faculties of the older universities in urban settings where such programs are concentrated are even weaker compared to the younger campus universities. The central Student Selection and Placement Test has thus inflicted collateral damage on upper educational levels in addition to its negative effects on lower educational levels.

From the mid-1990s on, a competitive environment developed in Turkish higher education, accompanying the increase in the number of private universities and the increased pace of globalization. Competition for students manifested itself in two opposite ways. Bilkent University, the oldest private institution in the country, founded in 1986, launched an immediate campaign to attract the largest possible number of students who ranked high in the central admission examination. Since the top students generally preferred bachelor-level programs that had the highest potential for producing future income, all of the leading institutions in the country started promoting their "brand-name" departments/programs. This development further intensified the compartmentalization of departments and Faculties and the fragmentation of curricula within individual universities.

Law No. 2547 stipulates a small number of compulsory courses, such as Turkish language and the history of the Turkish Republic; they may be taken as either credit or noncredit courses, depending on the preference of the institutions. With these exceptions, individual universities presently have full autonomy in determining curricula and course contents. Despite this freedom, there have been relatively few curricular innovations in bachelor-level programs in state universities. In contrast, a number of private universities have made use of this freedom to introduce core programs with significant liberal arts content and broad-based degree-programs.

Another innovation beginning in the mid-1990s was increased attention to academic evaluation and assessment, which had generally received little attention in university governance. Starting with the two state universities in which

English was the medium of instruction—Middle East Technical University and Boðaziçi University, and a third university, İstanbul Technical University—Turkish universities started outsourcing assessment to institutions abroad. Since then, many universities have undergone evaluation by the Conference of Rectors of European Universities (and its successor, the European University Association), and the U.S.-based Accreditation Board for Engineering and Technology (ABET).

In 2000, Turkey joined the Bologna Process at the Prague Ministerial Meeting, and quality assurance activities have since received new emphasis. One positive effect has been the systematic inclusion of liberal arts courses in engineering curricula as part of the Accreditation Board for Engineering and Technology requirements.

Examples of Liberal Arts Content

Sabancí University

Sabancí University was founded in 1996 and admitted its first group of students in the 1999–2000 academic year. In 2007–2008, the total enrollment was 2,934 students at bachelor-level programs, 381 students in master's programs, and 135 students seeking doctoral degrees. The university employed 43 full professors, 36 associate professors, 92 assistant professors, and 108 instructors, lecturers, and research assistants (ÖSYM, 2008).

Faculties in Sabancí University do not have a departmental structure. Students are admitted to one of the following three broad program groups: engineering and natural sciences, arts and social sciences, and economics and administrative sciences. All freshmen and sophomores are required to follow a compulsory core liberal arts program that includes basic courses in mathematics and natural sciences, social sciences, the humanities, and history, known collectively as the "university courses." Students in the social sciences areas, for example, do not have lighter mathematics and natural sciences loads, or vice versa. The total credits of the common core program correspond to roughly 40% of the degree requirements.

Required undergraduate university courses provide one of the foundations of the university's unique curriculum design (Sabancí University, 2009). These courses are devised with an interdisciplinary approach that seeks to establish correlations between the natural sciences and social science as well as correlations for the fields within these areas. These university courses have three goals: (a) to provide students with innovative and in-depth perspectives of the world, their country, their society, and themselves; (b) to equip students not only with fundamental knowledge but also with the tools of independent and critical thinking; and (c) to facilitate an informed and mature decision-making process for the choice of a major and career field.

In the first two semesters of their first year, students take six courses: (a) "Humanity and Society" (examples of free thought in world history); (b) "Principles of Atatürk and the History of the Turkish Revolution" (the bridge between the Ottoman and Turkish societies and the establishment of modern Turkey); (c) the language of 19th- and 20th-century Ottoman and Turkish literary texts; (d) "Science and Nature" (depicting physics, chemistry, and biology in a holistic frame); (e) "Mathematics" (an introduction to the culture of numbers and numerical thinking); and (f) English (enhancing communication, critical thinking, public speaking, and writing skills).

The first year of the liberal arts core program also includes "civic involvement projects." In the second year, a course on "major works" focuses on culturally significant Western and Ottoman art, culture, music, literature, and drama. The core program extends into the third year with a two-semester course on law and ethics, which examines these concepts in a modern society.

The goals of the "civic involvement projects" are to foster an awareness of the individual's role in society by encouraging involvement in civic and community organizations through a platform for participatory democracy and to broaden individuals' social and cultural perspective through such involvement while at the same time providing hands-on learning for basic managerial and team skills. All students work in teams on a project of their choosing that typically focuses on a topic such as environmental issues, child education, the elderly, women's issues, basic human rights, and health concerns, among others.

At the beginning of their first year, students provisionally indicate the specific degree program in which they eventually want to enroll. In their second year, students start taking courses in that program area, in consultation with their academic advisors. This process helps them to finalize the decision concerning their final program, which is made before the start of the junior year. At this stage, students are not bound by their freshman preference. Furthermore, it is even possible to switch from one broad program area to another.

Currently, the following bachelor-level programs are offered in three broad areas: (a) Engineering and the Natural Sciences: computer sciences and engineering, biological sciences and bioengineering, electronics, materials science and engineering, mechatronics, microelectronics, telecommunications, and production systems; (b) Arts and Social Sciences: social and political science, visual arts and visual communication design, and cultural studies; and (c) Economics and Administrative Sciences.

These degree programs are significantly different both in name and curricular content from programs that are normally offered in other Turkish universities. In this respect, the curricular pattern and the degree structure in Sabanci University come closest to the American pattern of choosing a major after completing a liberal arts core program.

Koç University

Koç University is a private university founded in 1993. In the 2007–2008 academic year, it enrolled 3,437 undergraduates, 364 master's candidates, and 30 doctoral-level students. The university employed 41 full professors, 26 associate professors, 64 assistant professors, and 137 instructors, lecturers, and research assistants (ÖSYM, 2008).

The university admits students to degree programs rather than to broad program areas. However, all bachelor's programs have the same curriculum structure: a liberal arts core program, area courses, and elective courses. All students are required to take a selection of courses from a common core program. The basic philosophy underlying the core program is that every Koç graduate must possess not just the depth of education that results from being trained in a particular academic discipline, but also a breadth of knowledge. The core program has been recently revised to give students the option of choosing courses in certain categories of the core. Thus, while students are required to take certain courses regardless of their majors, they are also able to choose courses from the core depending on their interests. Currently, the core curriculum with the requirements listed below applies to all freshmen.

Communication. These courses provide students, who are expected to be proficient in both Turkish and English, with the electronic and verbal means and skills for understanding modern oral, written, and computer-based communication.

The Humanities and Social Sciences. These courses enable the students to understand the modern world by presenting the cultures and events that have shaped our present societies. Basic concepts and methods of studying societies deal with the global context in general and Turkey in particular. Philosophical and literary works provide a comparative perspective on universal human issues. Humanities and social sciences core courses are organized in three groups: "Social and Cultural Studies and Human Behavior," "Historical Studies," and "Literature and Thought."

The Natural Sciences and Mathematics. These courses provide students with quantitative reasoning, general understanding of the natural world, and the foundations of sciences. They are offered in two groups: "Quantitative Reasoning: Mathematics," and "The Natural World: Science" (Koç University, 2009).

Bilkent University

In the 2007–2008 academic year, student enrollment at Bilkent included 12,079 undergraduates, 769 master's candidates, and 429 doctoral-level students. The university employed 98 full, 55 associate, and 189 assistant professors, and 1,048 instructors and lecturers (ÖSYM, 2008). As of October 2009,

Bilkent was the only university in Turkey to have received full accreditation from the Accreditation Board for Engineering and Technology (ABET) and the Association to Advance Collegiate Schools of Business for one or more of its programs.

According to information kindly provided by Professor Ali Doğramací, former Rector of Bilkent University, the university admits students to individual degree programs rather than to broad program areas but allows them the possibility of changing programs later. Each department has compulsory courses as well as electives. Liberal arts core requirements of Bilkent vary across Faculties and departments, and are implemented through the Faculty of Humanities and Letters. English language and literature are compulsory for all students.

The compulsory courses for students majoring in engineering, business, psychology, communication and design, English literature, and American culture and literature, include two courses in the humanities. These two courses aim to prepare students for a life of intellectual exploration and expression through reading the works of major thinkers and discussing challenging questions.

The first of these courses is readings on civilization, based on essential texts beginning with classics like *Gilgamesh* and *The Iliad* and coming up to modern works like Freud's *Civilization and Its Discontents*. The second course is an overview of modern thought based on readings in the Western tradition that helped shape the modern world by posing basic ethical, political, social, economic, religious, scientific, and technological questions that remain relevant today. Examples are Machiavelli, Shakespeare, Descartes, Pascal, Nietzsche, Marx, Dostoevsky, Kafka, Woolf, and such modern works as Koestler's *The Sleepwalkers*, and Friedman's *Hot, Flat, and Crowded*.

Students in the Faculty of Science and in the Faculty of Engineering additionally must take a minimum of two three-credit nontechnical electives from a wide range of offerings. Students majoring in law, education, political science, and international relations are required to take two courses in philosophy and two advanced courses in English language and literature. The two courses in social and political philosophy are also based on required readings of some of the same authors as the courses described above, but also including works by Aristotle, Aquinas, Augustine, Cicero, Plato, and Thucydides, while the second philosophy course expands the earlier reading list to include, for example, Bentham and Mill, Hobbes, Hume, Kant, Locke, Rousseau, and Mary Wollstonecraft. The two advanced language courses are taught in conjunction with the two courses in philosophy and aim to reinforce and develop students' academic English skills beyond the level reached in the freshman year.

The core liberal arts program at Bilkent for students majoring in natural sciences also includes two courses: "The Mediterranean World to 1600" and "The Mediterranean World and Beyond from 1600 to the Present." The first course begins with Fernand Braudel's general vision of the Mediterranean world; from there, both courses rely on chronology to organize information, establish causal relationships, and create thematic arrangements that include interpretation.

Students majoring in other areas are required to take courses in the history of civilization as part of their core liberal arts requirements at Bilkent. The courses again emphasize reading original texts in English translation from various historic periods and attempting to understand these documents within their historical contexts. The chronological divisions are: ancient, classical, and medieval periods (up to AD 1500) and the modern period (from AD 1500 to the present). The courses seek to develop students' written and oral critical thinking and analytical skills, in addition to giving them basic familiarity with these historical periods.

Programs Evaluated by ABET

Beginning in the mid-1990s, Middle East Technical University, İstanbul Technical University, Boðaziçi, and Bilkent universities had their engineering programs evaluated by the U.S.-based Accreditation Board for Engineering and Technology (ABET). ABET uses nine criteria: students, educational objectives, outcomes, continuous improvement, curriculum, faculty, facilities, support, and other program-specific criteria. According to Criterion 3, "Program Outcomes," engineering programs must demonstrate that their students attain competency in a number of outcomes, six of them in the liberal arts. ABET's Criterion 5 specifies "a general education component that complements the technical content of the curriculum and is consistent with the program and institution objectives" (ABET, 2009).

Between 1994 and 2006, ABET evaluated three engineering programs at Bilkent, six at Boðaziçi University, 21 at İstanbul Technical University, and 13 at Middle East Technical University and awarded them "substantial equivalency." This status means that the program is comparable in educational outcomes but may differ in format or method of delivery. Substantial equivalency is not accreditation, nor is it binding on colleges, universities, employers, or licensing agencies. ABET no longer conducts such evaluations; but İstanbul Technical University's architecture program has been evaluated by the U.S.-based National Architectural Accreditation Board, and its urban planning programs have been evaluated by the U.S.-based Planning Accreditation Board.

Middle East Technical University and Boðaziçi had little difficulty in meeting the general education components of ABET criteria because of their tradition of requiring students of engineering to take nontechnical electives, and neither did Bilkent University. İstanbul Technical University, however, deserves special attention (İTU, 2004). While the individual engineering programs at Middle East Technical University and Boðaziçi are organized as departments within the Faculty of Engineering, İstanbul Technical University is organized in the form of Faculties that represent the various engineering disciplines, with a separate Faculty of Architecture. Its traditional structure remained more or less intact after the reorganization of 1981.

İstanbul Technical University's history is distinguished by the fact that it was founded in the hope of revitalizing a declining empire. For many years, it was the only technical higher education institute in the country. Indeed, İstanbul Technical University literally built today's modern Turkey from scratch in terms of roads, dams, buildings, airports, telecommunication and energy infrastructure, and factories. But in its own way, the university as an institution became captive to its glittering past accomplishments, which hindered efforts to reform curricula.

This situation started to change with the appointment of Professor Gülsün Sağlamer, a reformist-minded rector of İstanbul Technical University (1996–2004) and the first woman to hold that position in the institution's more than 237-year history. According to information provided by Professor Sağlamer in March to April 2009, from the outset, it was apparent that running education and administration in multiple engineering Faculties resulted in severe compartmentalization. Departments were generally isolated units, lacking interdisciplinarity. To overcome this basic problem, curricula were radically revised across the institution by distributing credit hours among four main course groups: (a) a minimum of 25% of courses in mathematics and basic sciences; (b) a minimum 20% in engineering fundamentals; (c) another minimum 20% in humanities and social sciences courses; and (d) the remaining 25–35% in discipline-specific engineering design courses.

It was also during this period that departments in social sciences and humanities were established for the first time in the institution's history. Compulsory courses in the humanities and social sciences group include Turkish history, Turkish language, and English. Each program must offer one course in either economics or law. Other electives include foreign languages, linguistics, history, psychology, sociology, philosophy, anthropology, literature, political science, management, fine arts, and the history of science and technology.

Conclusions and Recommendations

In the previous section, I have outlined the liberal arts content in the curricula of three private and three state universities. Boðaziçi University, Middle East Technical University, and İstanbul Technical University are arguably the most prestigious institutions in the country as measured by student demand and the international reputation of their alumni. Both Boðaziçi University and Middle East Technical University have strong U.S. connections; the former began as a typical American liberal arts college, and the latter was modeled after U.S. land-grant universities. However, the liberal arts content of these two institutions' curricula diminished over time.

The case of İstanbul Technical University, on the other hand, shows how discipline-specific evaluations by the Accreditation Board for Engineering and Technology, the National Architectural Accreditation Board, and the Planning Accreditation Board and institutional evaluations by organizations outside the country such as the European University Association can be successfully used as agents of change to achieve radical curricular reforms that might otherwise have been difficult, if not impossible, in a conservative engineering school that has achieved so much in the past.

Sabancí University is unlike Koç and Bilkent in providing bachelor-level students with the opportunity to select an area of specialization based on their experience of completing a common liberal arts core program. Koç and Bilkent, on the other hand, admit students to individual degree programs, rather than to broad program areas. Koç has a common liberal arts core program for all disciplines offered in the university, with some options for students in different degree programs. Although Bilkent University has no common liberal arts core program, all bachelor's programs have significant liberal arts content.

Put in a historical perspective, the current Bilkent approach to liberal arts core curriculum seems to have been inspired by the Columbia General Education Program (1919–1936) and the Great Books and Chicago Plan (1930) (Lucas, 1994, pp. 213–219). In contrast, the approaches of Sabancí and Koç universities are similar to the current Harvard practice dating back to the Redbook Report of 1945: *General Education in a Free Society* (Lucas, 1994, pp. 250–251).

Aside from these six cases, the curricula of degree programs in technical fields have very little humanities and social sciences content, and those in social sciences and humanities fields have little, if any, natural sciences and mathematics content. A very high degree of compartmentalization and curricular conservatism persists across the country. Many academics attribute this circumstance to the reorganization of 1981 and the presence of a central board of governors—the Council of Higher Education. However, the only requirements that the Higher Education Law (Law No. 2547) imposes on university teaching and learning are the compulsory courses in the Turkish language and "Principles of Atatürk and the History of the Turkish Revolution," which may be offered as credit or noncredit courses at the discretion of each institution.

In the early stages of implementing this law, the Council of Higher Education specified the names of degree programs and also a very high percentage of course names. Even then, the content of the individual courses was determined so completely by the faculty members who taught them that many considered even the discussion of course contents in departmental meetings as an infringement on academic freedom. By about the mid-1980s, the Council of Higher Education's central control essentially became restricted to the names of degree programs and determining the annual undergraduate intake to each program. Thus, curriculum design today lies effectively within the authority of the individual universities, and nothing prevents them from introducing curricular innovation.

How they would undertake such measures depends on the structure and the traditions of the individual university. Older institutions with Continental European traditions see curricular alterations as the prerogative of the faculty and the central administration levels, while American-style universities like Middle East Technical University, Boðaziçi University, and the new private universities assign curriculum change to individual departmental councils made up of faculty members. Paradoxically, while central control on curriculum has relaxed over time, individual faculty members have become much more conservative. Many consider the courses they teach as their personal academic fiefdoms and resist any curricular change that may potentially decrease the weight of those courses in degree programs. In a governance system in which rectors and deans are effectively elected by faculty members on a one-person-one-vote basis, curricular conservatism by faculty members weighs heavily with university administrators. As a result, curricular innovation is currently possible only in American-style institutions, new private institutions with lay boards and appointed rectors, and, exceptionally, in the case of İstanbul Technical University, where Professor Sağlamer displayed remarkable leadership as rector (1996–2004).

The second factor that deters curricular innovation in Turkish universities is the lack of a national vocational qualifications framework and post-degree professional certification by professional bodies. For example, the curricular changes in engineering programs at Middle East Technical University, İstanbul Technical University, Boðaziçi University, and Bilkent University were prompted by the Accreditation Board for Engineering and Technology's evaluative activities between 1994 and 2006, rather than emerging from within academia.

The teaching-related outputs of national systems of higher education are difficult to measure. However, recent data from the Organization for Economic Cooperation and Development (OECD) makes it possible to analyze the relevance of higher education in general to the job market. The transition from education to work is a complex process, which depends not only on the length of the degree program, its curriculum, and the quality of teaching, but also on the general labor market and economic conditions in a given country—and now, given the forces of globalization, increasingly in the world. With this caveat, cross-country comparisons of the percentages of the cohort ages 20 to 24 and those ages 25 to 29 who have completed a tertiary-level degree and are seeking employment give an idea, however indirect, about the relevance of tertiary-level education to employment. The OECD collected data from 19 countries in 2006 about the 20–24-age cohort who had degrees but were unemployed. The all-country average was 8.2%. Australia led the ratings with only 3.0% of its degree-holding cohort in the job market unemployed followed by the United States with 3.9%. Turkey's position was 17th with 20.0% of its degree-holders in the job market but unemployed. For comparison purposes, its geographic neighbors showed a similar profile: 9.2 for Italy, 13.0 for Portugal, 21.4 for Greece, and 25.0 for Slovenia (OECD, 2008, Table C4.3; values of Turkey are for 2005 from OECD, 2007, Table C.4.3).

For the cohort age 25–29, based on data collected in 2006, the United States (1.9%) and Australia (2.0%) still had the lowest rates of unemployed university graduates. Turkey was 25th out of 26 nations, with 11.8% of this cohort of its degree-holding population unemployed. In this case, Greece's was 13.4, Italy's was 11.0%, Portugal's was 8.5, the OECD average was 8.2%, and Slovenia's was 8.1% (OECD, 2007, Table C4.3, pp. 337–338). Clearly, far higher percentages of Turks ages 20–24 and 25–29 with tertiary qualifications are unemployed than in the corresponding average OECD cohort.

The United States is obviously performing well, with the lowest unemployment percentages among those holding tertiary degrees in both age cohorts. It would be unrealistic to ascribe future employment to a single cause. I am, however, convinced that the typical U.S. pattern of pursuing a liberal arts core program, followed by specialization in a major and minor, which in turn is followed by an advanced professional degree, is best suited to the market requirements of the global knowledge economy, especially the service sub-sector. The flexibility of the American system prepares students for a labor market in which certain jobs and professional/vocational areas are becoming obsolete while new ones are being created by new technologies.

Two other characteristics of today's labor market are (a) its globalization, which extends to the whole world without requiring worker migration, and (b) the significant overlap in agricultural, industrial, and service areas. All of these features require curricula with a much broader epistemic base than in the past. For this reason, many countries in their efforts to reform their higher education systems are emulating the American model (Theil, 2008), and students in the international higher education market are demanding an Anglo-Saxon type of higher education, especially its American variant, delivered in the English language (Gürüz, 2008b). In my opinion, this trend is being hastened by the Bologna Process, which I see as a subtle attempt by European politicians to make changes which they could not accomplish by legislation with the goal of making their higher education systems more like the British–American system. Such an achievement will, in turn, enable them to compete more successfully for young minds and academic resources globally. Anne Corbett (2005) has referred to this possibility as the Bologna Process's "hidden Anglo-Saxon agenda" (pp. 195–196). The Bologna Conference of 1999 was preceded by the Paris Conference, convened in 1998 by the French minister of education Claude Allégre, with the British, Italian, and German ministers of education in attendance. In a statement to The Economist in 1997, Allégre had expressed his admiration for the American higher education system: "It was a pity that France had never succeeded in creating a Massachusetts Institute of Technology (MIT) or a Caltech" (quoted in "A Survey of Universities," 1997, p. 5). I believe that this statement by Allégre supports Corbett's view.

My recommendations for curricular reform in Turkey are also based on extensive exploration of the advantages of the American variant of the Anglo-Saxon system. The statistics I have presented on Turkish higher education show that most of the students enrolled in bachelor's programs are in business, economics, administrative sciences, social sciences, the humanities, the natural sciences, mathematics, and education. These are also the fields whose graduates encounter serious employment problems compared to those of engineering, law, and medicine. At the center of my proposals is a new Faculty of Basic and Applied Sciences that will comprise the various departments currently located within the Faculty of Sciences and Letters, and parts of the departments of political science and international relations currently located within the Faculty of Administrative Sciences.

I recommend keeping the first professional degrees in engineering, architecture, and medicine at the bachelor's level (the current arrangement) but I also recommend elevating the first professional degrees in law, teacher training for all levels, business administration, public administration, and diplomacy to the graduate level. Teacher training and law are crucial to sustaining a modern society. Teachers must first master the subject matter and then learn how to teach it effectively. Properly trained lawyers must have a broad worldview, an understanding of human nature, and a certain level of maturity, which can be achieved only by broad-based education spread over years.

I believe that the name "Faculty of Sciences and Letters," as it is commonly used in Turkey, is a misnomer that leads to a narrow interpretation of that Faculty's mission. Many in academia regard this Faculty as responsible only for basic science fields. I believe that this limited view arises from an incorrect interpretation of "art" carried over from the Faculty of Arts of the medieval university. A more useful definition includes all of the basic sciences and their applications as well as the fine arts. Such a usage also connotes acquiring skills by observation and by the application of basic knowledge for useful purposes, as in the art of doing something that is practical and useful, e.g., applying mathematics to banking and trade, or the history and the international relations of a country or region to doing business there. In support of my argument, I note that the etymology of "science" is *scientia*, from the Latin *scire* that means "to know." In the medieval period, the concept of science did not exist nor was it clearly defined. Prudence (*prudentia*) meant a judicious choice of means to meet needs based on preparation and foresight; wisdom (*sapienza*), encyclopedia (from the Greek *enkyklios*—general—and *paidea*—education), and *philosophia* (philosophy and history) were used interchangeably to evoke the meanings that we currently attach to "science." For centuries, "moral philosophy" meant the natural sciences and humanities; "natural philosophy" meant today's natural sciences. The title "doctor of philosophy" stems from the same roots.

The Faculty of Basic and Applied Sciences that I propose should, in general, comprise the following departments: mathematics, physics, chemistry, biology and life sciences, earth sciences, geography, computer sciences and informatics, statistics, sociology, philosophy, psychology, anthropology, history, art history, foreign languages and linguistics, economics, political science, and international relations. The degree structure should be based on a common liberal arts core curriculum, followed by the student's selection of a major and a minor. Major–minor combinations made up of different fields, such as economics and mathematics, should be encouraged. Upon completion of their studies, students should be awarded the bachelor of arts or the bachelor of science degree, depending on their major–minor combinations. My first recommendation to the Council of Higher Education would be to go no further than this point to avoid being regarded as prescriptive and to encourage individual universities to implement various means of faculty member participation in curriculum design and innovation. My second recommendation would be to provide more authority to departmental councils rather than to university senates and faculty councils in designing and implementing curricula and degree programs.

I strongly believe that such bachelor-level degrees from a Faculty of Basic and Applied Sciences will provide much better opportunities for Turkish degree-holders in the labor market of the global knowledge economy and also facilitate their entry into graduate-level programs that lead to first professional degrees in law, teaching, management, and public administration. It should also be possible for holders of bachelor of science degrees with the appropriate major–minor combinations to transfer to engineering, architecture, and medicine programs.

Except for the cases I have described, Turkey has no structured public discourse—either at the government level, by the Council of Higher Education, or at individual universities—about introducing a general education/liberal arts core curriculum to individual programs. The concept is completely alien, not only to the public at large, but also to the vast majority of academics. However, the issue reached the media in 2009 when the Council of Higher Education tried to prevent Sabancí University from allowing its students to switch their tentatively chosen programs after completing the required core curriculum. The university's influential benefactor, Sabancí Holding, resisted this dictum and took the university's case all the way up to the president of the republic. The council had no alternative but to relent. However, the media coverage and ensuing public debate did not deal with fundamental weaknesses of the undergraduate curriculum in Turkey and the resulting need for a liberal arts core program. Instead it focused on whether it was just to allow fee-paying students at a private university to change programs after admission.

In 1981, Turkish higher education was radically restructured, moving away from the Continental European model to a structure similar to that of statewide systems in the United States as in California and New York. The restructuring, however, was limited to the governance and reorganization of academic units. It was not accompanied by any curricular reform in state universities.

I conclude: Turkish higher education is in dire need of reforming its admission system, its curricular patterns, and its degree structure. Bold actions are urgently needed in the right directions.

References

ABET. Accreditation Board for Engineering and Technology. (2009). Retrieved in March to April 2009, from www.abet.org/Linked%20Documents-UPDATE/Criteria%20and%20PP/E001%2009-10%20EAC%20Criteria%2012-01-2008.pdf.

Barblan, A., Ergüder, Ü., & Gürüz, K. (2008). *Higher education in Turkey: Institutional autonomy and responsibility in a modernizing society—Policy recommendations in a historical perspective.* Observatory for Fundamental University Values and Rights. Bologna: Bononia University Press.

Corbett, A. (2005). *Universities and the Europe of knowledge.* Houndmills, UK: Palgrave Macmillan.

Ergüder, Ü. (2009, May 4). Some thoughts on universities and institutional autonomy. *Radikal.*

Freely, J. (2000a). *A history of Robert College* (Vol. 1). İstanbul: Yapý Kredi Yayýnlarý 1352.

Freely, J. (2000b). *A history of Robert College* (Vol. 2). İstanbul: Yapý Kredi Yayýnlarý 1353.

Gürüz, K. (2008a). *The Turkish national education system at the beginning of the 21st century: Historical perspective, international comparisons, fundamental problems and proposals.* İstanbul: Türkiye ÝÞ Bankasý Kültür Yayýnlarý. (In Turkish.)

Gürüz, K. (2008b). *Higher education and international student mobility in the global knowledge economy.* Albany, NY: SUNY Press.

Koç University. (2009). Retrieved in April 2009, from http://ais.ku.edu.tr/KUAIS/listCW.asp. Details provided by private correspondence with Professor Ersin Yurtsever, Dean of the Faculty of Letters and Sciences, Koç University.

İTU. İstanbul Technical University. (2004, February). *Self-evaluation report Ýstanbul Technical University: European University Association Institutional Evaluation Program.* İstanbul: İTU.

Lucas, C. J. (1994). *American higher education: A history.* New York: St Martin's Griffin.

OECD. Organization for Economic Cooperation and Development. (2007). *Education at a glance, 2007.* Paris: OECD.

OECD. Organization for Economic Cooperation and Development. (2008). *Education at a glance, 2008.* Paris: OECD.

ÖSYM. Student Selection and Placement Center. Öðrenci Seçme ve Yerleþtirme Merkezi. (2008). *Higher education statistics: 2007–2008.* Ankara: ÖSYM.

ÖSYM. Student Selection and Placement Center. Öðrenci Seçme ve Yerleþtirme Merkezi. (2009). *Higher education statistics: 2008–2009.* Ankara: ÖSYM.

National Ministry of Education. (2009). *National education statistics, 2008–2009.* Ankara: Author. Retrieved on January 30, 2011, from http://sgb.meb.gov.tr/istatistik/meb_istatistikleri_orgun_egitim_2008_2009.pdf.

Sabancí University. (2009). Retrieved in April 2009, from www.sabanciuniv.edu/eng/?ogrenim/ogrenim_kapak/ogrenim-kapak.html. Details also provided by private correspondence with Professor Üstün Ergüder, then director of İstanbul Policy Center of Sabancí University.

Student Selection and Placement Center. See ÖSYM. (1997, October 4). A survey of universities. *The Economist*, p. 5.

Theil, S. (2008, August 9). The campus of the future. *Newsweek*.

10

COMPARATIVE OBSERVATIONS

Problems and Prospects

Patti McGill Peterson

Introduction

Contemporary higher education in developing and transitional countries, regardless of national or cultural context, faces a similar array of challenges as it rises to meet the escalating demand of the 21st century. While this book acknowledges the important differences in each country's historical experience and current realities, there is a strand of interactive challenges facing all the countries featured in this project.

The complex interrelationship among key factors of access, equity, persistence, attainment, and massification readily creates the most serious challenge to the quality and effectiveness of educational programs. Aspiration often outpaces the ability to meet the increasing demand for higher education, whether from the vast populations and stronger economies of China and India or the newly empowered citizens and growing economy of South Africa. Differences in political and economic status notwithstanding, large segments of their populations are marginalized by their inability to locate points of entry into the education system. Finding ways to expand access to higher education while ensuring quality poses difficult decisions for those responsible for national budgets and the allocation of resources among competing priorities.

Forces at Work

Building higher education institutions for the 21st century and sustaining them at an acceptable level of effectiveness and quality is on the short list of priorities of every country that wishes to be competitive in the global marketplace and to raise its national standard of living. Space shortages for students, the lack of resources for teaching and learning, and the scarcity of well-qualified faculty work against that goal. In an environment of pressing issues and constricted resources, design of the curriculum for undergraduate students with a focus on the role of liberal education and its commitment to breadth of subject matter does not represent a high priority. Even though the curriculum is an important proxy for quality, it remains an area that is characterized more by inertia than activity.

In addition to the factors cited above, the case studies have pointed to an array of other variables that have a substantial impact on the climate for general education and the role of the liberal arts in undergraduate studies. While not all of these factors are present in all of the countries—or are present but at different levels of magnitude—they warrant review as additional reasons why there is so little holistic attention to the design of the curriculum and the role of liberal education.

As noted in this volume's first chapter, we are witnessing devolution of authority for higher education from government control to institutions and their governance boards all around the world. In some cases, however, the government retains considerable authority or at a minimum has a sufficiently significant bureaucratic role in institutional decision-making to thwart innovative ideas and curricular reform. While China can point to government-initiated reform that commands speedy implementation, other countries in this study report a very different experience. India and Pakistan are poster cases for huge bureaucracies that generate high-profile reform commissions whose recommendations, falling under the weight of the system, are rarely implemented.

Faculty members in Poland have the authority to propose the courses they wish to teach, but its Ministry of Education controls the overarching curricular framework. In all cases, the majority of institutions are still significantly dependent on the government for funding. The power of the purse can weigh heavily on curricular direction and dictate a primary emphasis on national development and workforce needs. This outlook in developing and transitional countries frequently results in support for more vocationally oriented and specialized professional education with little concern for a multipurpose, broad-based education for students.

The Role of the Faculty

It is important, however, to look beyond government power and purse strings to understand why the curriculum and general education for undergraduates do not get much attention from those directly responsible for students' education.

Relevant to this point are a number of issues that lie deep within institutions and the way they define their educational mission and practices.

The pressures of national development and workforce needs notwithstanding, the faculty in most places are the stewards of the curriculum and, even with government oversight, could advocate for institutional environments more conducive to providing students with both breadth and depth of subject matter in their studies. The opportunity presents itself as governments step back from their traditional role to allow more institutional autonomy. It is important, therefore, to ask ourselves: What are the forces militating against faculty taking a larger role in considering what curricular content will serve students well beyond their study of a specific field or discipline?

It is not just the government bureaucracies that can stymie curricular reform but academic bureaucracies themselves that are a stumbling block. The power of Faculties ("Faculty" as an academic administrative unit is capitalized while "faculty" refers to members of the teaching staff) has had a balkanizing effect on the bachelor's level curriculum and prevents a broader, more integrated view of knowledge that would include courses beyond the Faculties and the disciplines they represent. As noted in a number of the case studies, the Faculties tend to operate totally independent of one another. Academic separatism has real consequences for students and their programs of study. In Mexico, for example, this form of organization means, as just one important consequence, that virtually no common courses exist between Faculties. The impossibility of taking courses outside their Faculties means that students' programs resemble tunnels without side exits. Like Mexico, the Russian example cites the Faculties' tremendous degree of autonomy and independence from one another. Students are admitted not only into all-powerful Faculties but also into tightly circumscribed programs within the Faculties. A paradox of the post-Soviet period, in which Faculties have greater autonomy, is that an even more intense isolationism has developed, militating against the possibility of interdisciplinary offerings that would allow liberal arts-based general education. This same phenomenon is at work in post-Soviet Poland where faculty members, with a few notable exceptions, are not exercising newfound freedoms to consider new curricular possibilities. Even in countries with somewhat different academic structures, where departments are the principal organizational unit, such as Turkey and South Africa, similar silos are in evidence. In South African universities, faculty members within departments are described as relatively autonomous with no single integrating authority on curriculum development. In India, in 2004, the University of Delhi attempted to restructure its undergraduate program. The main resistance came not from the government but from the faculty themselves.

With more autonomy being given to Faculties, departments, and faculty members, it really is difficult to understand why there is so little institutional discourse among them about the curriculum. The author of the Turkey case study, who was formerly the head of its national Council of Higher Education, provides one answer. He notes a paradox: while central control on curriculum has relaxed over time, individual faculty members have become much more conservative. In his view, this condition is consolidated by a governance system in which rectors and deans are effectively elected by faculty members. Up-and-coming university administrators who advocate unpalatable reforms risk considerable backlash and the threat of no upward mobility within the academy. Faculty governance systems in other countries hold a similar capacity to control the curricular agenda.

Any inclination among faculty members to add general education, informed by the liberal arts, to the undergraduate curriculum would mean reaching across long-standing academic partitions. A willingness to see their work as deeply connected to students and the curriculum rests with how faculty members define their primary obligations in the academic workplace. Their attitudes and behavior will depend on whether their principal loyalty is to their Faculties and academic disciplines or mainly to the best interests of students. In fairness to the faculty, their own training and exposure to the way knowledge is organized and taught would not normally lead them in any direction other than a strong identification with their Faculties and, hence, to the exclusion of other loyalties. If they studied in a narrow band of subject matter within a Faculty somewhat akin to a medieval guild, the primary goal will be to replicate those patterns deemed important to membership in the guild. Mavericks are not rewarded with Chairs or whatever the equivalent may be in the developing and transitional countries of this study.

There is generally neither breadth of exposure to new ideas nor a reward structure that would encourage faculty members to be more student centered. This situation is underscored by conditions in countries like Mexico where our authors describe how the curriculum is defined by faculty preferences and not student needs. Academic positions and salaries are determined by teaching loads within each Faculty, which means that changes in curricular content have personal consequences and make curriculum reform and new undertakings unattractive to faculty members.

In many of our targeted countries, there is no significant experience with student-centered curricular development and pedagogy. Faculty members repeat in their expectations as teachers the practice of rote learning that they were expected to produce as students. The case study for Pakistan notes that problems of a narrowly focused curriculum are exacerbated by a pedagogical approach that typically remains teacher and textbook centered, unidirectional, and non-interactive. In the case of China, priority is given to memorization with less emphasis on analysis, innovation, and critical thinking. The authors for the Russian case study document a teacher-centered approach in which outdated lectures are read to students and rote learning is generally the modus operandi. Newer institutions in Russia are trying to change this paradigm but many faculty members remain embedded in a system that continues traditional modalities of teaching and interaction with students. The model of unassailable knowledge emanating from the lectern does not create a classroom climate supportive of student questions or critical thinking characteristic of the best models of liberal education.

While the background and experience of the professoriate in developing countries constrain their interest in curricular reform, so, too, do the conditions of their work. In a number of the countries under consideration, pay is low; and it is not uncommon for members of the faculty to hold positions in multiple institutions or other forms of employment. High teaching loads and the lack of incentives for participation in pedagogical and curricular reform also militate against the kind of faculty stewardship that would support new models of educating undergraduate students.

Special Cases and Unique Circumstances

Based upon the analysis above, the prospects for liberal education in developing and transitional countries appear at best uncertain. However, current developments in China present that country as an outlier on this subject. The examples of what is happening in the institutions of Hong Kong, a Special Administrative Region of the PRC, and in those of Mainland China, show exciting possibilities as well as some probable internal challenges. China, more than any of the countries under review, has declared that it intends to build a world-class higher education system. It is currently devoting vast resources to that goal by updating and reforming higher education, which it sees as critical to national development and to its international status.

In the reforms pursued by China's Ministry of Education (MOE), general education as a feature of undergraduate education is viewed as an integral aspect of making China a globally competitive country through a well-educated citizenry. As noted by the authors of China's case study, the introduction of general education throughout China, beginning in the 1990s, is designed to help prepare students to meet the demands of a rapidly changing, increasingly global environment.

While centralized control is changing somewhat, there is no question in this instance that the reports and recommendations of the MOE have been fundamental to the widespread embrace of general education in Mainland China. In Hong Kong, the University Grants Committee was responsible for mandating reform of undergraduate education for Hong Kong's eight baccalaureate-granting universities. Among the goals of the mandate are providing students with a broader academic experience and adding many of the elements of contemporary general education programs such as those more typical of U.S. institutions. In these instances, central directives have not fallen under the weight of government or higher education bureaucracies but have moved fairly swiftly toward implementation. This approach is serious. It is intentional. It is part of wanting to be the best.

China's National Plan for Medium and Long-Term Education Reform and Development (2010–2020) emphasizes that China seeks to become less dependent on foreign ideas and research. Nevertheless, ideas about liberal education and the results of undergraduate reform are generally borderless. And while both Mainland China and Hong Kong include an emphasis on Chinese culture (*wenhua suzhi jiaoyu* and Chinese heritage respectively), there is much that is Western and particularly American in the new Chinese models of general education. In Mainland China, distribution requirements, the focus on co-curricular life, and the development of student affairs units within universities reflects this influence. In Hong Kong the structure of general education programs includes in a number of the universities such things as internships, service learning, and a capstone experience—all features of the most creatively designed undergraduate liberal education programs in the United States. Hopefully, concepts and ideas that derive from *wenhua suzhi jiaoyu* will be equally borderless and enrich general education programs well beyond China's borders.

The most significant question for China is whether its general education goals, which seem very much like this volume's definition of liberal education, will have unintended consequences. Educating the whole person and truly exposing him or her to a broad spectrum of ideas from many cultures will invariably make students aware of other models of political and social life. This approach, coupled with a student-centered pedagogy that is typical of the best general education programs, will undoubtedly result in students assuming the habits of active inquiry, critical thinking, and the open expression of ideas. Well-executed general education programs can be a catalyst for rising expectations among students. It may make them more active and questioning participants in Mainland China's required series of political and military courses. These are the natural and expected by-products of educating students to have not only a strong sense of national identity but also a deeply informed perspective of the rest of the world.

Pakistan joins China as an outlier among the case studies of this project. It faces all the issues that limit the introduction of curricular reform and the prospects of general education informed by the liberal arts outlined at the beginning of this chapter. The unique issue that it presents is a national mandate for religious studies in higher education. This commitment has deep moorings in Pakistan's creation through the partition of India in 1947, and it has become a tenacious contemporary reality. Those responsible for educational policy have viewed the compulsory study of Islam as a uniting factor for the country. This resolution can be seen in such policy statements as: "The ideology of Islam forms the genesis of the State of Pakistan. The country cannot survive and advance without placing the entire system of education on sound Islamic foundations" (Government of Pakistan, 1998, p. 2).

This view has found its way into the curriculum via required Islamic studies (Islamiyat) at all levels of education in Pakistan. In addition, other subjects, such as social studies, have been "Islamized" with support from the State. According to the case study, the pedagogical premise of Islamyat is inculcation from the teacher and acceptance from the student. Rather than broadening the undergraduate curriculum and opening Islam to varying interpretations, comparisons to other religions, and critical inquiry, this approach has suppressed these possibilities.

Deeply integrated ideological views that pervade the curriculum and that are presented for automatic acceptance make it virtually impossible for the spirit of liberal education to gain traction and flourish. As outlined in the first chapter, liberal education and its curricular incarnation, general education, are dependent upon students' broad encounter with knowledge—cultural and ideological. In this framework, neither a predominance of Western thinking nor the absence of religious studies is a requirement. It presumes, however, a diversity of perspectives and a critical approach to subject matter. Mandates from governments or instructors that limit that possibility are tantamount to limiting the prospects of general education informed by the tenets of liberal education as an approach to teaching and learning.

Et Tu America?

The introductory chapter of this book includes a discussion of liberal education in the United States as part of the framework for a larger global discussion. The decision to provide the U.S. example as context was prompted by its status as a significant repository of liberal education. In its colleges and universities, the design of general education programs has generated a great deal of debate and the results have often led to curricular reform. This does not mean, however, that all is well. There are currently serious challenges to the form and role of general education as well as critiques of the overall effectiveness of undergraduate education in the United States.

The marketplace for higher education is a very competitive one. Student choices about academic programs are influenced substantially by the economic marketplace and perceived prospects of employment. As a reflection of these conditions, more than 20% of U.S. undergraduates study for a business degree. An ailing economy may well increase this trend. Federal, state, and institutional funding for the humanities, whose disciplines are critical to liberal arts programs, is also under fire. All of these factors have helped to fuel growing concern about the health and welfare of liberal education.

This concern was signaled recently by the Teagle Foundation in its call to the U.S. higher education community to produce proposals to improve undergraduate education. In describing the background and context for its Faculty Work and Student Learning in the 21st Century project, the foundation enumerated a series of challenges that had prompted the development of the program:

It has become clear that over-specialization in the disciplines, the fragmentation of the curriculum, the dominance of research in marking
faculty and professional achievement, the underperformance and low
attainment of many students, the economic stratification of education
opportunity, the displacement of liberal education by career studies, the
wide expectation for assessment of outcomes, and the heavy reliance on
part-time and adjunct faculty have created intense challenges for many
campuses and their faculties.

(Teagle Foundation, 2011)

The foundation came to this conclusion after undertaking a broad review of
the issues confronting the curriculum and the assessment of student learning
outcomes. Its ultimate hope is that the proposals it receives will provide
models for addressing these issues in creative ways so that undergraduate education can be revitalized.

In 2011, the publication of *Academically Adrift: Limited Learning on College
Campuses* was perhaps the penultimate indictment of the effectiveness of undergraduate education in the United States. One of the book's main findings was
that students whose progress was measured after two years of study (a period
when most would be exposed to some form of general education) showed no
significant improvement in critical thinking, complex reasoning, and writing. As
part of the general indictment, the authors pointed to an institutional culture
that ranks undergraduate learning low in priority (Arum & Roska, 2011).

Just as administrators in developing and transitional countries do not often
make curricular reform a top priority, their counterparts in the United States
suffer a similar reluctance. As an illustration, the book cites commentary from
Derek Bok, former president of Harvard University, who candidly asserts that,
while academic leaders have the authority to propose more attention to undergraduate instruction, they generally do not as a way to avoid opposition from
faculty and, hence, to preserve their careers. The authors, however, reserve
their greatest concerns for the faculty and their obligations to students and the
curriculum.

Reviewing earlier research by Ernest Boyer and Alexander Astin, they note
the negative impact on undergraduate education of faculty members' primary
loyalty to their disciplines and research. It is their premise that a shift in
loyalty and attention will be necessary if faculty members are to assume stewardship for the quality of instruction and the content of the curriculum:

At the core, changing higher education to focus on learning will require
transforming students' curricular experiences—not only the time they
spend sitting in their chairs during a given class period, but everything
associated with coursework, from faculty expectations and approaches to
teaching to course requirements and feedback.... Education is not a

process of simply accumulating facts, concepts and skills, but one that facilitates students' ever increasing grasp of the world.

(Arum & Roska, 2011, p. 131)

It is clear from this critique, and others like it, that undergraduate education and the goals of liberal education are not challenged only in developing and transitional countries. The United States of America, regardless of its status as the largest contemporary repository of liberal education programs, faces similar challenges in assuring vigorous and effective undergraduate education in its colleges and universities.

Concluding Observations

As we confront the challenges facing liberal education and its role in undergraduate education in developed and developing countries, we need to consider whether a substantial portion of those challenges stems from false dichotomies. Are we creating juxtapositions that result in a set of Solomon's choices? A litany of stark bifurcations is posed about the nature and purpose of higher education: human development versus economic development, enlightenment versus employment, individual development versus societal development, general education versus professional/vocational education, and teaching versus research—among others.

We need all of the above, and we must move beyond monochromatic oversimplifications of the alternatives that are often posed as choices. Countries need a capable workforce, but they also need a citizenry capable of participating intelligently in the polity for the betterment of society. Students need jobs, but they also need preparation for what we know will be many jobs constantly being shaped and reshaped by the forces of globalization. Beginning with the thought that careers last longer than jobs, Sandy Baum and Michael McPherson warn of the danger of the "either/or" *weltanschauung*:

> Dictionary.com tells us that education is development of the abilities of the mind (learning to know). Training is practical education (learning to do) or practice, usually under supervision, in some art, trade, or profession. The workforce of the future needs both education and training. Some individuals will do best concentrating on one process. Some will do better concentrating on the others. But there is a danger that current discussions of how best to increase the attainment levels of the population will lead to counterproductive polarization of these paths.
>
> (Baum & McPherson, 2010)

It is not just the "vocationalists" that pose a threat. Those advocates of liberal education who argue that it must adhere strictly to a narrow set of readings and authors in a traditional classroom setting are foreshadowing a very limited future for liberal education in a global setting. All-or-nothing-at-all stances and pristine definitions of the content and form of liberal education will sound a death knell for its global migration. What we need most is a flexible concept of liberal education such as the one offered at the outset of this volume, one that travels gracefully and adapts to differing circumstances. Its incarnations in post-Soviet Poland and post-apartheid South Africa will be different but still can be enormously effective if carefully integrated into the history and contemporary realities of those countries. But, above all, it is important to understand that one size does not fit all.

To choose only the vocational path for higher education, dictated by workforce analysis that will be quickly outdated and made irrelevant by the tides of globalization, is the equivalent of a dead-end street for citizenry and society. The importance of a blended choice was recognized clearly by Dr. Sarvepalli Radhkrishanan, Chairman of India's University Education Commission, as the country faced a newly independent future. The commission's report noted the need for vocational and professional education for economic development but the chairman also added that the aim of education is "not the acquisition of information, although important, or acquisition of technical skills, though essential in modern society, but the development of that bent of mind, that attitude of reason, that spirit of democracy, which will make us responsible citizens" (Government of India, 1948, p. 2).

One of the long-standing arguments against liberal education is that it is elitist. As pointed out in Chapter 1, a liberal education curriculum was offered to a narrow segment of society through much of its history. As we now move globally from elite to mass in higher education, the question is whether some form of general education will be part of all students' experience or still only for a chosen few. Students today are being educated in all kinds of institutions, some without walls, and through a wide array of pedagogies and technologies. One of the most important issues that we need to address is how to find different ways to balance their educational programs so that they can learn to know and to do. This can be done by developing creative ways to align liberal education with specialization, general education with professional education, and human development with workforce development. Attention to these kinds of alignments in higher education in every country, but especially in developing and transitional countries, will yield long-term benefits.

No country has the luxury of choosing one side of the educational equation if it aspires to be a leader in the community of nations. These are hard decisions when countries are faced with an extraordinary set of competing needs, but to take the narrow path of training to the exclusion of the broader path of education poses a fundamental danger to human and national development. The outcome has significant potential to influence not merely the progress of nations but the progress of humanity in the increasingly borderless world in which we live. For all of us who have contributed to this book, we hope that our perspectives will foster a discussion within and across national borders about the role of liberal education and its future in the education of undergraduate students everywhere.

References

Arum, R., & Roska, J. (2011). *Academically adrift: Limited learning on college campuses*. Chicago: University of Chicago Press.

Baum, S., & McPherson, M. (2010, July 14). Careers last longer than jobs. *Chronicle of Higher Education*. Retrieved on August 1, 2011, from www.chronicle.com/blogPost/ Careers-Last-Longer-Than-Jobs/25550/?sid=at&utm_source/.

Government of India. (1948). *Report of the university commission*. New Delhi: Author.

Government of Pakistan. (1998). *National education policy: 1998–2101*. Islamabad, Pakistan: Government of Pakistan, Ministry of Education.

State Council of the People's Republic of China. (2010). Outline of China's National Plan for Medium and Long-term Education Reform and Development (2010–2020). Retrieved in August 2010, from www.gov.cn/jrzg/2010–07/29/content_1667143. htm.

Teagle Foundation. (2011). *Faculty work and student learning in the 21st century: Request for proposals*. Retrieved on July 31, 2011, from www.teaglefoundation.org?grantmaking/ rfp/2011_faculty_rfp.pdf.

CONTRIBUTORS

Editor

Patti McGill Peterson currently serves as Presidential Advisor for Global Initiatives at the American Council on Education, the major coordinating and leadership body for United States higher education institutions.

She was Senior Associate at the Institute for Higher Education Policy (IHEP) from 2008 to 2011. The institute's mission is to increase access and success in post-secondary education around the world through research and programs that inform key policy-makers.

From 1997 to 2007, Dr. Peterson served as Executive Director of the Council for International Exchange of Scholars (CIES) and Vice President of the Institute of International Education (IIE). CIES coordinates international educational exchange with approximately 155 nations and has administered the Fulbright Scholar Program since 1947. It also manages foundation-funded higher education projects.

The Fulbright Scholar Program added notable dimensions during Dr. Peterson's tenure at CIES. In addition to its core exchange programs that annually involve over 1,600 U.S. and visiting scholars and professionals, new programs were developed to foster greater cross-cultural collaboration on topics of global significance and to encourage higher education development through academic exchange.

She was Senior Fellow at Cornell University's Institute for Public Affairs from 1996 to 1997. Her research focused on the nonprofit sector and its intersection with the for-profit sector in shaping public policy.

Dr. Peterson holds the title President Emerita at Wells College and St. Lawrence University where she held presidencies from 1980 to 1996. As a tribute to her leadership at Wells, an endowment was established for the Patti McGill Peterson Chair in the Social Sciences; and at St. Lawrence, the Center for International and Intercultural Studies was named in her honor. Her faculty appointments have included the State University of New York, Syracuse University, and Wells College.

She has held prominent international, national, and statewide leadership positions. She served as Chair of the U.S.–Canada Commission for Educational Exchange, the National Women's College Coalition, the Public Leadership Education Network, the American Council on Education's (ACE) Commission on Leadership Development and Academic Administration, and is a past President of the Association of Colleges and Universities of the State of New York. As a member of ACE's Commission on National Challenges in Higher Education she helped to identify priorities for government action on higher education issues for the President of the United States. She was a member of the Commission on Governmental Affairs for ACE, the Board of Overseers of the Nelson A. Rockefeller Institute of Government, and the Ford Foundation's International Fellowship Program. Her current board memberships include the University of Wisconsin's Board of Visitors, the Council for International Educational Exchange, the National Research University of Russia, HSE, the Roth Endowment, and the Mutual Funds Directors Forum. She serves as a trustee of the John Hancock Mutual Funds.

Dr. Peterson holds a B.A. degree from the Pennsylvania State University, an M.A. and Ph.D. from the University of Wisconsin and did post-graduate study at Harvard University. She has received numerous grants and awards including a Carnegie Fellowship at Harvard University.

Contributing Authors

Fatima Adam completed her Ph.D. on "Curriculum Reform in Higher Education in South Africa: A Humanities Case," and is a senior officer in the Academic Planning and Policy Implementation Division at the University of Johannesburg. Most of her experience is in project management and strategy development, largely in the area of science and technology education, predominantly at the school level. She has also been involved in higher education initiatives as Project Evaluator for the Council on Higher Education and as a member of the Commission on Racism established by the Ministry of Education.

Pawan Agarwal is now serving as Advisor (Higher Education), Planning Commission, Government of India, New Delhi. He is the former principal secretary to the government of West Bengal. Past contributions to higher education include service in the Indian government in higher education, as a Fulbright New Century Scholar on higher education (2005–2006), as a visiting scholar at the University of Melbourne's Endeavour Executive Award (2009), and as the author of studies for the World Bank, Inter-American Development Bank, Asian Development Bank, International Institute of Education (New York), South Asia Network of Economic Research Institution, and the Observatory on Borderless Higher Education. He is the author of *Indian Higher Education: Envisioning the Future* (New Delhi: Sage Publishers, 2009).

Jonathan Becker is Vice President for International Affairs and Civic Engagement and Associate Professor of Political Studies at Bard College in Annandale-on-Hudson, New York. He oversees Bard's dual-degree programs with St. Petersburg State University in Russia, the American University in Central Asia in Kyrgyzstan, and Al-Quds University in Palestine. He has written extensively on international education, Soviet and Russian media, and U.S./Russian relations, including *Soviet and Russian Press Coverage of the United States: Press, Politics and Identity in Transition*, rev. and exp. ed. (New York: Palgrave, 2003). He received his doctorate from St. Antony's College, Oxford, in 1993.

Michael Cross began his career as lecturer at the Faculty of Education, University of the Witwatersrand, in 1986, where he currently teaches educational leadership and policy studies. He has been awarded teaching and research fellowships and visiting scholar appointments in several institutions including the Johns Hopkins University, Northwestern University, Stanford University, Stockholm University, and Jules-Vernes University in Amiens. He is author and co-author of several books, book chapters, and numerous articles including *Imagery of Identity in South African Education, 1880–1990* (Durham, NC: Carolina Academic Press, 1999), which contextualizes some of the issues discussed in his chapter in this volume. He has served as an education specialist in several major national education policy initiatives in South Africa, such as the National Commission on Higher Education and the Technical Committee on Norms and Standards for Educators.

Wietse de Vries is originally from the Netherlands but has been living in Mexico since 1989. He is currently Professor and Director for Institutional Research at the Benemérita Universidad Autonóma de Puebla, where he is responsible for the institution's curricular reform and for tracer studies in which students and alumni evaluate the university's teachers and teaching practices, as well as their own learning. He is also involved in a European Union-funded international alumni study analyzing students' education received at institutions throughout Europe and Latin America and their later success in the labor market. Dr. de Vries has also conducted numerous international and comparative research projects on educational policies and their effects, evaluation, and funding, participated on several accreditation committees, evaluating both majors and institutions (in Mexico and Chile), and has consulted for the Undersecretaries of Higher Education in Mexico, Argentina, and Bolivia on institutional reform policies and curricular change. He held visiting professor appointments at the Pennsylvania State University (1995–1996) and the University of British Columbia (2003–2004).

Philip Fedchin is Associate Head in Curriculum Development and Information Resources at Smolny College of Liberal Arts and Sciences, St. Petersburg State University, Russia. He has a diploma in art history from St. Petersburg State University (1993) and an M.A. in International Studies, Limerick University (1996).

Zulfiqar H. Gilani, a psychologist by training, has served in Pakistan as Vice Chancellor of the University of Peshawar and as rector of Foundation University, Islamabad. His academic and research experience has been in the United States, Pakistan, and the United Kingdom. He was a Fulbright New Century Scholar (2005–2006) and also served as a visiting scholar in the Ontario Institute for Studies in Education (January 2007 to December 2008), and as a senior consultant in the Office of the Vice President for Research, both at the University of Toronto, Canada. His areas of interest in higher education are policy, leadership, reform, governance, and academic quality.

Kemal Gürüz, a retired professor of chemical engineering at Middle East Technical University, is former president of the Council of Higher Education, Turkey's national board of governors for all institutions of higher education. He has previously served as visiting professor of chemical engineering and Fulbright fellow at Worcester Polytechnic Institute, rector of Karadeniz Technical University, chairman of the Turkish Fulbright Commission, president of the Turkish National Science Foundation, and fellow at the Weatherhead Center for International Affairs at Harvard University. In 2005, he became the first recipient of the Chancellor John W. Ryan Fellowship in International Education at the State University of New York. He is the author of numerous articles and book chapters on higher education governance and research and development management, and *Higher Education and International Student Mobility in the Global Knowledge Economy* (Albany: SUNY Press, 2008). He holds an honorary doctoral degree from SUNY Binghamton.

Andrei Kortunov graduated from the Moscow State University for International Relations, has worked at the Russian Academy of Sciences, has led a number of national and international NGOs and foundations, and has served as visiting professor at Russian and U.S. universities. His current position is president of the new Eurasia Foundation, a social development agency in Moscow.

Ewa Kowalski, originally from Poland, is currently an independent scholar in Ontario, Canada. She obtained her Ph.D. degree in comparative and international education from the Ontario Institute for Studies in Education at the University of Toronto (OISE/UT). Her research and publications address a range of issues critical to understanding education transformation processes in Eastern and Central Europe in the context of democratization, globalization, and Europeanization. Her most recent works include "Reform of Technical and Vocational Education and Training in Poland's New Political and Economic Climate," in V. Masemann, N. H. Truong, and S. Majhanovich (Eds.), *Clamouring for a Better World: A Tribute to David N. Wilson*, The World Council of Comparative Education Societies (Rotterdam: Sense Publishers, 2010), and (2008), "Representations of Linguistic and Ethno-Cultural Minorities in Poland's Education Policy, National School Curricula and Textbooks," *Journal of Multilingual and Multicultural Development*, 29(5), 364–379.

Manli Li is a professor in the Institute of Education, Tsinghua University, Beijing, China. Her teaching and research focus on higher education and human resources education. As a Fulbright scholar at the Center for International Studies at MIT in 2007–2008, she conducted a research project on liberal education and engineering education excellence.

Kathryn Mohrman became the first director of the University Design Consortium at Arizona State University, where she is a professor in the School of Public Affairs. Before this position she was executive director of the Hopkins-Nanjing Center, a Sino-American academic joint venture based in China. She served as president of Colorado College and dean at several institutions; she has also taught in China and Hong Kong. Her research involves the examination of world-class university phenomena based in part on work conducted as a member of the New Century Scholars program supported by the U.S. Fulbright program.

José Francisco Romero is currently Coordinator for Educational Management at the Vicerrectoría de Docencia of the Benemérita Universidad Autónoma de Puebla, Mexico. He holds a B.A. in psychology and an M.A. in management of educational institutions. His master's thesis on the link between universities and industry won the National Association of Universities (ANUIES) National Award for best dissertation in the field of education and was published as a book in 2008. Besides his work as an administrator, Mr. Romero has published several papers on accreditation, public policies, and funding.

Jinghuan Shi, Professor and Executive Dean of the Institute of Education, Tsinghua University since 2002, previously had worked in Beijing Normal University for 20 years as the deputy dean of the Department of Education and as director of the Institute of Educational History and Culture. She was a Fulbright professor at the University of Maryland at College Park in 1996 and a specially appointed professor at Hokkaido University of Japan in 2006. She is now the chairperson of the Beijing Association of Women Professors.

Rajashree Srinivasan is a faculty member at the Azim Premji University at Bengaluru and was earlier a Senior Lecturer in education at Lady Shri Ram College for Women, India's premier women's liberal arts institution, where she served as the head of her department (2006–2008), with primary responsibility for time assessment and reform of the undergraduate curriculum. In addition, she has served as Convener of Lady Shri Ram's "Reaffirming Equity, Access, Capacity, and Humanism" (REACH) project to provide liberal arts access to students from economically and socially disadvantaged backgrounds.

Index

Page numbers in *italics* denote tables.